CW00409433

OUR FOOD OUR FUTURE

To Heston

Food for thought, the
whole industry needs to
work together for the future
you and I hope will emerge!

Warmest
Alan

OUR FOOD
OUR FUTURE

Eat Better, Waste Less, Share More

ALAN WATKINS & MATT SIMISTER

Urbane
PUBLICATIONS

First published in Great Britain in 2017
by Urbane Publications Ltd
Suite 3, Brown Europe House, 33/34 Gleaming Wood Drive,
Chatham, Kent ME5 8RZ

A CIP catalogue record for this book is available
from the British Library.

ISBN 978-1-911583-43-1
MOBI 978-1-911583-44-8
EPUB 978-1-911583-45-5

Design and Typeset by Michelle Morgan
Cover by The Invisible Man

Printed and bound by CPI Group (UK) Ltd,
Croydon, CR0 4YY

urbanepublications.com

If you are worried about food, escalating population and sustainability – read this book. An exposé of the wicked problem of food together with an inspiring vision of how, with the right people and a clear intent, we can waste less, feed more and protect the planet.

Dave Lewis, CEO Tesco

A brilliant book. It explores the complexities of the global food system and how we can fix the challenges. If you care about access to quality, affordable food then read this book.

Heston Blumenthal, 3-star Michelin Chef, Founder of Fat Duck Restaurant

The world is changing at a speed like never before. And the food industry is no exception. This book shows sleek and brave ways of dealing with the solutions for a new world! If you are interested in the food supply for the decades to come, this book will enlighten you.

Alvaro Munoz, CEO AMC Fresh Group

Providing healthy, nutritious food for the world's 9.7 billion people in 2050, while improving our natural environment, is the challenge of our time. This book articulates the scale of the challenge and imagines a future that will make you think and, more importantly, act.

Richard Swannell, Development Director, WRAP

This book gives an excellent overview of how our food system works, shedding light on the inner workings of this huge and very complex industry. Encouragingly Alan and Matt point to how people are starting to come together to make the important changes that we need to make to secure our collective future.

Lindsay Boswell, FareShare

At last – a book that addresses the real issues around food quality and supply. With shocking but important facts throughout, Our Food Our Future reminds us that a collaborative approach is the only way to make the global improvements that are needed. Everyone must read it.

PB Jacobse, Chief Executive Officer, CEO Rhubarb

Alan and Matt's book highlights the moral duty for all in the food industry to set precedents for ethical trade and sustainability. This is a must read for anyone who has an interest in our planet, humankind and the future of food. If we all work together, we will have a voice loud enough to move mountains.

Tom Redwood, Founder and CEO Babease Ltd

As someone embedded clinically and commercially in human health, food innovation, generation and waste resolution, I found this book to be a fabulous transcript, capturing the very zeitgeist of human needs, science and commercial reality – a substantial task. If you are involved at any level in the generation, supply and ingestion of food, then this should be on your reading list!

Michael Ash, Managing Director Clinical Education

Table of Contents

Contents

Foreword
by Ken Wilber

One of the co-authors of this book (Alan Watkins) and I wrote a work entitled *Wicked and Wise: How to Solve the World's Toughest Problems*. In that book, we point out that the main reason wicked problems are almost impossible to solve is that they are staggeringly complex and interwoven, with virtually every component of the wicked problem itself being another wicked problem. Our standard models and approaches to these problems are nowhere near wicked enough themselves - that is, they cannot come close to matching the complexity, sophistication, and convolution of the problems. Wicked problems, we point out, are multi-dimensional, involve multiple stakeholders, have multiple causes, multiple symptoms, multiple solutions, and are constantly evolving. None of our existing models come anywhere near addressing each and every one of those convolutions in one consistent framework.

With at least one major exception - that known as Integral Metatheory. Dr. Roger Walsh maintains that "Integral Metatheory is the most comprehensive, most successful metatheory now in existence." It began as an attempt to do a type of big-data analysis on literally thousands of the world's major cultures across all of human history - including premodern, modern, and postmodern - and use each of the major maps of reality that each of those cultures created in a way that would fill in the gaps found in any of them. The result was a massively comprehensive map - a "supermap" if you will - that gave one of the most sophisticated, complex, and complete overview maps or integral frameworks of the full human condition and its many territories.

Because this integral supermap contained most of the human potentials that have been suggested by virtually any human culture anywhere, its overall complexity and sophistication made it ideal for addressing wicked problems. It actually has elements or components that deal with multi dimensional realities, involve multiple stakeholders, recognize multiple causes, multiple symptoms, multiple solutions; and it recognizes its own dynamic as constantly evolving. In the book itself, we use climate change as a significant example of a wicked problem, and we show, step by step, how the wicked model of Integral Metatheory can effectively address issues as complex and wicked as global warming.

Of course, implementing solutions to wicked problems depends not only on a theoretical (or metatheoretical) adequacy, it demands, perhaps above all else, a collective political will - and that is a wicked problem in itself (containing an almost infinite regress of similar problems). None of the world's wicked problems can be claimed to have been solved until this political will component falls into place, by whatever means. What can be done, while waiting for that will to emerge (or perhaps taking steps oneself to help with its emergence), is to continue moving forward with a planning of the metatheoretical overview or integral approaches that are a crucial aspect of addressing the many wicked problems that are now the greatest threats to humanity's survival. Among the least sexy, and most profoundly important, is the world's food supply.

Welcome to *Our Food Our Future*. This book takes an integral approach and applies it carefully and systematically to the problem of feeding humanity - and in a way that fully addresses and embraces all of the many dimensions of a wicked problem itself.

So you will find problems identified, and solutions offered, that span the entire spectrum of human possibilities - technological and economic, psychological and spiritual, cultural and social, individual and collective, legal and environmental, belief systems and worldviews and value needs. All of these various dimensions are carefully reviewed and included in a coherent and consistent fashion, with each partial solution clearly interwoven with all the other partial solutions, coming as close as possible to a whole solution that might indeed adequately address this looming and devastating wicked issue.

Most of today's truly nasty problems facing humanity are both wicked and global, and in a certain sense, it's the globalness that drives the wickedness. Any wicked problem that is prominent today - climate change, food supply, water resources, world governance, terrorism, global financial systems, military hyperdrive, trafficking, worldwide epidemics, weapons of mass destruction (nuclear, biological, chemical), poverty, inequality - is also a global problem. Even 50 years ago, if a nation were facing a particularly nasty problem, it could generally take steps itself that would in large measure address the specific problem. But today, that's just no longer true. Most of the major problems faced by any nation today are worldwide problems, and require many (or perhaps most) other nations also to take steps to help alleviate it. If the United States halted its carbon emissions entirely, this would come nowhere near being able to end global warming. As the Paris Accords acknowledge, virtually all nations everywhere have to sign on board in order to make any action in this area truly effective (though America's absence from this is unforgivable). But it's the global nature of the problem - running across and including dozens and dozens of various fields, disciplines, areas, and aspects - that make them truly wicked. When you've got a problem that is deeply threatening to America, Sudan, Honduras, and Malaysia, you have a real problem; and when you fully define that problem, you've got a pretty good definition of a wicked problem.

The point is, in today's world gone global, most of our problems have likewise gone wicked. And they categorically will not be solved unless our solutions become equally wicked. When the world passed over into an age that could be called "global", then from that point forward (i.e. from now on), all of our solutions had to be integral - or truly inclusive, comprehensive, all-embracing. The narrow, partial, siloed, piecemeal, and fragmented approaches that have dominated the world through most of its history became instantly outmoded and outdated, and belong now only in the museums of the dusty and dated past. To the extent that any such partial and limited approaches are applied today, they simply populate the storage bin of the dismally failed and faded. As numerous writers have noted, the Global Age is the Integral Age - in other words, the Age of Wicked Problems is the Age of Integral Solutions - and there is no turning back on any of those.

And make no mistake, global nutrition is a wicked, wicked problem. Close to a billion people worldwide are in danger of starvation. Another two billion lack sufficient vitamins and nutrients. Malnutrition causes almost 50 percent of the deaths in children under five. In some countries, such as Somalia, fully half of its population are near-starving. The problem is so wickedly severe that the malnutrition part of the food problem runs in the other direction, too: if one billion people are close to starving, almost two billion are significantly overweight - the food quality is so bad it feeds directly into obesity. If wealthy countries, such as America, have relatively few people openly starving, fully two-thirds of the population are overweight and a staggering one-third are clinically obese. This is not adequate nutrition, it's deeply inadequate - a stunning 3.4 million people a year die from medical problems related to being overweight.

Most of the efforts surrounding food or malnutrition problems focus exclusively on starvation, and clearly that is a major focus. Yet the deeper issue is that fully one in three of all human beings now alive on this planet have a severe problem with food. The inadequate nutrition they are getting leaves them either near starvation or severely overweight. Which of those would you rather die from? Does it really matter? Something is badly, badly broken with humanity's relationship to food.

And addressing this issue means addressing not only exterior factors such as calorie counts, farmable land, and food distribution mechanisms, but also interior factors such as the development of human values, worldviews, and collective beliefs. All of these simply must be addressed if humanity's food problem - this truly wicked problem - is actually to be solved in any sort of enduring, sustainable, and effective fashion.

Welcome to the types of solutions of wicked problems that will become commonplace in the future - the "Global Age" future - but are, at this time, still properly called "leading edge". Alan Watkins and Matt Simister are uniquely qualified to present such a wicked, integral, and leading edge solution to this profound crisis. Watkins is the CEO of a rather extraordinary leadership consultancy, Complete Coherence, which applies fully integral approaches to leadership and business issues, and thus traces all of the multiple dimensions that define wicked problems as they appear in companies and their leaders, as outlined in his book *Coherence* (and exemplified in *Wicked and Wise*). His TEDx talks have attracted close to four million viewers. Simister is now responsible for Tesco's business in Central Europe, and Tesco is the third largest retailer in the world (a good deal of it involving food). Simister was part of the reorganization of Tesco that occurred three years ago and part of the team credited with salvaging the company. Together they bring a bright and brilliant approach to one of the most utterly fundamental and foundational issues that could ever face humanity.

The point is that humanity's relationship to food is fundamentally broken, and that relationship is as basic as basic can get. We see this even going back to premodern times, with the rise of the Great Religions, since virtually all of them subscribed to the "Great Chain of Being", which was a view of reality that, as Arthur Lovejoy pointed out, has been held by the majority of humans for most of their history. It gives a layered view of reality, stretching from dimensions that are the most fundamental but least significant (most foundational but least meaningful), to ones that are the most significant but the least fundamental (most meaningful but least foundational). A typical example of the Great Chain in the Christian tradition is: matter, body, mind, soul, spirit. In all of the Great Traditions, food is seen as part of the lowest level, the material or physical level. The food drive or hunger drive is even lower than sex (which emerges with the second level, that of the living or biological body). So if you don't eat, you will die; but if you don't have sex, you won't die (although the species will). Food, in other words, is more fundamental, more foundational (and less meaningful, less significant).

This also means that, since food is the most basic level, all of the higher levels depend upon adequate food being present in order for them to be able to operate in the first place. We see this all the way to today's models such as Abraham Maslow's needs hierarchy, which is an updated version of the Great Chain, and runs from physiological needs to safety needs, to love and belongingness needs, to self-esteem needs, to self-actualization needs, to self-transcendent needs - and here, once again, food is on the bottom (a major contributor to physiological needs) - which also means, every one of the higher needs can only emerge if and when hunger needs are met (starving people don't worry about self-actualization). Maslow called them "prepotent" - a higher emerges only after the lower has been met.

Thus, to say that fully one third of all human beings have problems with food, is to say that they are having problems with the most fundamental drives that human beings have. And problems with that level mean that their access to all higher levels of human needs and meaning becomes profoundly compromised. When you violate and destroy food needs, you are simultaneously destroying safety and belongingness and self-esteem and self-actualization. You are literally gutting a human being's overall development, you are tearing out the core of what it means to be a human, you are destroying any chance of a greater future for that person (and very likely any future at all). There's nothing meaner you can do to a human being.

And we have done this to one out of every three people now alive on this planet. And continuing as we are, this shows no signs of getting any better and every sign of continuing to get worse. And thus the extreme ugliness and wickedness of this wicked problem becomes glaringly obvious.

Instead of engaging in yet another limited, partial, and fragmented approach to this staggering crisis, please join Alan Watkins and Matt Simister in a wonderfully wicked ride through this global mess, as they strike forward looking for truly comprehensive, integral, and fully wicked solutions to a problem that continues to kill not only human beings themselves, but their higher motivations, needs, and ideals as well. As we saw, humanity's relationship to food is the most basic and fundamental relationship that a human being can have, and getting that right is absolutely necessary as a genuine foundation and ground floor for all that is to come. Get that right, and our future is open; get it wrong, and a curtain of darkness automatically falls on any higher tomorrow. Please consider joining with Alan and Matt to open that future for everybody, and to do so in ways that finally have a real chance of actually succeeding.

Ken Wilber
Denver Colorado, Summer 2017

Our Food Our Future

Chapter 1:

The Problem with Food

Watching the nightly news can be a depressing experience and a stark reminder of the difficulties people face all over the world. Beamed live into our houses, we frequently see images of famine in developing countries and obesity at home. In the first quarter of 2017 Somalia is in the middle of acute food shortages brought about by severe drought, crop failure and weak governance after years of conflict. Mothers are being forced to walk hundreds of miles in search of food, water and sanctuary, foraging for anything edible en-route and boiling up weeds as their only meal! According to the UN, six million people - over half the population - are in urgent need of food assistance[1]. In total 20 million people are at risk of starvation in Somalia, South Sudan, Yemen and Northern Nigeria. In Malawi, Sudan, Afghanistan, DRC and Syria millions more don't have enough food to feed their families[2].

At the other extreme, obesity and diabetes are reaching epidemic levels across the world. 65 million adults suffer with diabetes in India, 98 million in China, nine million in Indonesia and seven

---

[1] UN New Centre (2017) UN migration agency launches $24.6 million appeal for drought-hit Somalia http://www.un.org/apps/news/story.asp?NewsID=56286#.WNU00OSsn4h

[2] Oxfam International (2017) Hungry in a world of plenty: millions on the brink of famine https://www.oxfam.org/en/rights-crisis-famine-south-sudan-west-africa-crisis-crisis-yemen/hungry-world-plenty-millions-brink

million in Pakistan. These are not countries normally associated with such health issues yet changing diets and, ironically, greater affluence together with genetic disposition are creating a 'perfect storm'. 382 million people are living with diabetes worldwide, often in places where many cases go undiagnosed and untreated[3]. In the West, diagnosis may be more likely but escalating numbers are putting huge additional stress on an already stretched public health system. In the UK, 3.8 million people have diabetes and it costs the NHS £10 billion per year[4].

In addition to this diet of bad news about food, we are also given frightening statistics about impending climate disasters, disappearing ice caps and methane time bombs as the frozen tundra thaws under the unrelenting rise in temperature. This is as well as other climatic disasters such as earthquakes, typhoons or tsunamis. All we can do is watch horrified and helpless as Mother Nature demonstrates her power. As if natural disasters, often accelerated by our desire to burn fossil fuel, weren't depressing enough, we then have the on-going migrant crisis – millions of people fleeing their homes due to conflict and war. Others simply seeking a better life and willing to risk everything in makeshift smugglers' boats to get it.

It would be easy to think of these news stories as distant and disparate issues with little in common, but all of them impact people's most fundamental need – their need to survive. And at the core of the ability to survive is the access to safe, healthy food and water.

Changes to climatic conditions and the unpredictability of weather has a profound impact on the production of food. Many

---

[3] Lipska K (2104) The Global Diabetes Epidemic The New York Times
     http://www.nytimes.com/2014/04/26/opinion/sunday/the-global-
     diabetes-epidemic.html?_r=0

[4] Diabetes UK (2014) Diabetes UK responds to obesity and Type 2
     diabetes report https://www.diabetes.org.uk/About_us/News/Diabetes-
     UK-responds-to-obesity-and-Type-2-diabetes-report/

of the natural disasters we see on the news devastate food production in the affected areas for years.

War is also bad news for the food chain. Areas of conflict become uninhabitable, land is destroyed. Nations have used the disruption of the food supply chain as a strategy of war for centuries. Before the Second World War, the UK imported 70 per cent of its food. One of Hitler's principal strategies was to attack food supply ships bound for Britain in an effort to starve the nation into submission. When land has been destroyed by a weather event or conflict then the people have to move. If there is no food, there is no choice.

And for the first time in human history, lifestyle diseases such as diabetes, heart disease and some cancers are killing more of us than infectious disease *and* they are killing more of us than starvation and malnutrition. Attempts to cure these modern conditions cost a fortune. In the US more than one-seventh of GDP is spent on healthcare dealing with the problems of modern life[5].

Figure 1.1 Maslow's Hierarchy of Needs

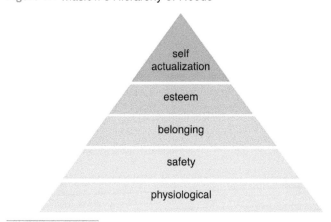

---

5   Bittman M (2011) How to Save a Billion Dollars *The New York Times*
    http://opinionator.blogs.nytimes.com/2011/04/12/how-to-save-a-trillion-dollars/?_r=0

In the 1940s Abraham Maslow presented the 'hierarchy of needs' (see Figure 1.1). This simple diagram indicated stages of our growth and development in terms of what we need as human beings.

First are our 'physiological' needs – in other words, we need food, water and shelter. This is purely a survival issue. We need food and water to stay alive – it is the basic requisite for life. Shelter also makes survival more likely and certainly more tolerable. And yet, according to the United Nations Food and Agriculture Organization (FAO), an estimated 795 million people in the world do not get the food they need to live a healthy life, estimated to be, on average, the consistent consumption of at least 2,100 calories[6]. That's nearly one in nine suffering from chronic undernourishment in 2014-2016[7]. Even more startling is that these numbers only relate to protein-energy malnutrition i.e. the lack of adequate levels of protein and food that provides energy. Some reports suggest a further two billion people lack sufficient vitamins and minerals, in particular vitamin A, iodine, iron and zinc, all of which are essential for optimal health[8]. Hunger kills more people each year than AIDS, malaria and tuberculosis combined[9].

The cost of living and income swings can significantly affect the poor and hungry. When prices rise, consumers often shift to cheaper, less-nutritious foods, heightening the risks of micronutrient deficiencies and other forms of malnutrition, which can have long-term adverse effects on people's health,

---

[6] World Food Programme – What is Hunger? http://www.wfp.org/hunger/what-is

[7] The State of Food Insecurity in the World 2015 http://www.fao.org/3/a-i4646e.pdf

[8] Business and Sustainable Development Commission (2016) Valuing the SDG Prize in Food and Agriculture http://s3.amazonaws.com/aws-bsdc/Valuing-SDG-Food-Ag-Prize-Paper.pdf

[9] The State of Food Insecurity in the World 2015 http://www.fao.org/3/a-i4646e.pdf

development and productivity[10]. When we think of malnutrition we tend to think of starving children but obesity is also frequently a malnutrition issue. These individuals are 'overfed but undernourished'[11]. They may be consuming more than enough food and calories, but that food contains too many macronutrients such as fat, sugar and carbohydrate while lacking the vital minerals and vitamins we need for physical and mental health.

Poor nutrition causes 45 per cent of deaths in children under five – 3.1 million children each year in low and middle income countries (LMICs)[12]. According to the UN more people on the planet are obese than underweight. Worldwide obesity has more than doubled since 1980 and in 2014 more than 1.9 billion adults were overweight. Of these over 600 million, or 13 per cent of the global population, were obese, and a staggering 3.4 million people die each year because of excess weight issues[13].

Malnutrition, in one form or another, now directly affects billions of people around the world. Lack of food leads to poor physical, mental or emotional development or lack of immune resistance. Lack of suitably nutritious food leads to excess weight and related complications, as well as the increased risk of chronic diseases which facilitates an endless downward cycle[14].

---

[10] The State of Food Insecurity in the World 2015 http://www.fao.org/3/a-i4646e.pdf

[11] Ezra Taft Benson who served as United States Secretary of Agriculture during both presidential terms of Dwight D Eisenhower and stated, "... we are an overfed and undernourished nation digging an early grave with our teeth...".

[12] Maternal and Child Nutrition Executive Summary The Lancet http://www.thelancet.com/pb/assets/raw/Lancet/stories/series/nutrition-eng.pdf

[13] Noori z (2016) 11 things to know about global obesity World Economic Forum https://www.weforum.org/agenda/2016/10/11-things-to-know-about-global-obesity?utm_content=buffer4b899&utm_medium=social&utm_source=twitter.com&utm_campaign=buffer

[14] Global Nutrition Report 2016: From Promise to Impact, Ending Malnutrition by 2030 http://ebrary.ifpri.org/utils/getfile/collection/p15738coll2/id/130354/filename/130565.pdf

According to the United Nations, the world does produce enough food to feed everyone[15]. However, too many people still don't have sufficient income to purchase enough nutritious food or access to land to grow enough food. The food that is produced is not always distributed to or accessible by those who need it, and certainly in the Western world an unbelievable amount of food is wasted. Considering how many people go to bed hungry this wasted food is a travesty. If the challenge of supplying the world with enough nutritious food at an affordable price wasn't difficult enough, it will only get worse as the global population increases. The UN predict that there will be 8.5 billion people on the planet by 2030, and a staggering 9.7 billion by 2050[16]. With these sorts of numbers there is no guarantee that we will be able to produce enough food to feed everyone.

There is little doubt that reliable access to safe, nutritious food is a serious problem for humanity, affecting half to two-thirds of the planet in one form or another. What makes it so challenging to solve is that it is a wicked problem.

Food - a Wicked Problem in Desperate Need of a Wise Solution

At the heart of the *Wicked & Wise* book series, of which this is the third, is the growing sense many of us share that there is something seriously wrong with the world; from climate change to poverty, to escalating inequality, to affordable healthcare, to education or the increasing failure of democracy and political systems to wisely steer our nations' futures. It is clear that the solutions that have been proposed by societies' leaders are not really working.

---

[15] Feeding the World Part 3 FOA http://www.fao.org/docrep/015/i2490e/i2490e03a.pdf

[16] World population projected to reach 9.7 billion by 2050 http://www.un.org/en/development/desa/news/population/2015-report.html

We believe they have not worked because there is a failure to genuinely appreciate the true nature of the problems we face. The problems mentioned above, and there are many more examples, are 'wicked problems' – a term coined by Professor Horst W J Rittel to differentiate between 'tame', solvable problems and the intractable super-complex problems that seem to have no clear or obvious solution. These problems are not 'wicked' in the sense that they are somehow evil, although those affected by these issues could be forgiven for thinking otherwise. But rather that the problem is wickedly complex, that our knowledge and appreciation of the problem is incomplete; the nature of the problem appears contradictory and is constantly changing.

In this book, we will explore the wicked problem of food – or at least safe, secure and adequate access to the food we need to survive and thrive. Of course, food and water are not just essential for our physical nourishment, providing us with fuel to function as a human being. The right food and good quality nutrition is essential for nourishing our brain and allowing us even the opportunity to progress through Maslow's hierarchy of needs to self-actualisation. It is, after all, misguided to worry about being the best we can be when we haven't eaten in three days. Securing enough food will always take precedence over every aspect of human existence. Only when we have access to enough food and water will we even consider our safety needs- and so on up the hierarchy toward self-actualisation.

The Definition of a Wicked Problem for the 21st Century

If we want to solve any problem, especially a wicked one, we must first be able to define that problem. A thorough definition of the challenge we face ensures we have a complete understanding and appreciation of exactly what we are up against. When elements or perspectives of the problem are unknown, underestimated, unappreciated, ignored or just a little fuzzy then we always run the risk of being blindsided in our attempts to find a workable solution. It is therefore useful to look at the wicked problem of food through the lens of the six key properties of a wicked problem (see Figure 1.2). A wicked problem:

- Has multiple stakeholders
- Has multiple causes
- Has multiple symptoms
- Has multiple solutions
- Is multi-dimensional
- Is constantly evolving

Figure 1.2 Definition of Wicked Problems

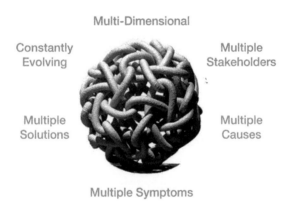

Multi-Dimensional

Constantly Evolving

Multiple Stakeholders

Multiple Solutions

Multiple Causes

Multiple Symptoms

If we stand any chance of successfully solving the wicked problems of the world, including food, we must first appreciate the complexity of the challenge we face so that we can mirror that complexity in the wise solution we propose.

1st Aspect of a Wicked Problem: Multiple Stakeholders

Wicked problems are wicked mainly because they involve people - usually a lot of people. Unfortunately, they are notoriously challenging to work with because everyone is different. Each person sees the world in their own unique way based on where they were brought up, their personal situation and experiences, what culture they live in, what language they speak, their religious and political convictions, and so forth. People have different values; they have different cognitive capabilities, different levels of emotional intelligence, and different levels of maturity, different belief systems and therefore different ideas about the problems we face and how to tackle them.

Each stakeholder group views the problem differently based on the issues that directly affect them in the food supply chain. As a result, they experience a different reality because of their objectives and priorities. Invariably, they will therefore advocate a version of 'the truth' that explains their perceived problems, while often dismissing, minimising or simply not appreciating the other, often conflicting, interdependent problems experienced by other stakeholder groups. There are definitely multiple stakeholders in the wicked problem of food, each perceiving the challenges they face individually and the challenges the industry faces collectively very differently. The main ones are:

- Consumers
- Retailers and food service
- Wholesalers and distributers
- Processors and manufacturers
- Agribusiness and agricultural commodity traders
- Farmers and growers
- Government

- Environmental groups
- Media

Consumers

We are all consumers. Whether we are in the developing world or the developed world we all want and need access to safe, nutritious, affordable food.

Beyond that, the food we buy is based on what's important to us individually and collectively. For consumers in the developing world or low income families in developed countries, the main considerations may be access and price. If a family is struggling financially they are looking for affordable options to feed their children and themselves.

However, price is not just important to those with less money to spend. The primary drivers of where people choose to shop, certainly in the UK, are location, ease of parking/shopping and price. Consumers are also increasingly 'shopping around' to get the best deals, facilitated by technology which is creating greater price transparency. If anything, price sensitivity is increasing, with consumers seeing no real wage growth and feeling increasingly uncertain about the general economic situation around them. Busier lifestyles also mean that people are looking for easier, faster ways to shop, hence the growth of online shopping, home delivery and 'click and collect'. In addition, people are spending less time cooking. 'Food to go' is the fastest growing category in 'out of home' consumption (5.3 per cent per annum between 2012-2015). 'Prepared food' is the fastest 'in home' growth area (2.6 per cent per annum)[17].

Consumers with children tend to focus on fewer, bigger main shops, whereas those who don't have children or no longer have their children living at home tend to shop more frequently, investing more time on specific shopping missions with more

---

[17] ONS Allegra: Consumer Insight

top-up shopping. As the population ages, the number of one to two person households in the UK has increased from just over 50 per cent in 1980 to 64 per cent now. During the same time period, the number of solo eating occasions has increased from 33 per cent to 44 per cent[18].

One of the other macro trends is healthier eating. The vast majority of UK consumers are interested in eating better and living healthier lifestyles, but their behaviour and engagement with health varies quite widely. Food businesses do extensive research to segment and target consumers accordingly, differentiating dieters from those seeking to age more healthily; those striving for the family to eat and live better; people lacking inspiration or knowledge; those who love looking after themselves and for whom food is just one part of a holistic healthy lifestyle; and the passionate chefs who love cooking from fresh, wholesome ingredients.

For some consumers, traceability or how and where their food is raised or produced is important and they will actively seek products that support their buying choices. Some consumers have concerns about highly processed food because of the additives and preservatives often found in those products and the impact those ingredients may be having on their family's health. The assumption for many consumers is that the more processed a food is the less healthy it becomes. And whilst manufacturers are seeking to address this perception and creating healthier, processed options, some consumers still prefer to eat more fresh fruits and vegetables and make their own meals from staple ingredients. For other consumers, 'heat and eat' meals, stir-in sauces and tins provide welcome convenience when they don't have time to cook or don't want to cook. Some are looking for a happy medium and may cook but purchase ready-prepared ingredients to save time.

---

[18] ONS (2014) Future Customer Needs, Customer Insight; nVision research

Some consumers with health issues or food intolerances will specifically seek out 'free from' products such as gluten free, or will deliberately purchase 'organic' products because of the way the products have been grown, or because they perceive them to taste better. For other consumers, such considerations are less important and the price difference often associated with organic produce is simply too much in comparison with the visibly equivalent products on display alongside. Some worry about the air-miles their food has travelled, or the impact of excessive packaging on the environment. In many developed countries consumers are more ethnically diverse than ever and are looking for access to their own cultural ingredients.

Christian Hansen, a global bioscience company that develops natural solutions for the food, nutritional, pharmaceutical and agricultural industries, undertook a project to discern the long-term, structural trends that would affect its industry and the value drivers that would influence consumer decisions over the coming ten years. This work involved extensive expert and industry interviews, investigation into technological practices, and ethnographic studies. The project identified five value drivers (tasty, healthy, convenient, authentic and safe) – all constrained by affordability – that consumers use to make decisions about food consumption and purchases.

What Christian Hansen discovered is that these five value drivers are all very important, and consumers must make unwanted trade-offs or 'dilemmas' when making food and health purchases.

As consumers, we are often encouraged to eat well and look after our health via government advice but this can be confusing. In the UK, the government promote the Eatwell Guide (see Figure 1.3).

Figure 1.3 The UK Government Eatwell Guide (2016)

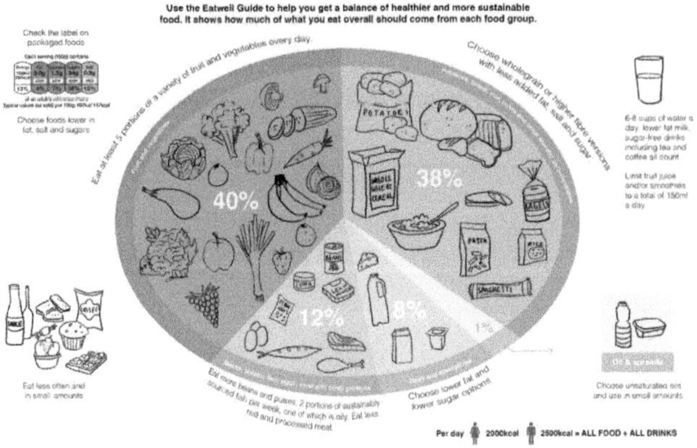

Modified from Original Source: http://bit.ly/2pNAFe7

According to UK government dietary recommendations adults should be eating:

	Male	Female
Energy (kcal per day)	2500	2000
Protein (grams per day)	55.2	45
Fat (grams per day) [less than]	97	78
Saturated fat (grams per day [Less than]	31	24
Polyunsaturated fat (grams per day)	18	14
Monounsaturated fat (grams per day)	36	29
Carbohydrates (grams per day) [At least]	333	267
Free sugars (grams per day) [Less than]	33	27
Salt (grams per day) [Less than]	6.0	6.0
Fibre (grams per day	30	30

Original Source: http://bit.ly/2ooQ6Zb

Interestingly, UK government data from the Defra Family Food Survey 2013 indicated that consumers are not eating anywhere near the recommended amounts of each category (see Figure 1.4). The only category that was close to recommended levels was protein, the rest were either too high or too low.

Figure 1.4 2013 UK Household Purchases Versus the 'Eatwell Plate' Ideal*

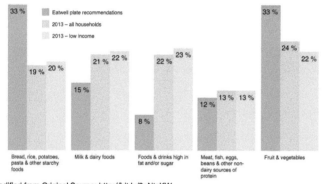

Modified from Original Source: http://bit.ly/2pNtsKW
*Eatwell Plate was superseded by the Eatwell Guide in 2016

In the US, the United States Department of Agriculture (USDA) have traditionally had a food pyramid but in 2010 they introduced new guidelines for proper dietary nutrition called 'MyPlate' (see Figure 1.5).

Figure 1.5 ChooseMyPlate.gov

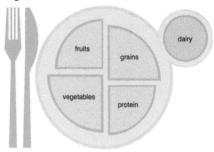

Modified from Original Source: http://bit.ly/2oHO6wA

These guidelines, developed by the USDA in conjunction with the Department of Health and Human Services are designed to serve as the "cornerstone of Federal nutrition policy and nutrition education activities". According to US government dietary recommendations adults should be eating:

	Male (31-50 age)	Female (31-50 age)
Energy (kcal per day) (moderately active)	2400 - 2600	2000
Protein (grams per day)	56	46
Total Fat (% of calories)	20 - 35%	20 - 35%
Saturated fat (% of calories)	< 10%	< 10%
Carbohydrates (grams per day)	130	130
Fibre (grams per day	31	25

Original Source: http://bit.ly/2ojLgwV

Even between government recommendations there are variations in advice, and there are always differing ways in presenting the information, which adds to the confusion. The UK government use a more useful 'grams per day' of fat for example, while the USDA recommendations state percentage of calories which is much harder to ascertain. There is also a sizeable difference in the recommended carbohydrate intake. As consumers, we are often left perplexed about what really is best for us. Do we look at calories or fat? Should we be worried about additives and preservatives or not? Is too much salt really a problem? For most of us healthy means balance. This is why, even despite the differences both the US and UK government recommendations both include high proportions of fruits and vegetables. Even high school Anatomy, Physiology and Health tells us there is more to good nutrition than macronutrients such as protein, fat and carbohydrate, and yet most of us, including medical doctors who receive virtually no nutritional training in their medical career, know very little about the complexity of vitamins and minerals and their critical importance for health, their interconnectivity and their role and interaction with healthy gut bacteria. The 'Eatwell Guide' or the 'MyPlate' graphic is therefore designed to help consumers understand the relative proportions of food types they should be incorporating into their diet in order to achieve a healthy balance, as determined by the respective government advice at the time.

The idea behind these dietary graphics is that if we focus on a diverse mix of food types while cutting back on the stuff we already know to be bad for our health such as sugar, excess salt and saturated fat, then we will improve our health. Of course, when we are buying pre-prepared foods or processed foods it can be challenging to apply these types of illustrations to the food we eat. In an effort to cut through the complexity of nutritional information many products now use a macronutrient 'traffic light' system. Red is considered 'high' or potentially 'bad' and therefore the consumer should not eat too much of that food; and green is considered 'good' and the consumer can be assured that they can eat more of that food.

Ultimately, the consumer's primary objective is always to feed themselves and their family. They also want choice, convenience and access to year-round tasty produce. Many consumers, especially when asked to consider it, also want to support local farmers, animal welfare and for the countryside to be well-manicured and also support wildlife. However, when faced with associated price premiums and the day-to-day challenges of modern life, shopping behaviour doesn't always reflect all of these good intentions.

Retailers and food service

Of course, consumers need to buy their food from somewhere. When buying food for the home we tend to purchase those goods at large grocery retailers or from local shops. When eating out we will purchase our food from service outlets such as restaurants or take away establishments.

Grocery retailers sell a huge selection of food from the fruit, vegetables and meat produced by the farmers and growers to value-added products such as bakery items, ready meals, canned and packaged food and snacks. Retailers also supply non-food products (health and beauty, household, clothing and general merchandise) that are wanted by many customers to satisfy a broader shopping mission. In the UK, the food market is worth £196.6 billion a year ('in home' represents £112.7 billion and the rest is 'out of home')[19].

Retailers provide us with choice, variety and a range of quality options. They often operate across multiple channels e.g. hypermarkets; supermarkets; convenience stores and online, serving multiple customer groups and multiple shopping missions such as breakfast/lunch/dinner; food for now/for later/ special occasions.

This stakeholder group faces many unique challenges. Primarily, they must satisfy the ever increasing and fragmented needs of a dynamic customer base, in an extremely competitive market place characterised by very low margins. They are amongst the biggest employers in the country and frequently play an important role in local communities. Their objective is to provide a diverse range of products and services that the consumer wants at accessible price points whilst building brand and shareholder value. Most responsible retailers also acknowledge that they have a role to play in encouraging healthier choices – better value fresh produce; products with less sugar, salt or saturated fat; and healthier meals. However, they can't tell people what to eat, and must also cater for what the consumer wants to buy, including products that are not that healthy. If the customer wants certain products and they are not available in store or online, the consumer will simply shop elsewhere. The big FMCG manufacturers (eg Nestlé, Coca-Cola, Kraft, Mondelez and Unilever) are essentially channel agnostic, and will seek to increase the market penetration and share of their brands wherever they can. In addition to creating

---

[19] UK Government Food Statistics Pocketbook 2014 https://www.gov.uk/ government/uploads/system/uploads/attachment_data/file/423616/ foodpocketbook-2014report-23apr15.pdf

emotional desire for their products directly with consumers they often employ elaborate pricing/incentive mechanisms to encourage retailers to support promotions and additional displays to increase sales, regardless of how healthy the product is for their end consumer. Despite this encouragement from the FMCG companies some supermarkets have chosen to forego short-term commercial benefits for longer term customer loyalty. For example, although confectionery is still available in the main store they are not always available at the checkouts to tempt an impulse buy; or catch the eye of insistent children at the end of a stressful shopping trip. Giving out free fruit to children at the store entrance can introduce kids to healthier snacking choices while also making it easier for the parent to get their shopping done. But getting the balance right for everyone, on every trip, is not always easy. For example, the busy worker on a short lunch break looking for a good value meal deal (sandwich, snack and drink) doesn't want to have to navigate half the shop to pick up three items.

Food service outlets also face a similar challenge. They too offer a selection of food options with each restaurant or food outlet often specialising in a particular type of cuisine or dining experience to appeal to different consumers. We all have our favourite take out joint or favourite local restaurant. Again, as consumer awareness and expectations increase around what is in food, and the service options available to them, the food service industry will also have to rise to the challenge of delivering better value, healthier alternatives whenever and however customers want them. Neither retail or food service is short of new entrants seeking to grab market share by offering better value, and/or better service propositions, through disruptive physical or online business models.

Many of the big retailers also have significant property interests that present unique strengths and challenges. For example, given the importance of location for big basket main shops, the opening and development of superstores fuelled a large part of retailers' growth strategies in the eighties, nineties and early noughties. However, the switch to internet shopping over the last 10 years, together with more frequent top-up shopping missions, has fundamentally challenged the economics of the big stores. Where some retailers created a significant competitive advantage through securing the best out of town hypermarket locations, shifts in consumer behaviour have seen that advantage become, to some extent, a bit of a liability as they realised they may actually have too much of the wrong sort of retail space. Retailers (and manufacturers) have also been challenged by wage inflation, rising rents and increasing overheads. The need to automate to reduce costs whilst delivering the increasing service required by more demanding consumers is a very real challenge for most. All this on top of the usual reputation and trust issues that come with stocking tens of thousands of products from all around the world, and serving millions of people on a daily basis.

Retailers have to deal with the very significant problems of consistency of service standards from multiple outlets, managing thousands of employees, the volatility of demand, customer expectations and competitor activity, whilst trying to meet the short and long-term expectations of their shareholders.

Running a successful supermarket chain or large food service operation is far from straightforward and the complexity they face is exacerbated by also having to meet the needs of their own complex and varied stakeholder groups. These will include, customers, staff and suppliers in addition to shareholders. All of whom want and expect something different from their relationship with the supermarket or restaurant. All this adds even more complexity. For example, what few of us probably think about is that food is a huge area for institutional investors. In practice this means all of us - through our pension funds - need supermarkets to be profitable. Our employee pension funds frequently invest in corporations connected to the food industry because it is often seen as a stable, blue chip investment opportunity that can add to pension value (after all, everybody needs food and toilet paper!)

As a result, retailers, whether stores or food service outlets, are themselves confounded by their own various stakeholder groups, each with potentially different objectives and thus amplifying the overall complexity still further.

Wholesalers and Distributers

Wholesalers and distributers are intermediaries between the farmers and growers and the businesses that manufacture and sell the huge variety of food we have come to take for granted.

Commonly, large national grocery retailers have direct relationships with food processors and manufacturers. Many smaller, or more locally structured food businesses with smaller volumes and/or less developed operational capability will rely on wholesalers to meet their supply requirements.

Wholesalers assemble, sort, break bulk, repack and redistribute products in smaller lots to a wide selection of customers, including retailers, cash and carry stores, industrial, commercial, institutional or other professional business users. Traditionally, wholesalers have been closer to the markets they supplied than the source of the products.

Distributors often run a network of stocking points, regionally or nationally, where they can hold, pick or cross-dock for customer deliveries, in the temperature regime that is required to maintain the right shelf life and quality for the relevant group of products. A broader product portfolio might mean a better solution for the end customer, but also more complexity for the distributor, often requiring many multi-temperature facilities and delivery vans.

Given the nature of the role they play wholesalers must be very competitively priced, but increasingly are seeing more demand to increase the service that they provide to their customers, including greater order flexibility, shorter fulfilment windows, new product/menu development, and increased supply chain transparency and integrity.

Key concerns that keep this stakeholder group up at night include managing volatility and variability in supply and demand, managing stock risk and costs, and controlling overheads in a fiercely price competitive market.

Processors and Manufacturers

Food processors and manufacturers take what's produced by farmers and growers directly (or through wholesalers and distributors) and turn these ingredients into finished products that are subsequently sent into retail or food service in the format they require for onward sale to consumers.

In some product sectors, raw materials will need both primary and secondary processing. For example, live animals will be sent to a slaughter-house, where they are killed, de-boned and then butchered into individual primal cuts. These primal cuts are then delivered in vacuum packaging into meat packers, the secondary processors (situated closer to their customers or their distribution centres), who will slice, dice, mince and pack the meat into retail-ready packaging. Food hygiene standards, traceability systems and controlled temperature storage facilities are often very important in food processors in order to preserve shelf life, maintain product safety and integrity, manage stock and order quantities, and ensure that the right products are delivered to the right specifications for retailers to meet their customers' requirements.

Meat processors face particular challenges because they may not need or want all the parts of the animal they buy from producers. Take pig meat, for example. The UK is a big importer of pork loins for bacon and legs for hams and gammons; we export ribs to the US, bellies to Japan and heads/trotters to China. The UK consumer has a high demand for chicken breasts, but not for chicken feet, which are also exported to China. Around 45 per cent of meat and meat products consumed in the UK are imported into the UK, and around 24 per cent of

British production is exported[20]. It is therefore clear that for UK meat processors to be efficient and profitable they must not only regularly and consistently kill 'in balance' at a scale appropriate to their abattoir facilities, but they must be effective in developing and managing export volumes as well as domestic customer channels. Changes to trading conditions can therefore have a profound impact on this stakeholder group.

Significant investment is also required in plant and machinery to build and run high quality, efficient food processing facilities, so it is important that manufacturers develop strong relationships and volumes with their customers and supply chains that will enable them to meet their respective specifications and order profiles. Manufacturers will constantly look for procurement, production, storage and distribution efficiencies to compete on cost; in addition to seeking differentiation to create and add value to their portfolio of products, brands and services. Effectively managing all of this complexity is necessary if the manufacturer is to drive sales and increase profitability.

Food manufacturers will supply customers' own label products, their own proprietary brands, or often a combination of the two, in order to optimise their businesses. In food, brands are more commonly found in processed products, where it is easier to develop, market and sustain a consumer price premium. Fresh produce, meat, dairy commodities and freshly baked bread tend to be predominantly supplied and retailed as own label products. Products with more complex formulations, or sold in pots, jars, tins, bottles, boxes and bars, are often branded. Thus, the more processed a food substance is the more likely it is to be branded and marketed. This is necessary to create the perception of added value. Such a perception is itself necessary to sustain the additional margins required to ensure highly processed foods are profitable.

---

[20] Overview of Current UK Meat Import and Export Trade The International Meat Trade Association http://www.imta-uk.org/images/stories/pdf_docs/imports_paper/Overview%20of%20Current%20UK%20Meat%20Import%20and%20Export%20Trade.pdf

Processors and manufacturers will often play the role of customer to the primary producers and food suppliers. They will also be the supplier to retail and food service customers. The competitive forces that they face in terms of supply and demand, and the capabilities that they need to develop to compete effectively, will vary based on the sectors in which they specialise and the channels they choose to serve. Both supply and demand conditions will vary tremendously from local factors, to national, regional or even global influences in many agricultural commodities.

Processors and manufacturers need to meet various regulations that govern their operations including health and safety, hygiene, ingredient declarations and food labelling. In addition, they need to stay ahead of consumer demand and invest in research and product development to meet changing consumer tastes and requirements.

Agribusiness and agricultural commodity traders

There are four dominant global agricultural traders, referred to as the ABCDs (ADM, Bunge, Cargill and Louis-Dreyfus). They were established as private, family-owned grain traders as far back as the 1800s, but have now grown into large global companies operating across a number of food (and energy) commodities and a range of activities upstream in the value chain. These activities range widely from simple land ownership, to planting and growing, or they may provide independent growers with finance. They also provide post-harvest storage, milling, processing and distribution services. The ABCDs are recognised as expert risk managers in an increasingly volatile world of food commodities. There are a number of other large players, such as Wilmar in Asia, and Olam in food ingredients, but in the industry the term ABCDs is used generically to describe the big food commodity companies.

Other important agribusinesses would include the big seed and agrichemical providers like Syngenta, Monsanto, DuPont and Bayer, as well as big farm equipment suppliers like John Deere.

Much of the structural and technological development in our most important, core food commodities, is down to these companies and they play a vital role in the production of food across the world.

Agribusinesses comprise of multiple stakeholder groups often under one umbrella corporation. Individually they are affected by the various challenges of each individual stakeholder group. They are however also so large that they need to concern themselves with macro issues of economy, food and fuel commodity volatility, risk management, changing regulations and geo-politics.

Farmers and Growers

These are the people who raise the animals for meat or grow the crops that are either sold to consumers in their original form or turned into a huge variety of food products sold indirectly or directly through food service or retail.

Even within this stakeholder group there are differences of opinion depending on type and size of farming system, geography and inherent weather patterns. In the UK for example there is a huge difference between production methods and the objectives of producers with a few hundred acres and producers with several thousand acres. Large producers are more concerned with volume production and differentiating their products and services. Smaller producers will struggle to compete on price so will be more likely to seek to differentiate their product based on provenance - what, how or where it was produced. For example, they may concentrate on a specific breed of beef that is highly sought after in restaurants, or they may promote the locality of where the product was grown or reared.

Ask farmers and growers what their perspective is regarding the main problems they face and they are likely to complain about the weather or how much they are paid for their produce. This is largely because food producers must commit to a whole season's cost and hard toil, with little or no control or influence on some of the key factors that will determine their success or failure. The prices they get at market, in addition to their controllable costs, ultimately determine the profitability of their farming activities and this often varies considerably from one season/year to the next.

It is this volatility, and resulting impact on individuals and farming enterprises, which has driven much of the ill sentiment in agricultural supply chains. This volatility is also the main argument for subsidies. A good year for a lamb farmer in the UK for example might mean £75 per lamb (£3.55 per kilogram - paid to a maximum of 21 kilograms)[21]. A bad year might mean £35 per lamb (£1.63 per kilogram)[22]. In November 2016, the average lamb price paid to UK farmers was £3.50 per kilogram while the average retail price for the same period was £6.92 per kilogram[23]. In potato production, a good year in the UK might mean £290 a tonne (equivalent to 29p per kilogram)[24]. A bad year might mean £100 a tonne or 10p per kilogram while the retail price remains relatively stable at 80p per kilo. These are extreme differences when factored over a whole flock or yield and can often make or break the producer. It's no surprise, therefore, that when farmers see imports sitting next to their produce on their local shops' shelves they find it inflammatory.

Of course, consumers, and therefore the retailers who serve them, have a different perspective. Lamb for example, is the most expensive of all the readily available meat options and though many consumers love it, they don't always consider it good value for money, especially when set against alternatives such as pork or chicken. As a result, consumers may only purchase lamb on a special occasion such as Easter or Christmas. For retailers, competitive pressures in the six weeks leading up to these two

---

[21] http://www.fwi.co.uk/business/prices-trends/

[22] Dafydd LO, (2015) Farmers hold crisis summit over 'critical' lamb price fall BBC News http://www.bbc.co.uk/news/uk-wales-33804496

[23] AHDB Beef and lamb UK Farm to Retail Data http://beefandlamb.ahdb.org.uk/wp/wp-content/uploads/2016/12/UK-farm-to-retail-091216.xlsx

[24] http://pages.fwi.co.uk/pdf/market-prices/FWMP_Potatoes.pdf

key seasonal periods can result in them buying lamb legs for over £8/kg and selling them for less than £5/kg. These sales periods can represent over 20 per cent of annual lamb sales or over 60 per cent of annual leg sales. In these instances, lamb is considered a 'loss leader' for the retailer. In other words, the retailer feels that they need to sell the lamb at a loss to ensure they don't lose customers to other retailers who may be running a similar promotion. As the centrepiece to the special meal, customers are more likely to choose where they shop based on this headline product and retailers cannot afford to lose the entire food basket for one of the most important shopping occasions in the annual calendar. Considering the typical lambing season in the UK is Spring, there is normally no, or very little, British lamb for the Easter market, and limited supply for the Christmas market. Retailers will therefore often source the lamb from New Zealand which can, depending on the time of year, be anywhere up to 50 per cent cheaper than domestic supply. It is perhaps no great surprise that a large percentage of lamb leg joints purchased in the UK are from New Zealand. Although consumers are not always just interested in price and wish to support domestic suppliers there are clear challenges for British lamb producers in the battle to remain viable. It's therefore quite easy to appreciate the wickedness of this particular problem in relation to the sustainability of individual domestic agricultural sectors.

This example highlights a dimension of trade that we touched on in the producers and manufacturers section. As consumers, we prefer certain parts of the animal over others. Modern eating habits in more developed countries have moved from cheap yet highly nutritious offal and less well known cuts to the 'best' part of the animal. Combine income constraints and cultural eating preferences elsewhere and the inevitable result is greater demand for certain parts of the animal over other parts, with little thought or regard for what happens to the rest. For a lamb or pig - the key cuts are the leg, the loin, the shoulder, the belly and the '5th quarter'. Clearly, it's impossible for farmers to raise animals with only the parts we like to eat. Meat processors must therefore buy the whole animal and seek to optimise "the value of the carcass". Thus, they kill animals in balance, importing cuts where there is more demand, and seeking to export, or further process (into ready meals, for example) cuts where there is less domestic demand. For sheep meat, whilst the UK might typically import legs from New Zealand, we also export shoulders to France. The UK currently imports nearly 18 million legs of lamb per year. For the UK to be self-sufficient in lamb legs domestic production would have to increase by 66 per cent. Many farmers would see this as a huge opportunity, but for one very important consequence – what to do with the additional 132,113 tonnes of other cuts and edible elements that would also come from the nine million additional lambs required to supply those 18 million legs. In case you are wondering, a leg of lamb is only ever the two hind legs - so each lamb can only supply two legs of lamb, not four. This additional lamb product is however unlikely to be absorbed by domestic or export markets considering total exports currently run at 79,000 tonnes[25]. Obviously, each cut is priced according to its individual supply and demand factors. For example, legs are more expensive because UK consumers want and value them; offal or unusual cuts are cheaper because hardly any consumers want them. This too impacts the price farmers are paid as the buyer must figure out the volumes and returns they can achieve for each cut, across domestic and export markets, across retail, processors, manufacturers or food service customers, against the assets and overheads they employ – all of which ultimately determines optimum kill levels and therefore their demand for finished animals from farms into their slaughterhouses.

The annual battle with the weather is also a major concern for producers all over the world. It's often the weather that will determine yield, year on year. This, of course, also impacts farm gate prices as the economic forces of supply and demand come

---

[25] Overview of Current UK Meat Import and Export Trade The International Meat Trade Association http://www.imta-uk.org/images/stories/pdf_docs/imports_paper/Overview%20of%20Current%20UK%20Meat%20Import%20and%20Export%20Trade.pdf

into play. A poor growing season due to weather reduces yield which reduces supply and therefore increases price. A good growing season increases yield which increases supply and pushes prices down.

Regulation is also a major part of food production – certainly in Europe. Directives comes out of Brussels about farm and land management, livestock rearing and movement as well as environmental considerations. What few people realise however is that directives are then individually interpreted by respective governments – each making decisions on a different set of factors, from a different perspective. On the ground, there is therefore considerable variation in how directives are implemented between countries - even countries operating within the same economic area. The regulations, legislation and documentation required for the production of meat in the UK is for example very different from that required in Greece or France simply because the UK government has often chosen the 'Gold Standard' implementation of specific directives. While some regulation is essential to maintain a high quality, safe food supply chain, most farmers and growers would claim that the amount of regulation is arduous, that there is considerable unnecessary duplication and that it takes a great deal of time to stay up-to-date. This regulation can also add costs to the supply chain that are not present in different parts of the world, often making 'home-grown' products more expensive. In addition, how subsidies are distributed in each country often goes to the very heart of consumer irritation in the idea. For example, while other EU countries institute a cap on payments, the UK doesn't[26].

Government

Government policy has had a profound impact on the food chain around the world, from the implementation of subsidy systems

[26] Deardon N (2017) Scrapping EU rules won't save UK farming. Supporting small farmers will The Guardian https://www.theguardian.com/commentisfree/2017/jan/05/scrapping-eu-rules-uk-farming-small-farmers-andrea-leadsom

to help farmers maintain a fair level of return to supply our food, to helping consumers to understand what is good and bad for us when it comes to food. The Department for Environment Food & Rural Affairs (DEFRA) in the UK for example states that it, "aims to play a major role in people's day to day lives, from the food that we eat, the air we breathe, to the water we drink" through safeguarding the environment, supporting the food and farming industry and sustaining a thriving rural economy.

The food industry is responsible for producing safe food. Government agencies are responsible for setting food safety standards, conducting inspections, ensuring that standards are met and maintaining a strong enforcement program to deal with those who do not comply with the defined standards. Government economic policies influence the demand for foods (through taxation for example), whilst educational strategies hope to stimulate particular food choices.

Many consumers look to government health advice to inform us what we should be eating more or less of in an effort to improve or maintain our health. And yet, government advice that we should eat fewer eggs or consume less cholesterol - or even that a low-fat diet is a good way to lose weight - have all been debunked or at least questioned in recent years[27].

What consumers are not always aware of is that lobby groups sometimes find their way onto working committees and advisory boards and therefore may unduly influence the 'advice' coming out of these groups – often in favour of the food they are lobbying for. Take for example the The American Pizza Community (APC), a coalition formed in 2010 to advocate for policies affecting pizza companies and operators including menu and labeling information. This lobby group succeeded in getting Congress to class pizza as a vegetable in school lunch programs in the US and

[27] Teicholz N (2015) The Government's Bad Diet Advice The New York Times http://www.nytimes.com/2015/02/21/opinion/when-the-government-tells-you-what-to-eat.html

is doing all it can to make sure that US pizza restaurants don't have to put calorie labels on their menus[28]. A study published in PLoS Medicine provided significant documentary evidence of sugar industry manipulation of research on dental cavities in the 1960s and 1970s. The archive of 319 industry documents, which were uncovered in a public collection at the University of Illinois, revealed that a sugar industry lobby group representing 30 international members had accepted the fact that sugar caused tooth decay as early as 1950, and adopted a strategy aimed at identifying alternative approaches to reducing tooth decay so they could continue their commercial concerns unabated[29].

As consumers, we need to be mindful that the advice coming from government can often change depending on the political party in charge and the advice itself may be significantly influenced by what action will gain votes. That said, government advice is probably more reliable than most sources.

Government as a stakeholder group is further complicated by the political system itself and how decisions are made[30]. Political appointments may change and decisions on food policy may be subject to competing interdepartmental priorities. For example, the Ministry responsible for Agriculture may be influenced by the farming lobby and their desire to see 'fair' domestic farm gate prices and local/national sourcing policies. The Ministry responsible for the economy may be focused on the interests of the broader population and prefer to see the prices of core food products lower, be they imported or domestically produced. The Ministry responsible for health may be focused on how the food

[28] Nestle M (2013) Food Politics: How the Food Industry Influences Nutrition and Health University of California Press

[29] Kearns CE, Grantz SA, Schmidt LA (2015) Sugar Industry Influence on the Scientific Agenda of the National Institute of Dental Research's 1971 National Caries Program: A Historical Analysis of Internal Documents http://journals.plos.org/plosmedicine/article?id=10.1371/journal.pmed.1001798

[30] Watkins A and Stratenus I (2016) Crowdocracy: The End of Politics Urbane Publications, Kent

we produce affects public health and whether private businesses can help provide healthcare services, and the Ministry for the environment may be focused on different objectives again, such as conservation. Of course, without an understanding of how to effectively reconcile these different perspectives decisions may be changed repeatedly or even overturned adding to the potential chaos, confusion and inefficiency in the system.

Environmental Groups

For environmental groups, two of the primary issues with food are the destruction of our planet to make way for food production, and the welfare of people and/or species that are impacted in the process. Food production is one of the primary causes of biodiversity loss through habitat degradation, overexploitation of species such as overfishing, pollution and soil loss.

This loss of biodiversity is a global issue. Brazil, sometimes referred to as "the grower of the world" is, amongst other things, one of the world's top soybean producers. In the nine states of the Brazilian Amazon, an area globally significant to climate change, the land mass under intensive mechanised agriculture grew by more than 3.6 million hectares between 2001 and 2004 alone[31]. According to ecologist Philip Fearnside, considered one of the foremost authorities on deforestation in the world's largest tropical forest, while soybean has offered great economic opportunities for Brazil, soybean monocultures wipes out biodiversity, destroys soil fertility, accelerates climate change, pollutes freshwater and displaces communities – all to produce agrofuel and livestock feed[32].

[31] Morton DC et al (2006) Cropland expansion changes deforestation dynamics in the southern Brazilian Amazon Proceedings of the National Academy of Sciences USA (PNAS) vol. 103 no. 39

[32] Fearnside, P.M. (2001) 'Soybean cultivation as a threat to the environment in Brazil', Environmental Conservation, 28(1), pp. 23–38. doi: 10.1017/S0376892901000030. https://www.cambridge.org/core/journals/environmental-conservation/article/soybean-cultivation-as-a-threat-to-the-environment-in-brazil/191311DBCD27A85DBF078 2E989956867#

According to the WBCSD, a global organisation of over 200 leading businesses and partners working together to accelerate the transition to a sustainable world, our food system is broken. It contributes to climate change, water stress, desertification and ecosystem degradation. It's also a vast contributor to global emissions[33].

Whilst acknowledging the problems inherent in the existing food supply structures the World Wildlife Fund (WWF), who are arguably the environmental group with one of the broadest perspectives on the food industry and its associated impacts, also see an opportunity to influence the development of food production and consumption through holistic strategies to build more integrated healthy agro-ecosystems. In addition to the physical system thinking that is clearly required, encouragingly WWF also acknowledge the need for changes in human systems. Trillions of decisions and actions take place every day with visible and invisible impacts on society and the Earth. WWF understand that complex problems will not be solved with superficial solutions and are developing partnerships with other parts of the food value chain to work together on wiser answers.

There are also cultural and socio-economic issues and challenges that increasingly surface as a result of the globalisation of food. Environmental groups are frequently very active in these areas, often applying pressure to brands in developed countries to try to leverage and accelerate change in supply chains, often in less developed countries. They highlight some of the significant inequalities across regions, but also differences in consumer preferences and priorities. For example, the differences in animal welfare standards required to satisfy Brazilian chicken exports into the UK versus Asia, Africa and the Americas, as well as other parts of Europe. Or, modern slavery on Thai fishing

---

[33] Bakker P (2016) Two Degrees for Food: Rebuilding the Global Food System http://www.wbcsd.org/Overview/News-Insights/Insights-from-the-President/Two-Degrees-for-Food-Rebuilding-the-Global-Food-System

boats, ultimately supplying into richer Western nations where consumers, quite rightly, find such practices abhorrent. Or different methods employed to catch tuna, and the implications for the unwanted by-catch. The issues are many and varied, and often they personify the wickedness of the food problem, where comprehensive sustainable solutions are rarely as simple as they might initially appear to be. For example, UK grocery demand for shrimp or chicken might only represent one or two per cent of the demand from some of the complex Thai or Brazilian supply chains highlighted above. This is not enough of a market to warrant a wholescale change in production practices.

Your perspective on acceptable trade-offs, whether in the UK, Brazil or anywhere else where the environment and food production potentially clash, will depend almost entirely on what stakeholder group you most strongly identify with and what you value most.

The Media

The media, as a stakeholder group, exert a huge amount of influence on the myriad of issues around food. Some would argue that the media are however driven by a desire to entertain or dramatise in order to drive sales or ratings, rather than to educate. As consumers, it would appear we can't get enough of food – and the media, whether print, online or TV provide us with endless stream of content. In the UK, 14 million people tuned in to watch the final of the 2016 Great British Bake Off. There are cooking channels and many nations have a plethora of 'celebrity chefs' – many with their own shows. But it's not just cooking. It seems we are interested in all things food with TV shows such as *Truth About Food. Trust Me I'm a Doctor* and *Tomorrow's Food* that explore various dimensions of the food industry. Even rural interest shows like *Countryfile* or *Landward (UK)*, which seek to educate consumers about rural issues and food production, prove surprisingly popular across non-rural demographics.

There is clearly an appetite for food in the media and they wield huge power to influence public opinion. In the early 1980s for example, UK MP Edwina Curry famously stated that, "most of the egg production in this country, sadly, is now affected with salmonella". Her poorly educated statement led to a 60 per cent crash in the demand for eggs[34].

In a modern media world where all that matters are online click throughs, real journalism, investigation and education are giving way to 'click-bait'. More and more in-house writers are being paid a small monthly retainer together with a fee for each set number of clicks their story generates. This often leads to the dumbing down of a story together with a sensational, provocative and even blatantly false headline in order to attract attention. For example, tentative early science linking microbial gut bacteria to obesity was pounced on by various newspapers with headlines such as "Fat? Blame the bugs in your guts"[35]. Although before the true 'click-bait' era, this type of sensational journalism presents what the newspaper believes will sell newspapers or gather online 'clicks' rather than informing readers about what the science actually found[36]. This is challenging both to the media who lose credibility over time and also consumers who are confused about who and what to believe.

Even taking a whistle stop tour of these stakeholder groups it's very easy to appreciate the staggering complexity of wicked problems like food where each stakeholder group will passionately defend an entirely defendable, but frequently opposing position based on competing priorities. It would be safe to say that none

[34] Doughty E (2015) Edwina Currie: 'I never stopped eating eggs' The Telegraph http://www.telegraph.co.uk/food-and-drink/news/edwina-currie-eggs-salmonella/

[35] Highfield R (2007) Fat? Blame the bugs in your guts The Telegraph http://www.telegraph.co.uk/news/science/science-news/3295620/Fat-Blame-the-bugs-in-your-guts.html

[36] Yong E (2016) Gut reaction: the surprising power of microbes The Guardian https://www.theguardian.com/science/2016/aug/25/gut-reaction-surprising-power-of-microbes

of those stakeholder groups see the challenges the same way and certainly don't all agree on how to manage them.

Making real headway in tackling wicked problems such as food production and supply is especially thorny because the responsibility for finding a workable solution almost always cuts across many groups of people who may not naturally all be aligned on the problem, the cause or the solution.

The solutions for most stakeholders therefore comes down to a matter of judgement about what is 'better', 'worse', 'good enough' or 'not good enough'. If we can't define the problem or the definition varies depending on the stakeholder we ask, then it is difficult to generate an accepted objective definition of the problem let alone the quality of the solution. Finding solutions when there are so many stakeholders with such different views is almost impossible and more often than not negotiations or discussions end in deadlock.

2nd Aspect of a Wicked Problem: Multiple Causes

Not only do wicked problems involve multiple stakeholders they also have multiple causes. Of course, different stakeholders hold different views about the causes of any problem. The conversation is more about creating an integrated understanding of all the various factors that may be at play in the genesis of any problem rather than taking an overly simplified single factor view. Such a shift in the focus of the conversation drives us in the direction of precision and balancing the complexity of different causes rather than coming up with oversimplified sound bites.

This more nuanced approach doesn't mean it's impossible to rank the degree of contribution of any single factor. For example, a crowd of stakeholders may take the view that in the debate about food the top two 'big issues' are quantity and quality. Do we have enough food to feed a growing global population? And if we do, is that food sufficiently safe, nutritious and accessible to ensure that we solve the planet's malnutrition problem once and for all – whether too little food or not enough of the right type of food.

Of the two issues, quality is much more complicated and involves many different factors including the nutritional value of the food, calorific value of the food, food purity, likely interactivity between certain food and gut flora, and so on. Ultimately what may be considered important in the nutritional quality debate is whether the food we eat delivers the nutrients we need to thrive and/or does the food we eat contain any ingredients that are actively harming us? This is a considerably more complicated issue than many who raise the quality issue would like us to believe.

With some problems, it can help significantly to understand the cause of the problem in its historical context. This is certainly true of many health-related issues[37]. It's also true for food. If we really want to find a wise solution to the ongoing challenges we need to solve in the food supply chain we need to appreciate as many of the causes or potential causes for those challenges as possible.

When looking at the food industry many observers would consider the passing of the Agriculture Act in 1947 as one of the most significant changes to the industry in the last seventy years, certainly in the UK. Deliberate bombing of food and supply ships bound for Britain during WWII highlighted the UK's lack of food security and the Agriculture Act was passed to increase self-sufficiency and lower the amount of food imported into Britain. In 1962, the Common Agriculture Policy (CAP) implemented a system of agricultural subsidies and other programmes. Some sort of government support for food producers is now operational in many places including the countries in the European Union, the US, Canada, South America, Africa and parts of Asia.

---

[37] Le Fanu, J (1999) The Rise and Fall of Modern Medicine Little, Brown and Company, London

Although there are signs of change in various subsidies systems, most of the initial incentives rewarded producers for focusing on increased yield. This frequently meant production moved from traditional crop rotation to large-scale monoculture. Different crops thrive best in different types of soil with different nutrient content. Crop rotation is when a producer grows one crop one year and a different crop the next year and so on – rotating what's grown on a specific piece of land. With rotation, a crop that utilises one type of nutrient ratio during the growing process is followed by a crop in the next growing season that utilises a different nutrient ratio thus allowing the soil to replenish. Crop rotation also mitigates the build-up of pathogens and pests that can occur when one crop is continuously grown. This approach helps to maintain soil structure and fertility by increasing biomass from varied root structures.

However, at a time when increased yield was the primary objective crop rotation fell out of favour and monoculture or the continuous growing of one crop took precedence. It was much more efficient. Hedgerows were pulled up to create larger fields that could accommodate the new equipment that could harvest the crops quicker, chemical fertiliser was added to return at least some of the nutrients to the soil (predominantly nitrogen, phosphate and potassium) and pesticides were used to temper the pathogens.

In meat production, animal breeds were changed to those that grew more quickly and intensive farming methods emerged. Large agribusinesses entered the food production industry around the world to capitalise on subsidies and maximise potential profits.

As a solution to food security and lack of food, introducing subsidies and incentivising food production and productivity worked but there is growing evidence that the focus on yield has decreased the nutrient content and purity of the food produced which may be having a significant knock-on effect on our health[38]. In addition, large landowners, whether estate owners or agribusiness, started to make serious money from subsidies and stories of six and seven figure payments, quite rightly, incensed the general public[39].

This type of outcome is typical in wicked problems where the solution to one challenge increases the risk of gamification which can unintentionally create new problems. Blindness to such potential distortions or knock on 'domino' effects can have very negative consequences as we all experienced following the global financial crisis of 2008.

In the US subsidies are frequently cited as a cause for escalating childhood and adult obesity. Congress and the Department of Agriculture are spending more than $1.28 billion annually to subsidise a handful of crops including corn and soybean used as additives in cookies, confectionery, fizzy drinks and other high calorie low nutrient 'junk food' – the primary contributors to obesity. The famous 'Twinkie' contains 14 ingredients made with highly subsidised processed ingredients, including corn syrup, high fructose corn syrup, corn starch and vegetable shortening – none of which would be considered remotely healthy by a qualified nutritionist. Of the $277 billion spent on US subsidies between 1995 and 2012, about $81.7 billion went to subsidise corn and $26.3 billion went for soybeans. In contrast, the government provided only $637 million to support fruit or vegetable growers[40].

Clearly, subsidy systems around the world need constant review to ensure the balance is appropriate. In Europe, there is some

---

[38] Dirt Poor: Have Fruits and Vegetables Become Less Nutritious? Scientific American https://www.scientificamerican.com/article/soil-depletion-and-nutrition-loss/#

[39] BBC News (2012) Rich landowners paid millions in farming subsidies BBC website http://www.bbc.co.uk/news/uk-17225652

[40] Pianin E (2012) How Billions In Tax Dollars Subsidize The Junk Food Industry The Fiscal Time Business Insider http://www.businessinsider.com/billions-in-tax-dollars-subsidize-the-junk-food-industry-2012-7?IR=T

appetite for change. In the UK change is inevitable post Brexit. Considering that in 2015, the top 100 recipients of the CAP received £88 million in agricultural subsidies then change is definitely needed. Especially when those recipients were already wealthy landowners such as the Queen, a Saudi Prince and the Duke of Westminster.

The danger is a regulatory 'race to the bottom' as highlighted by a stark report from the parliament's environmental audit committee warning that Brexit could "carry a triple jeopardy for UK farmers": loss of EU subsidies, trade barriers, and competition from "countries with lower food standards, animal welfare standards and environmental protection"[41].

Sensible solutions that reduce or eliminate subsidies, while maintaining our existing high standards, diversity and sustainability and encouraging new entrants into an aging industry are all needed for a thriving agricultural sector. In the US change may be harder to achieve as powerful lobbies seek to maintain the status quo. Of the $277 billion mentioned above a staggering 75 per cent went to just 3.8 per cent of producers – almost exclusively agribusiness[42].

If you ask farmers or growers what has caused the problems in food, many are likely to point to large-scale commercialisation and the emergence of powerful global agribusinesses and supermarket chains. They would wholeheartedly agree with the UN paper, *Agribusiness and the right to food* which points out, "Due to the deeply unequal bargaining positions of food producers and consumers on the one hand, and buyers and

---

[41] Deardon N (2017) Scrapping EU rules won't save UK farming. Supporting small farmers will The Guardian https://www.theguardian.com/commentisfree/2017/jan/05/scrapping-eu-rules-uk-farming-small-farmers-andrea-leadsom

[42] Pianin E (2012) How Billions In Tax Dollars Subsidize The Junk Food Industry The Fiscal Time Business Insider http://www.businessinsider.com/billions-in-tax-dollars-subsidize-the-junk-food-industry-2012-7?IR=T

retailers on the other hand, the latter can continue to pay relatively low prices for crops even when the prices increase on regional or international markets, and they can continue to charge high prices to consumers even though prices fall"[43]. This stakeholder group are likely to suggest that we may have more food as a result of global agribusiness and food manufacturers but we don't necessarily have better food. Not everyone would agree with those sentiments but they do exist in this stakeholder group.

Many of the large supermarket chains are in fact developing their approach – keen to foster strong, mutually beneficial long-term collaborations with farmers and producers as well as supplying partners. Clearly, it's easier to build strong, integrated relationships with a relatively small number of manufacturing partners and larger producers rather than each of the sometimes thousands of individual smaller producers. Considering these products will originate from tens of thousands of farms across different agri-sectors, across the world, as the growing calendar moves with the sun, it's easy to appreciate how challenging this might be. Hence the advent of 'producer groups' such as Tesco's Sustainable Dairy Group, which facilitates a 1:700 relationship where the retailer forms closer working relationships with 700 dairy suppliers, and the use of internet based supplier networks that now facilitate 1:1000s relationships via desktop and mobile app. This delivers against the simple premise that you can't trust anyone that you've never met or had any contact with, and the wider approach allows for greater understanding up and down the food chain, facilitating the sharing of common problems, information, insight and potential solutions across a broad set of stakeholders.

In their defence, global agribusiness will argue they have fed the world. Manufacturers would argue that it's them that have

---

[43] UN General Assembly (2009) Report of the Special Rapporteur on the right to food, Olivier De Schutter Agribusiness and the right to food https://www.globalpolicy.org/images/pdfs/SocEcon/2009/Hunger/agribusiness_and_the_right_to_food.pdf

transformed food and given us much more choice and variety than we used to have. They have created products for the modern world and allowed us to feed ourselves conveniently and without a great deal of effort or fuss. Retailers will argue that they have helped bring us those products, provided better quality at affordable prices, and made them available in one convenient location so we can save time and get on with our lives. Far from being part of the problem these stakeholder groups all passionately believe they are part of the solution – bringing consistency to the food supply chain and giving us year-round choice and predictable, affordable quality.

Shifts in social and technological trends have also contributed to changes in the food industry. What we as consumers want changes what is produced. More women are now in full-time employment. The idea of cooking a meal for the family after a long day at work isn't very appealing to many people, this is also true of those who live alone. Increasingly those individuals are turning to ready-meals and cook-in sauces as a convenient way to feed the family or themselves quickly. Those against our escalating reliance on processed food will argue that these foods contain too many preservatives and are usually too high in salt, fat or sugar. Such modern conveniences may be impairing the nutritional content of these foods and negatively impacting our health. We live in a society where millions of us watch cooking shows but the numbers of people who actually cook a meal from scratch is declining – especially in the west[44]. It's unlikely that is going to change and telling people to cook isn't going to help. We need better solutions.

Technology and innovation is also playing a role, not just in how we buy and source our food but the food supply chain itself. Many innovations have transformed the shelf life of the products

---

[44] Bevis E (2012) Home Cooking and Eating Habits: Global Survey Strategic Analysis Euromonitor International http://blog.euromonitor.com/2012/04/home-cooking-and-eating-habits-global-survey-strategic-analysis.html

we take for granted from ready-meals to fresh fruit. For example, retailers are increasingly consolidating and date coding the produce close to its origin, rather than its destination. Full trucks of fruit are now delivered directly from Spain, for example, which then by-passes additional pack-houses in the UK. This can add two days of freshness for the customer, helping to improve quality and reduce waste. These types of innovations can also reduce cost significantly, which again helps them to reduce prices, increase sales velocity and freshness, and encourage consumers to eat more healthy produce.

SmartFresh is used on a wide range of fruits and vegetables in over 26 countries to extend shelf life. *NatureSeal* adds 21 days to the shelf life of processed fruits and vegetables. Sliced apples don't turn brown, pears don't become translucent, melons don't ooze and kiwis don't collapse into a jellied mush, instead appearing fresh and natural. When we plump for the healthy option of a tub of fresh fruit from the petrol station we may, however, not be getting exactly what we imagine. But it's not just fresh fruit – manufacturers frequently use scientific tricks and innovations to provide a certain quality they require. *Microlys®* is a cost-effective speciality starch that gives "shiny, smooth surface and high viscosity". *Pulpiz*™, Tate & Lyle's tomato 'pulp extender' provides the same pulpy visual appeal as an all-tomato sauce, while using 25 per cent less tomato paste[45]. While many of these innovations are no doubt incredibly helpful and have their place in the food chain, they are usually classed as processing agents so they don't appear on the label. As a result, consumers tend not to know about them and we don't know if there are any long-term health impacts from these types of additives and innovations.

The point here is that, like all wicked problems, the causes of the food challenges we face very much depend on what stakeholder

[45] Blythman J (2015) Inside the food industry: the surprising truth about what you eat The Guardian https://www.theguardian.com/lifeandstyle/2015/feb/21/a-feast-of-engineering-whats-really-in-your-food

group you ask. Again, all of these points are true – at least partially. Remember, with wicked problems no one is 100 per cent right and no one is 100 per cent wrong – all perspectives usually contain some truth. The challenge is to find a way forward that can embrace as many views as possible rather than trying to privilege the view of one or two particular stakeholders. We need to see the entire system and take a system's view if we are to manage the complexity effectively never mind find a wise inclusive solution.

The simple truth is that every stakeholder group from 'farm to fork' and beyond has contributed to some extent to the situation we now find ourselves in. From the farmers and growers relentless pursuit of yield to maximise subsidy, to agribusinesses scale that has on occasion come at the expense of food purity, nutritional value, animal welfare or the environment, to processors and manufacturers making products that have contributed to our obesity crisis, to retailers promoting meat or short shelf life products aggressively to attract customers, to poor government policy unduly influenced by powerful lobbies inside the food industry, to the media more interested in a controversial headline than providing information for the consumer. We have all played our part. We buy our food without really thinking about what's in it or how it was made and, certainly in the West, we waste way too much of the food that we buy.

Collectively we have caused this problem and collectively we must find a way to come together and solve it.

3rd Aspect of a Wicked Problem: Multiple Symptoms

Not only do wicked problems involve multiple stakeholders, and have multiple causes that no one can agree on, but they also have multiple symptoms, i.e. the wicked problem manifests in a multitude of different ways. It is often these multiple symptoms that muddy the water when it comes to the various causes of the problem, and certainly can be very distracting to the media who have a penchant for reacting to the latest symptom of wicked problems. Reactivity may make for a powerful 'sound bite' or 'Tweetable moment', but too often the information is over-simplified or taken out of context. It represents a nibble of the corner or the problem. A *mange-bouche* of the real issue, not least because many of the symptoms of one wicked problem are also wicked problems in their own right.

For example, if you think about poverty and poor education, both are wicked problems and each is a symptom of the other. Poverty can be a symptom of poor education because unless an individual can gain at least a basic education where they can read, write and count, then it becomes much harder to secure a well-paying job.

Conversely poor education can also be a symptom of poverty because if a child is continuously sent to school without food because the parents can't afford breakfast, then that child will probably not have the concentration necessary to attain a good education that could help lift them out of poverty. In many developing countries, there may not be a school near-by, or the children may be removed from school and sent out to work to supplement the family income because the family is so poor. Of course, those children then never get the education that could help them break the poverty cycle.

Wicked problems are incredibly challenging to handle partly because of the deep interdependencies between causes, symptoms and potential solutions. We now live in a world where we are profoundly connected to each other and our actions impact on others whether we intend that impact or not. We are genuinely interdependent. Of course, if we don't understand the reality of our interdependency, it is easy to conclude that all problems are either your fault and your problem or my fault and my problem. If we consider that the problem is yours this makes it easier, at least in our minds, to ignore the problem or wash our hands of it because it has nothing to do with us. If it is 'my' problem, then 'I' am likely to wade in believing 'my' view is the only right definition and solution. Either way the problem persists because we don't collectively appreciate the connectivity between causes, symptoms and how proposed solutions can have an unintended knock-on effect in areas far removed from the original problem.

Take the emergence of global agribusiness as a case in point. When corporations moved into food production, manufacture and distribution their focus on efficiency and productivity created bigger yields which solved the problem of 'enough food' – certainly for the developed world. The unintended consequence of the move to large scale agriculture has seen the loss of close to four million mainly family owned farms in the US alone. Smaller farming operations tend to support local economies by providing jobs and spending money in local businesses. A University of Minnesota study showed that small farms with gross incomes of $100,000 or less made almost 95 per cent of farm-related expenditures within their local communities. These types of operations have a multiplier effect: for every dollar the farm spends, a significant percentage remains in the local economy, contributing to the economic health of that community. In contrast, large farms with absentee owners or agribusinesses with gross incomes greater than $900,000 made less than 20 per cent of farm related expenditures locally. This has a significant knock-on impact on economic prosperity within rural areas which affects jobs, local prosperity, other businesses in the community and job opportunities for local people. For example, the rural workforce employed on US farms dropped by about 50 per cent in the 1980s and 1990s[46]. Seeking to solve a food supply problem has therefore often exacerbated an employment and economic prosperity problem further deepening the rural/urban divide – albeit unintentionally.

---

[46] Food Economics http://www.sustainabletable.org/491/food-economics

It may be easy to turn our back on wicked problems, ignore the causes and pretend the symptoms don't exist, but the escalating interdependencies inherent in these issues means that they are not your problems or my problems– they are universally *our* problems, and pretending otherwise will simply mean they remain unresolved until enough of us realise the flaw in our isolationist mentality. We simply can't afford to stick our head in the sand indefinitely - we need to come together to find workable solutions.

4th Aspect of a Wicked Problem: Multiple Solutions

Clearly if a wicked problem involves multiple stakeholders, has multiple causes that no one can agree on, and displays multiple symptoms, then there will inevitably be multiple potential solutions.

There is a myriad of possible solutions to every wicked problem; which one is decided upon will depend on the stakeholders, their level of development, their agenda, their conviction in the root causes of the problem, and which symptoms they are seeking to alleviate first. There are also possible solutions that are never even considered.

In food, what is considered a solution will primarily depend on what part of the food problem you think is more important. If a stakeholder group believes that the over-riding challenge is one of access – just making sure we have enough food for the world to eat then the solution they propose is likely to involve streamlining food production systems, minimising waste or the pursuit of technology innovations such as precision farming or GMO.

If, however, a stakeholder group believes that the primary problem is food safety and nutritional content then the solution they are going to propose would be very different. They are likely to support at least a partial push back to organic production, cutting back on poor quality processed food, or finding ways to improve the nutritional content of highly processed food, encouraging a cooking revival and educating people how easy it is to make nutritious quick meals from scratch.

The possible solutions would change again if the stakeholder group was more concerned about the impact farming and agribusiness has had on our environment. They may believe that the countryside needs more protection and it's not even just about the production of food.

Ultimately whether a solution is 'good enough' or not will largely depend on the social context and who is making the assessment and the stakeholder's interdependent values and objectives. The interconnected nature of the causes and symptoms also means that binary 'right' and 'wrong' assessments are impossible. When it comes to wicked problems we need answers that represent the wisest way forward for now. Perhaps, instead of seeking a perfect solution we go for what is workable and better than the solutions we have now. Especially for wicked problems where there is no perfect solution. No single solution for food will solve all the issues we face; rather we need to assess all possible solutions and create a tapestry of workable initiatives that address all the challenges of the wicked problem.

5th Aspect of a Wicked Problem: Multi-Dimensionality

On top of the fact that wicked problems involve multiple stakeholders, have multiple causes and multiple symptoms which present multiple potential solutions they are also multi-dimensional.

All problems, including wicked ones are multi-dimensional. Understanding what 'multi-dimensional' really means and how it shapes all wicked problems (as well as all our lives) is absolutely key to being able to solve wicked problems such as food.

Figure 1.6 Ken Wilber's All Quadrants All Lines (AQAL) Model

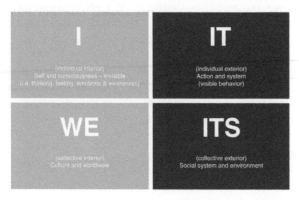

Every aspect of human experience - and every second of that experience - exists or is occurring in one or more of four critical dimensions. These dimensions were first identified by US philosophy Ken Wilber as individual interior ('I'), collective interior ('WE'), Individual exterior ('IT') and collective exterior ('ITS') (see Figure 1.6).

This may seem like an academic distraction in a book about solving the issue of food but it is absolutely crucial to understand the multi-dimensional nature of reality. Why? Because it is the lack of this understanding that is one of the primary reasons that we never solve the problem.

Allow us to explain these dimensions because if you can appreciate their existence it may just change the way you approach this or frankly any problem. Right now, as you read the words on this page thoughts may bubble up. Thus, you might be thinking, "What have these dimensions got to do with food?" Whatever thoughts and feelings you are having right now they are your own personal invisible inner response. No one else knows what you are thinking or feeling at this moment. You are having a subjective experience to what is written. This is your interior dimension of 'I' or 'being'.

In addition to this inner subjective experience you are simultaneously doing something. For example, you may be reading this book on the train to work. As you approach your stop you will probably put the book or e-reader away and make your way toward the exit ready to disembark. You can be seen leaving the train. This is your observable behaviour and that is happening while you are still thinking. As you get off the train your experience is both individual interior 'I' and individual exterior 'IT'. This 'IT' dimension is what you are personally 'doing'.

When you exit the train, you might bump into two of your colleagues and you start talking to them. This conversation is observable so there is an 'IT' or social convention that you are all doing. But while you are chatting what cannot be seen is the unwritten social rules that exist between you and your colleagues. The norms of social interaction, the acceptable level of banter that exists in your group and the degree of trust between you - the interior of your relationships. None of this can be seen. This is the 'WE' dimension of 'relating'.

Of course, each individual experiences the cultural norms or 'WE' in your group slightly differently through their own subjective 'I' experience. But you all know exactly who your colleagues are; you know who belongs and who doesn't belong. You can't see this 'WE' connection 'out there' in the exterior world; just as your interior 'I' experience can't be seen 'out there' in the objective world. But none of your colleagues doubt the existence of this shared knowledge. No one doubts the existence of the shared dimension that makes up the relationship. Each 'I' being in that 'WE' group feels connected, strongly or weakly to every other 'I' in the group through the 'relating' dimension.

Every single moment of our lives occurs simultaneously in all dimensions; 'I', 'WE', 'IT', and 'ITS'. The problem is that we just don't realise this. Or if we do, we certainly don't see the relevance or importance of this insight. This deceptively simple frame allows us to understand a good deal of the complexity of the modern world, and explains why some of the most intractable wicked problems have become so intractable.

The reason this is extremely important is that all problems, and particularly all wicked problems have an 'I', 'WE' and 'IT(s)' dimension. The 'IT' or 'doing' dimension includes all observable interactions plus all objective systems and processes. The 'WE' or 'relating' dimension embraces the unseen interpersonal dynamics, degrees of trust, depths of understanding, quality of rapport that exist on the inside of our relationships rather than the fact that there is a relationship.

When we search for solutions to the challenges we face the common tendency is to focus almost exclusively on the exterior objective dimensions. In other words, we only consider behaviour ('IT') or systems and processes ('ITS') in the world of 'doing'. What are people doing about the problem? What systems and structures do we need to put in place to make this situation better?

Most efforts to solve a problem, including the issues surrounding food are focused on exterior solutions. Either changing individual behaviour – "We need to educate people about obesity" or "We need to encourage people to cook more". These are 'individual exterior', 'IT' or 'doing' manoeuvres trying to change individual behaviour. But on their own they will not solve the problem. In the doing dimension the alternative to targeting individual behaviour is to target the system itself and try to improve food production processes, minimise waste and streamline distribution. These are 'collective exterior' 'ITS' manoeuvres. Again, these 'ITS' solutions are also an important part of a coherent approach but they will not work in isolation either.

The approach to complex and wicked problems is often to focus almost entirely on exterior 'doing' ('IT'/'ITS') and completely ignore the dimensions of 'being' ('I') and 'relating' ('WE'). This is despite the fact that all wicked problems are essentially human problems deeply rooted in the 'I' and 'WE' dimensions. Everything from escalating terrorism to global warming to corruption to poverty to the dysfunction of the world's governance systems or the inadequacy of the world's food production and distribution systems all require individuals to change what they are 'doing' in significant numbers. But this only happens if we change our inner beliefs and evolve our values. We also need to connect much more effectively with others whether they are like-minded or have diverse opinions from ours. In the end, it is individuals who start to think differently about a problem, because they feel differently and this allows them to connect differently and this causes them to push through the change that alters what we all end up 'doing' in the world. We can already see this phenomenon in the food supply chain, certainly in the West, with more people thinking differently about food and developing greater awareness of where our food comes from, how it's produced – including a growing demand for transparency and higher animal welfare.

We can't solve what we don't appreciate
A lack of awareness of the multi-dimensional nature of the challenges we face from the very start means that our attempts to solve wicked problems will continue to fail. If we keep taking a one dimensional, partial approach to multi-dimensional issues then we should not be surprised by our lack of progress.

Part of the complexity is tied up in the way we think about a problem. Many people tend to operate from an "I'm right, you're wrong" mindset. This makes it difficult to connect successfully with others as they also think the same way. The result is an argument about who is right rather than seeing the value of each person's perspective.

Unfortunately, such a binary approach fails to recognise that no one is smart enough to be right 100 per cent of the time. Which equally means no one is wrong 100 per cent of the time either. It's much more likely that both parties bring important considerations to the table – thus illuminating more of the complexity of the problem which invariably gets us all closer to a wiser solution. Being able to engage with the wicked problem with some humility and preparedness to open up to other people's views is vital for success. And by this we do not mean lip service. We mean genuine open-hearted interest as to why someone thinks differently or even oppositely from our own position.

Such openness is especially important because there are no clear simple or obvious answers to wicked problems. There are layers of complexity and interdependencies. No one person's solution is going to be 100 per cent correct or 100 per cent incorrect. We simply have to remain open to ideas from others, be able to seek out the value in diverse views and effectively integrate multiple perspectives to define a wise way forward. And the diverse views we must integrate have to address all dimensions of the problem, the 'I', 'WE', and 'IT'/'ITS' or they will continue to fail.

Take Ukraine, as an example. The country is deeply divided with the west of the country leaning towards the European Union and the east of the country leaning towards Russia. One of the many issues currently facing the country is security. If you are working in a government building in the unstable east of the country you might think the best way to address the security of the building is to erect a fence and place armed guards on the gates. This 'gates, guards and guns' approach is clearly the 'IT' answer to the security problem. But it does very little to reduce the feelings of fear for the people working in the building. In fact, when they look out and see all the guards they are quite likely to feel more fearful. Taking a simplistic 'IT' approach fails to address the much wider relationship problems between Ukraine and Russia and the West. Thus, you cannot solve an interior problem (fear) by only employing an exterior solution (gates, guards and guns). Neither can you solve an exterior problem, like people attacking the building, by telling people to "stop worrying" (a particularly poor attempt at an interior solution).

The difficulty in solving wicked problems is amplified by complexity in each dimension. The 'IT'/'ITS' dimensions are for example, affected by global megatrends often described using the PESTLE acronym (Political, Economic, Social, Technical, Legal and Environmental).

Political Complications

This external lens can be applied to any topic including food. Food is most definitely a political issue although how much depends on the country you live in and the political mileage food has with the electorate. For example, Pew Research found that 71 per cent of Chinese consumers considered food safety to be a major issue and looked to government to improve quality standards[47]. This pressure led to China's revised Food Safety Law, enacted in October 2015, which is intended to strengthen the regulation of food companies in China and enhance oversight along the supply chain[48].

Government policy in any area can and does have a profound impact on legislation which ultimately affects all stakeholder groups from consumers to the various businesses up and down the food supply chain. Needless to say, powerful lobby groups working on behalf of these stakeholder groups seek to get to the ear of politicians so they can influence that policy and legislation and protect their own commercial interests.

Economic Complications

The economic consequences created by our food challenges represent losses of gross domestic product (GDP), each year, of 10 per cent—far greater than the annual percentage loss in world GDP due to the global financial crisis of 2008–2010[49].

---

[47] Wike R, Parker B (2015) Corruption, Pollution, Inequality are Top Concerns in China http://www.pewglobal.org/files/2015/09/Pew-Research-Center-China-Report-FINAL-September-24-2015.pdf

[48] China's Food Safety Law (2015) http://gain.fas.usda.gov/Recent%20GAIN%20Publications/Amended%20Food%20Safety%20Law%20of%20China_Beijing_China%20-%20Peoples%20Republic%20of_5-18-2015.pdf

[49] Horton, S., and R. H. Steckel. 2013. "Malnutrition: Global Economic Losses Attributable to Malnutrition 1900–2000 and Projections to 2050." In How Much Have Global Problems Cost the World? A Scorecard from 1900 to 2050, edited by B. Lomborg, 247–272. Cambridge, UK: Cambridge University Press.

As mentioned earlier, malnutrition and poor diet are key drivers of the global burden of disease and it's a burden born by both societies and individuals. In the United States, for example, when one person in a household is obese, the household faces additional annual health care costs equivalent to eight per cent of its annual income[50]. In China, a diagnosis of diabetes results in an annual 16.3 per cent loss of income for those with the disease[51]. All of these figures mean that the economic burden of malnutrition falls heavily on all of us, whether we are personally affected or not. The NHS costs of treating overweight patients and those affected by obesity, and related morbidity in England alone have ranged from £479 million in 1988 to £4.2 billion in 2007[52]. Estimates of the indirect costs i.e. those costs arising from the impact of obesity on the wider economy such as loss of productivity, range between £2.6 billion[53] and £15.8 billion[54]. It's not all bad news though – these figures present a huge opportunity. Preventing malnutrition delivers $16 in returns on investment for every $1 spent[55].

Social Complications

In addition to the political and economic impact of food, social changes are also influencing what food we buy. Certainly, in

---

[50] Su, W., J. Huang, F. Chen, W. Iacobucci, M. Mocarski, T. M. Dall, and L. Perreault. 2015. "Modeling the Clinical and Economic Implications of Obesity Using Microsimulation." Journal of Medical Economics 18 (11): 886–897.

[51] Liu, X., and C. Zhu. 2014. "Will Knowing Diabetes Affect Labor Income? Evidence from a Natural Experiment." Economics Letters 124 (1): 74–78.

[52] Butland B, Jebb S, Kopelman P, et al. Tackling obesities: future choices – project report (2nd Ed). London: Foresight Programme of the Government Office for Science, 2007.

[53] National Audit Office. Tackling Obesity in England. London: The Stationery Office, 2001.

[54] Butland B, Jebb S, Kopelman P, et al. Tackling obesities: future choices – project report (2nd Ed). London: Foresight Programme of the Government Office for Science, 2007.

[55] Global Nutrition Report 2016: From Promise to Impact, Ending Malnutrition by 2030 http://ebrary.ifpri.org/utils/getfile/collection/p15738coll2/id/130354/filename/130565.pdf

the West, economic pressures on the family mean that both parents are often in full-time work. Limited time and energy after a long day at work has fuelled a global trend towards fast, easy and convenient food. Of course, these social norms often vary considerably from place to place which adds another layer of complexity to the issue.

Another social trend that is influencing food is our attitude to waste. We live in a consumer, 'throw-away' society which encourages us to buy new rather than repair. This mindset has also flowed into food and many of us have become too comfortable with food waste, and don't see it as a huge problem. We have certainly become better at recycling to aid the environment so there is no reason why we couldn't become better at wasting less food, particularly if we were more informed about the impact that waste is having on the planet and our ability to feed everyone.

Technological Complications

Technical innovations have made a huge impact on both the production, manufacture, storage and distribution of food. Scientific innovations such as precision farming that allow growers to monitor a range of variables in their crop to better utilise resources and improve output are increasingly widespread and show distinct further promise. Other innovations such as Genetically Modified Organisms (GMO) may also prove beneficial in the long term but they are highly controversial.

GMO is a polarising issue. On one hand the results of a long-term research study indicate that GMO does not necessarily increase yield or require less pesticides to produce – two of the central arguments for their introduction and continued use[56]. Those concerned about food safety and against GMO will point

---

[56] Hakim D (2016) Doubts About the Promised Bounty of Genetically Modified Crops The New York Times http://www.nytimes.com/2016/10/30/business/gmo-promise-falls-short.html?smid=tw-nytimes&smtyp=cur&_r=0

to this study and ask the question, "If GMO is not increasing yield or reducing our dependency on chemical pesticides then why use GMO at all?" And it's a legitimate question – especially if the study is scientifically verified.

But GMO isn't just about better crops it is also about human health. The World Health Organization (WHO) state that GM foods currently available on the international market have passed safety assessments and are not likely to present risks for human health. In addition, no effects on human health have been shown as a result of the consumption of such foods by the general population in the countries where they have been approved[57].

Human beings have been changing animals and plants through selective breeding for generations, so the idea itself is not new. What's new however is the name 'Genetically Modified Organisms' and the fact that companies now own the patents to these new crop breeds. This means there is a much stronger profit motive driving change. Of itself this is not a bad thing, a strong profit motive is an engine that drives innovation but it certainly means we need to be much better informed and assess GMO with absolute, independent rigour. Given the likelihood that effective commercial operations could lead to the very widespread adoption of GMO technology, which would, if problems arose mean the problem could instantaneously become global with little recourse to reverse the spread of GMO material around the world.

Much of the resistance to GMO is down to the fact that it sounds scary and many people don't really understand the technology or the risks. Eating something that is 'genetically modified' simply doesn't sound great – so there is a real marketing and branding nightmare for those involved in the area. Second, the distaste

---

[57] WHO Frequently asked questions on genetically modified foods http://www.who.int/foodsafety/areas_work/food-technology/faq-genetically-modified-food/en/

around GMO also comes from the widely reported litigious business practices of some of the companies who create these new plant breeds[58].

If we are to meet the demands of a growing population however, we will almost certainly need to wrap our head around GMO. We may need to get over the label 'GMO' and separate the science fact from the science fiction. We will also need to address any personal dislike we may feel toward the companies at the forefront of this technology in order to make enough food for everyone on the planet.

At this point, there are probably bigger issues than GMO to address. Since a great deal of animal feed, already contains GMO it is already in the food chain and there is no going back. And that is true, even in Europe where legislation on GMO in food for human consumption is still tightly regulated.

On the upside, the experts and scientists we interviewed for this book all believed that our fears around GMO are completely overplayed in the media and tend to get mixed up in the negative press around the companies that create them[59]. GMO is almost certainly part of our future food solution, especially when little tweaks in genetics can make seeds more likely to grow in certain geographic areas with different climates, resist insect damage or viral infections or deliver higher nutrient content. In the future GMO are likely to include plants with improved resistance against drought, which could be increasingly important if we don't address the other wicked problem of climate change.

---

[58] Organic Seed Growers and Trade Association, et al., v. Monsanto Company, et al. Supreme Court Case No. 13-303.
RT (2013) US farmers challenging Monsanto patent claims appeal to Supreme Court https://www.rt.com/usa/monsanto-patents-lawsuit-supreme-court-487/

[59] Interviews conducted in December 2016

Legal Complications

The legal issues surrounding food are immense. The regulation that governs food production varies considerably from country to country. Many of the stumbling blocks in 'free-trade' agreements congregate around different regulation. The Transatlantic Trade and Investment Partnership, more commonly known as TTIP was roundly criticised by the consumers in Europe because European legislation is considerably stricter than US legislation. In the US, a substance can be used until it's proven unsafe whereas in Europe a substance has to be proven safe before it can be used. As an example, the EU currently bans 1,200 substances for the use in cosmetic production whereas the US currently bans 12[60]. Through the TTIP the US are pushing for 'regulatory convergence'. The fear is that this convergence is actually a euphemism for the lowering of EU standards and would lead to products currently not allowed into EU being allowed to enter the single market. For example, US beef raised using growth hormone and an over reliance of antibiotics in intensive rearing systems is currently banned in Europe but this could change.

This issue is now even more relevant in the UK following the 2016 referendum vote to leave the European Union. As a sign of things to come, Conservative MP Jacob Rees-Mogg said regulations that were "good enough for India" could be good enough for the UK – arguing that the UK could go "a very long way" in rolling back high EU standards[61]. There is now a very real possibility that many of the hard-fought and often constructive EU environmental and safety standards could be swept aside along with much of the draconian red tape madness that has caused so much ill-will toward European bureaucrats. There is

---

[60] Williams L (2015) What is TTIP? And six reasons why the answer should scare you The Independent http://www.independent.co.uk/voices/comment/what-is-ttip-and-six-reasons-why-the-answer-should-scare-you-9779688.html

[61] Stone J (2016) Britain could slash environmental and safety standards 'a very long way' after Brexit The Independent http://www.independent.co.uk/news/uk/politics/brexit-safety-standards-workers-rights-jacob-rees-mogg-a7459336.html

little doubt that too much regulation can cause more harm than good and it can stifle innovation and growth but used correctly it can also be a powerful force for good, protecting the environment and people who may not be able to protect themselves. Surely a more rigorous look at individual regulation, potential duplication and their respective interdependencies along with their positive and negative consequence, unintended or otherwise is a much wiser way forward than the carte blache reduction in regulation or mirroring regulation in countries where the very lack of regulation has already caused significant environmental and food safety problems or workforce exploitation.

Regulation is an incredibly complex and thorny issue in food production and presents additional complex challenges to producers, manufacturers and retailers seeking to streamline global food supply systems.

Environmental Complications

Finally, there are also significant and varied environmental concerns in relation to food production. For example, deforestation is a major issue in Asia and South America – where huge tracts of forest are cleared to make way for crops such as soy, palm oil or to rear cattle. This repurposing of land can destroy animal habitat and often also significantly increases greenhouse gas emissions.

Given that food systems - growing food and animal feed, making and transporting food, cooking, eating and throwing food away - accounts for just under a third of greenhouse gas emissions, food alone has the potential to use up the entire Paris climate agreement's carbon budget to keep climate change to well below two degrees centigrade[62]. According to the World Resources Institute if food loss and food waste were its own country it would be the third largest greenhouse gas emitter after

---

[62] Benton T (2016) What will we eat in 2030? World Economic Forum
     https://www.weforum.org/agenda/2016/11/what-will-we-eat-
     in-2030?utm_content=buffer5ac1f&utm_medium=social&utm_
     source=twitter.com&utm_campaign=buffer

China and the United States. It is these types of conflicts – our escalating demand for food to feed an expanding population and our simultaneous need to tackle climate change that add still more levels of complexity to the food problem.

On top of generating emissions, food production and distribution puts additional pressure on already scarce resources of land, water and energy. Other environment issues that are causing concern are land grabs by wealthy countries aware of their impending food shortage, buying up cheap land in developing countries[63].

Considering that each of these PESTLE lenses can also be viewed from the multiple dimensions of 'I', 'WE', 'IT' and 'ITS', it becomes very easy to see just how challenging it is to solve these wicked problems. However, taking a multi-dimensional approach can profoundly improve our ability to solve them because it allows us to better identify all the issues that make the problem wicked and therefore must be addressed to create a successful solution. This complete, integrated approach was used by Foundation Paraguay - consistently voted as one of the top two or three organisations in the world for effectively ending poverty[64].

Founder Martin Burt, former Chief of Staff to the President of Paraguay, started looking at poverty; and the first thing he noticed in all of the existing programs around the world was how narrowly they defined poverty. Again, most of them were focused almost exclusively on the 'ITS' quadrant in some version of the PESTLE framework. Instead, Burt gathered evidence of what poverty looks like *in all four quadrants*. This gave him, not just the standard half dozen or so PESTLE type items, but 50 elements, each explored from all four dimensions. The result was 200 'characteristics' of poverty. He then searched extensively for

---

[63] The Oakland Institute (2011) Land Grabs leave Africa Thirsty https://www.oaklandinstitute.org/land-deal-brief-land-grabs-leave-africa-thirsty

[64] http://www.fundacionparaguaya.org.py/?lang=en

programs and systems that showed some capacity to handle all 200 characteristics to create a total interwoven integral approach. Foundation Paraguay's success in tackling poverty and their recognition in the field is a direct result of employing this more inclusive and comprehensive methodology.

6th Aspect of a Wicked Problem: Constantly Evolving

Of course, all this means that wicked problems are also constantly evolving. The stakeholders involved in solving the wicked problem are constantly changing. The political will behind these problems also changes with regime change or cabinet re-shuffles. When Teresa May succeeded David Cameron as UK Prime Minister in 2016, she appointed Angela Leadsome as Secretary of State for Environment, Food and Rural Affairs. It has become her job to re-assess the subsidies system in the UK following Brexit amongst other things. Thousands of primary producers feared the worst when, displaying a worrying lack of awareness of ecology or hill farming she suggested, "It would make so much more sense if those with the big fields do the sheep, and those with the hill farms do the butterflies[65]." Whilst this may sound great to the environmentalists realistically we have competing priorities to manage in a constantly evolving political, economic and geographic landscape. And this is true for all countries around the world.

The stakeholders themselves are also personally evolving as their understanding, views and opinions change or hopefully develop over time. The causes are also constantly evolving: new causes are identified and new symptoms manifest.

---

[65] Tyrell K (2016) Dark days ahead for British agriculture? Or green shoots of a brighter future? Ecologist website http://www.theecologist.org/News/news_analysis/2988057/dark_days_ahead_for_british_agriculture_or_green_shoots_of_a_brighter_future.html

Each solution usually highlights a new, different and often conflicting aspect of the nature of the problem, so there is no end point. We will never reach a point where we can, for example, tick off 'poverty' as a task that has been completed and a wicked problem that has been eradicated. The problem-solving process as well as the problem itself is constantly shifting and evolving. It only ends when we run out of resources, be that time, money or the desire to solve it. Successive governments, for example, may shift their focus from one area to another because of their political persuasion, but the problems themselves are still there.

Tackling wicked problems is like playing that 'whack-a-mole' game at a funfair. As soon as you whack one mole, another two pop up somewhere else! But we must try. And we will only succeed if we are able to solve and re-solve them over and over again while taking their multi-dimensionality into account.

Wicked Problems Require Wicked Solutions

If we are serious about solving and re-solving wicked problems, we must recognise that the solution needs to be every bit as wicked as the problem it is designed to solve.

It has been suggested that there is no obvious answer to wicked problems but there is an obvious answer - the solution must match the nature of the problem. If the wicked problem involves multiple stakeholders, then the solution must involve and collaborate with all those multiple stakeholders. If the wicked problem has multiple causes, then the solution must take those multiple causes into account and expect and even anticipate multiple far-reaching repercussions. If the wicked problem has multiple symptoms, then the solution must address all those symptoms so as to ensure that at the very least the solution doesn't exacerbate those symptoms or create new, potentially worse symptoms! If the wicked problem has multiple potential solutions, then we must accept that we will need to implement multiple solutions before we can make any real progress. If we are facing a wicked problem that is multi-dimensional, then the solution must be multi-dimensional and address all dimensions. Finally, if the wicked problem is constantly evolving, then the solutions we implement must also constantly evolve.

Like all wicked problems, the challenges we face in the food supply chain are not simple to fix. Solutions in one direction will invariably cause separate challenges elsewhere. Different stakeholder groups will passionately defend their territory. The truth is that blame for the current food situation could be laid at all our doors. But the causes are nowhere near as important as the solutions and our collective will to find those solutions and make them work.

Many of the proposed solutions to humanity's food problem could easily be viewed as counterintuitive or even contradictory; but inclusive solutions are needed for wicked problems. Simplistic solutions don't work. Instead we need to remain open to finding a tapestry of answers that when taken together address as many of the issues we face as possible.

Tim Benton, Professor of Population Ecology and the UK Champion for Global Food Security at the University of Leeds makes an inspiring prediction around what we will be eating in 2030... "Although there are signs of a push-back against globalisation, its many benefits suggest that increasingly the historical divide between the 'developed' and 'developing' world will break down, and the issues, for every country, will be how to ensure access to culturally acceptable, healthy diets, that are affordable by the poor. This will involve both locally produced food and food traded from afar. Food systems are likely to diversify as markets simultaneously grow for local 'real food' as well as nutritious 'convenience food'. We won't have an 'organic world' or a 'big ag' world, we'll have both. But we must have better nutrition, less waste, and more sustainability

– otherwise we simply stack up ever more problems for the future[66]."

Surely, that's a vision we can all get behind.

Remember, the wicked problems we face are *shared problems*. We need to appreciate that we *are* all in this together and solving them and resolving them will need all of us, individually and collectively, regardless of what stakeholder groups we belong to or prioritise. We will need to coherently integrate all aspects of who we are and work together in this crucial endeavour. When we do, we can alleviate the suffering that flows from this and many other unresolved wicked problems.

However, we feel it's only fair to warn you that this book really is a book of two halves. The first three or four chapters can make for challenging reading as we dig into the problems we face in terms of food production and distribution. Don't give up! Chapter five pivots the book as we acknowledge those issues but also the converging forces of hope that indicate that we can collectively solve the problem. The final chapters take a closer look at how we might do that, through innovation and systems ('IT/S'), what we are personally going to do ('I') and the need for innovative inclusive collaborations ('WE'). A final wrap up chapter should help inspire you to embrace the challenge ahead and encourage others to do the same.

---

[66] Benton T (2016) What will we eat in 2030? World Economic Forum https://www.weforum.org/agenda/2016/11/what-will-we-eat-in-2030?utm_content=buffer5ac1f&utm_medium=social&utm_source=twitter.com&utm_campaign=buffer

Chapter 2:

Productivity and Escalating Food Inequality

The problems looming large in the future of food include how to ensure adequate production, supply, distribution, affordability, how to improve health, ensure quality and reduce waste. And, many of these issues take on greater significance depending on geographic location. Basically, getting enough food to survive and flourish is potentially going to be harder as the population rises and it's almost certainly going to be harder for some people more than others.

Although the UN state that we currently produce enough food to feed every man, woman and child on the planet those that really need it, often still don't get it[67]. The average amount of available food fit for human consumption (and after allowing for waste, animal-feed and non-food uses), per head globally improved to 2,860 calories per person per day in 2015 (see Table 2.1 for comparisons). Thus, there is currently enough food produced globally to go around. The problem is that it is not getting to those who need it or the right type of food is not getting to those who need it. Food inequality is already here and is a reality for billions of people around the world, in both the developing and developed world.

---

[67]   Feeding the World Part 3 FOA http://www.fao.org/docrep/015/i2490e/ i2490e03a.pdf

Table 2.1: Per capita food consumption (kcal/person/day[68])

	New historical data					Projections			Comparison 1999/2001	
	1969/ 1971	1979/ 1981	1989/ 1991	1990/ 1992	2005/ 2007	2015	2030	2050	New	Old
World	2 373	2 497	2 634	2 627	2 772	2 860	2 960	3 070	2 719	2 789
Developing Countries	2 055	2 236	2 429	2 433	2 619	2 740	2 860	3 000	2 572	2 654
-excluding South Asia	2 049	2 316	2 497	2 504	2 754	2 870	2 970	3 070	2 680	2 758
Sub-Saharan Africa	2 031	2 021	2 051	2 068	2 238	2 360	2 530	2 740	2 136	2 194
Near East/North Africa	2 355	2 804	3 003	2 983	3 007	3 070	3 130	3 200	2 975	2 974
Latin America and the Caribbean	2 442	2 674	2 664	2 672	2 898	2 990	3 055	3 200	2 802	2 836
South Asia	2 072	2 024	2 254	2 250	2 293	2 420	2 590	2 820	2 303	2 392
East Asia	1 907	2 216	2 487	2 497	2 850	3 000	3 130	3 220	2 770	2 872
Developed Countries	3 138	3 223	3 288	3 257	3 360	3 390	3 430	3 490	3 251	3 257

Original Source: http://bit.ly/2pwNCtt

Some 2.3 billion people still live in countries where food consumption is less than 2,500 calories per day and about half a billion live in countries where consumption is less than 2,000 calories per day. This problem is mainly felt in developing countries where reliable, consistent access to safe, nutritious food is not always possible.

At the other extreme some 1.9 billion are in countries consuming more than 3,000 calories per day. Without a corresponding increase in activity via exercise or a physically demanding job the consistent intake of more calories than the body needs will lead to weight gain, obesity and ill-health[69]. Although obesity is often viewed as a predominantly 'first world problem', obesity

---

[68] Alexandratos, N. and J. Bruinsma. 2012. World agriculture towards 2030/2050: the 2012 revision. ESA Working paper No. 12-03. Rome, FAO. http://www.fao.org/docrep/016/ap106e/ap106e.pdf

[69] World Agriculture Towards 2030/2050 The 2012 Revisionhttp://www.fao.org/docrep/016/ap106e/ap106e.pdf

rates tend to track with a nations prosperity, this often masks the truth – obesity is often a poverty issue not a wealth issue[70]. Obesity is more prevalent in low income areas, exacerbated by the reality that too many people are living in locations classified as 'food deserts' – a term used to describe an area that does not have ready access to affordable fresh, healthy and nutritious food due to lack of retail opportunities, availability or distance (see Figure 2.1).

Figure 2.1: **Food Deserts in the US**

23.5 million people live in urban neighborhoods and rural towns with limited access to fresh, affordable, healthy food, according to the USDA.

2.1
million households do not own a vehicle and live more than 1 mile from the nearest grocery store.

People of the poorest socio-economic status have
2.5 times
the exposure to fast food restaurants compared to those living in the wealthiest areas.

Low income zip codes have
30%
more convenience stores, which tend to lack healthy items, than middle – income zip codes.

150 – 200
jobs can be created by a large retail grocery market.

Modified from Original Source: http://bit.ly/2pcU1wN

If this is the reality now what happens when there are even more people on the planet?

Sir David Attenborough has frequently talked about the frightening explosion in human numbers. In 2016, he went further and stated, "We are a plague on the Earth. It's coming home to roost over the

---

[70] Levine JA (2011) Poverty and Obesity in the U.S. American Diabetes Association http://diabetes.diabetesjournals.org/content/60/11/2667.full

next 50 years or so. It's not just climate change; it's sheer space, places to grow food for this enormous horde. Either we limit our population growth or the natural world will do it for us, and the natural world is doing it for us right now[71]."

Looking at Figure 2.2 of the rise in human population now and projected into the future it's easy to appreciate his concern.

Figure 2.2: Population Growth

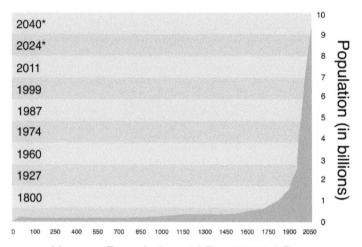

Human Population 1AD – 2050 AD

Modified from Original Source: http://bit.ly/2ojCRJR

The most obvious steps we could take to ensure we can feed everyone is to curb population growth. The best way to achieve that would probably be fertility education and access to safe and reliable birth control but this option is highly controversial due to religious belief. So controversial in fact that it's extremely

---

[71] Gray L (2016) David Attenborough - Humans are plague on Earth The Telegraph http://www.telegraph.co.uk/news/earth/earthnews/9815862/Humans-are-plague-on-Earth-Attenborough.html

unlikely population growth, which is another wicked problem, will be curbed via a change in policy from religious leaders. And this leaves us with the very real prospect of a world of 9.7 billion people in 2050.

If we refuse to tackle population growth, then we need to look elsewhere for a solution. Production is the logical next step. In order to produce more food to feed an escalating population there are really only two main strategies: increase yield and/or expand the amount of cultivated land used to produce food. There are also essentially two schools of thought regarding our ability to deliver on those goals – let's call them the optimists and the pessimists.

The pessimists believe that the world's agriculture resources are overstretched and incapable of meeting the population growth needs. This viewpoint usually gets more media attention because it makes for more sensational headlines. The pessimists will point to deep rooted environmental trends such as soil erosion or land productivity, desertification of cropland and the increasing conversion of arable land to non-farm uses such as urbanisation, falling water tables, rising temperature and the slowing of production capacity[72].

One of the ideas driving the pessimists is that they think we have already banked the majority of gains in food production and yield. In the last 50 years, aggregate food production has increased by 170 per cent. This has been down to greater efficiencies, improved breeding and husbandry techniques, mechanisation, increases in yield, higher cropping intensity from improved cropping techniques, fertilisation and irrigation[73]. For example, between 1960 and 2000, production of rice, maize (corn) and wheat grew by 66 to 88 per cent in Asia and Latin America. This

[72] Gardner B (2013) Global Food Futures Bloomsbury Academic

[73] Feeding the World Part 3 FOA http://www.fao.org/docrep/015/i2490e/i2490e03a.pdf

three-fold increase in yields of cereal crops was achieved by the introduction of high yield varieties, the application of chemical fertilisers and advances in crop management techniques[74]. In 1935 America, average corn yield was about 1.6 tonnes per hectare. By 2015 the average US corn yield was 11 tonnes per hectare, which is an astonishing increase of 687.5 per cent[75]. All these numbers are impressive and yet it is our previous success that makes the pessimists so concerned about our ability to feed the planet come 2050. They believe that we have already achieved the bulk of the gains we can expect. They tend to think that production capacity will slow down and may even fall away, especially considering the government and consumer pressure to phase out or at least reduce the use of chemical fertilisers, pesticides and herbicides.

In contrast, the optimists believe that a combination of science, technology, improved efficiency and husbandry together with reduced waste can and will meet the demand. They acknowledge that whilst many productivity increases may already have taken place, in some regions particularly, there is still plenty of opportunity to solve the problems we face if we work together. Global warming, competing demands for land, water and energy and escalating urban pressure will certainly create additional hurdles to jump but improved plant varieties, innovative production techniques, precision farming and irrigation together with more sophisticated land management may converge into a workable solution for the benefit of all.

Both of us are optimists although we readily acknowledge 9.7 billion people is a lot of mouths to feed! If enough of us start to think about the issue differently and work more effectively together then we can create a sustainable food supply and help protect the planet at the same time.

---

[74] Sanchez, P.A. (2010) Tripling crop yields in tropical Africa. Nature Geoscience, 3, 299

[75] Nature & US Chamber of Commerce

Let's explore our ability to increase production in more detail.

Production

The widely cited and much reported figure taken from Food and Agriculture Organization of the United Nations (FAO) research suggests that we will need to produce 70 per cent more food than we produced in 2005-2007 in order to meet the demands of such a huge population. That's a scary statistic. When digging around in this research it's interesting to note however that even the FAO acknowledge that this 70 per cent figure has taken on a life of its own. It has frequently been taken out of context to imply that increase should be in one food group over another or that this is what's required to feed the planet when actually the figure relates to the projected increases that are required to match the projected demand as they think those demands may develop (food, feed or biofuel), not what is "required to feed the projected world population or to meet some other normative target". Their revised figures suggest closer to 60 per cent of 2005-2007 levels but this 60 per cent is not just reflective of the demand for food for human consumption, it's demand for feed for animals and biofuel too[76]. While feed for animals is indirectly food for us, biofuel is not. As a result, there are considerable concerns around this type of energy generation, especially when people are still starving or don't have access to enough food.

These estimates also simply extrapolate our current consumption out into the future but if we appreciate what we are up against and take steps to tackle the problem properly then we may very well require an even smaller percentage increase in production. For example, even if we just reduce or eliminate the majority of food waste we will solve a huge part of the potential problem (more on that in the next chapter). The FAO acknowledge this

---

[76] World Agriculture Towards 2030/2050 The 2012 Revision http://www.fao.org/docrep/016/ap106e/ap106e.pdf

and point out that while this metric goes some way to highlight the scale of the challenge, its usefulness is limited. The volume index adds together very dissimilar products (oranges, grain, meat, milk, coffee, oilseeds, cotton, etc.) using price weights for aggregation.

What's also a little misleading about these often-quoted statistics is that they focus on aggregate world production increases. But considering we already produce enough food to feed the planet and that food doesn't reach the people who need it then these aggregate increases don't necessarily guarantee adequate production increases in the most vulnerable regions of the world. Hence the potential for continued food inequality.

According to the Global Agriculture Productivity (GAP) Index each region, with the exception of Latin America and the Caribbean, shows insufficient growth in total factor productivity (TFP) to meet future estimated food and agriculture demand. If current trends continue to 2030, the gap in East Asia will be 33 per cent; in South and Southeast Asia, 13 per cent; and in Sub-Saharan Africa, 82 per cent. And yet these are the very regions that are the most vulnerable[77]. Therefore, food inequality may get even worse.

It seems especially tragic that it is in the least prosperous and currently least agriculturally productive countries where TFP growth is most needed. This, of course, leaves those countries vulnerable to changes in the import market as they seek to import food to make up the shortfall. This can be costly depending on the market at the time. In 2008, the international food price index rose 54 per cent (compared with 2000) which meant that the food import bill for sub-Saharan Africa was estimated to have increased by close to 20 per cent[78]. This vulnerability is especially

---

[77] 2014 GAP Report® – The Global Agricultural Productivity (GAP) Index http://www.globalharvestinitiative.org/index.php/gap-report-gap-index/2014-gap-report/2014-gap-report-the-global-agricultural-productivity-gap-index/

[78] Gardner B (2013) Global Food Futures Bloomsbury Academic

pronounced in areas that are also more acutely impacted by climate change. As global weather patterns change it is often the countries that are already struggling to make enough food that are worse hit through extended droughts, flooding or other extreme weather events.

The Impact of Climate Change

Which option each country or region employs in order to increase food production (increase yield or increase cultivatable land) usually depends on which route is most viable or the availability of cultivatable land. In land-scarce regions of south Asia for example the bulk of increases in output will have to come from increased yield or increased crop intensity (growing crops more often). Where it is easier to reclaim cultivated land that approach may be employed first. Both options are however profoundly affected by climate change.

There is little real doubt that we are heating up the planet somewhere near 300 times faster than at any other time in our history. John Schellnhuber from the Climate Research Institute in Potsdam put it this way: "The possibility of a tipping point in the Earth system as a whole, which prevents the recovery of stable equilibrium and leads to a process of runaway climate change, is now the critical research agenda requiring the concentration of global resources in a 'Manhattan project' style of engagement." He concluded: "All other work on impact assessment, mitigation and adaptation depends on the outcome of this over-arching issue."[79] However, the consequences of this dramatic temperature change are far from straightforward. Extreme weather events, rising sea level, ocean warming and acidification, shrinking ice sheets, declining arctic ice, decreased snow cover and increased disease all impact our ability to produce food – certainly in the quantities that will be required to meet future needs. And these

---

[79] Wasdell, D presentation (2013) Sensitivity, Non-Linearity & Self-Amplification in the Global Climate System. The Annual Conference of the Club of Rome, Ottawa: 20th September 2013.

impacts are almost certainly going to be more severe in the places that are already struggling!

Extreme weather events

Not all extreme weather events are symptoms of climate change, but many are. There have and always will be storms and heatwaves and droughts, but the amount, frequency and severity of these extreme events are increasing[80].

The number of 'record high' temperature events have been increasing around the world. There is more rainfall and there are more storms. Hurricanes and other tropical storms get much of their energy from warm ocean water, and as the ocean gets warmer, the storms get more frequent and more violent - with stronger winds and heavier rainfall.

If you look at the US alone the number of annual billion-dollar climate catastrophes has risen sharply in the last few years. According to The National Centers for Environmental Information (NCEI), the US' scorekeeper for putting severe weather and climate events in their historical perspective, North America has sustained 200 weather and climate disasters since 1980 where overall costs reached or exceeded $1 billion (including CPI adjustment to 2016). The total cost of these 200 events exceeds $1.1 trillion. In 2016, there were 15 weather and climate disaster events with losses exceeding $1 billion each across the United States. These events included a drought event, four flooding events, eight severe storm events, a tropical cyclone event, and a wildfire event. Overall, these events resulted in the deaths of 138 people and had significant economic effects on the areas impacted. The 1980–2016 annual average is 5.5 events (CPI-adjusted); the annual average for the most recent five years (2012–2016) is 10.6 events (CPI-adjusted). Fifteen events, in 2016 alone represented the 2nd highest total number of events

---

[80] The Third US National Climate Assessment http://nca2014. globalchange.gov/highlights/report-findings/extreme-weather#submenu-highlights-overview

surpassing the 11 observed in 2012. The record number of events in one year (since 1980) is 16, as observed in 2011[81].

When these storms strike, higher sea levels result in greater storm surges and coastal flooding and damage. Increased temperatures and evaporation also means that tornados are more frequent and stronger. Of course, these storms cause significant damage, destruction and loss of life. They can also decimate crops.

As the Arctic warms up, wind patterns are also becoming disrupted, altering the course of the jet stream - making it 'wavier' with steeper troughs and higher ridges[82]. It was this alteration of the jet stream that plunged the UK into a nationwide 'white-out' in January 2013 when a NASA satellite image showed the entire British Isles under snow.

Figure 2.3: Map of Anticipated Impact on Agricultural Productivity

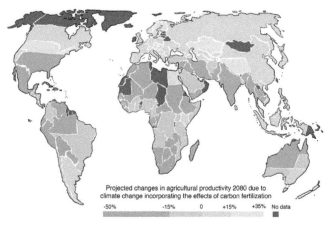

Projected changes in agricultural productivity 2080 due to climate change incorporating the effects of carbon fertilization

-50%   -15%   0   +15%   +35%   No data

Modified from Original Source: http://bit.ly/2ojCRJR

---

[81] Billion-Dollar Weather and Climate Disasters: Overview https://www.ncdc.noaa.gov/billions/

[82] Mulvaney K (2013) 10 Signs Climate Change is already happening http://news.discovery.com/earth/global-warming/10-signs-climate-change-is-already-happening-130422.htm

Weather systems are also moving more slowly, which in turn increases the chances of longer lasting extreme events like droughts, floods, extreme snow, heat waves and wildfires. These changes are also almost certainly going to be most severe in the Southern Hemisphere. This is because the Southern Hemisphere is already warmer so further increases in temperature become destructive faster thus diminishing the amount of sustainable land available for cultivation still further and further compounding food inequality for those areas.

Climate change will likely reduce acreage of productive farmland, decrease amounts of consumable water and reduce the amount of human habitable land - all of which will put even further pressure on areas that are already struggling to produce enough food.

Ocean warming, acidification and rising sea level

Another symptom of climate change is rising ocean temperatures and acidity which negatively impact marine life. Coral is dying and fish stocks are dwindling, which has a knock-on effect for the people who rely on either for their livelihood. In developing nations, fishing provides an income and food source for many who are then adversely affected when fish stocks diminish.

Rising sea levels are also causing problems. Using core samples, tide gauge readings and satellite measurements, it has been deduced that the Global Mean Sea Level (GMSL) has risen by four to eight inches (10 to 20 centimeters) over the past century. However, the annual rate of rise over the past 20 years has been 0.13 inches (3.2 millimeters) a year, roughly twice the average speed of the preceding 80 years[83]. This is causing coastal erosion and loss of land mass. This trend is, of course, extremely worrying - especially if you live near the sea! Thousands of coastal cities, like Venice, which witnessed historic flooding in 2008, face serious

---

[83] Sea level Rise National Geographic http://ocean.nationalgeographic.com/ocean/critical-issues-sea-level-rise/

problems. In Indonesia, 24 islands have already disappeared off the coast of Aceh, North Sumatra, Papua and Riau. In the capital city of Jakarta, the main international Soekarno-Hatta Airport could be below sea level as soon as 2030[84].

As well as the loss of land mass for cultivation or housing, rising sea levels can have a devastating impact on coastal habitats, polluting fresh water aquifers and agricultural soil, as well as causing the loss of plants, fish and birds. This of course also has a negative impact on food production.

Shrinking ice sheets and decreased snow cover

Clearly if the planet is warming up then the cold parts of the planet become warmer and ice sheets melt, which in turn increases the sea level. The Arctic Ocean around the North Pole is covered in ice all year around, although there is obviously some thaw in summer. However, the amount of summer ice is now the smallest it's ever been since scientists started measuring the ice with satellites in the 1970s. The ice is also significantly thinner.

In 1995, the Larsen-A ice shelf on the Antarctic Peninsula, collapsed. Sixty kilometres to the north, the Prince Gustav ice shelf collapsed and several more have disappeared in the last decade. The Antarctic Peninsula, the region that reaches northward toward the tip of South America, is the most rapidly warming part of the Southern Hemisphere, in which temperature increases of about 2.7 degrees Celsius over the last 50 years. In fact, in the Antarctic Peninsula, the degree of melting is a unique phenomenon in at least the last 1000 years[85]. During the second half of December 2016 British Researchers reported that a rift threatening the Larsen-C Ice shelf had grown by a further 18 kilometres. Only a final 20 kilometres of ice now connects

---

[84] BBC (2014) Indonesia: Rising sea 'threatens 1,500 islands' http://www.bbc.co.uk/news/blogs-news-from-elsewhere-26337723

[85] Mulvaney K (2013) 10 Signs Climate Change is already happening http://news.discovery.com/earth/global-warming/10-signs-climate-change-is-already-happening-130422.htm

an iceberg one quarter the size of Wales (about 5000 square kilometres) to Larsen-C[86].

These massive ice sheets and snow-covered land mass reflect a lot of sunlight back out to space, therefore preventing the planet from overheating. Shrinking ice sheets and less snow cover means that the earth is now absorbing that extra energy and exacerbating the problem. This is an example of a positive feedback loop, where warming causes changes that lead to even more warming.

The loss of snow cover on land also impacts fresh water supply. Snow that forms in the winter, melts in the summer and fills up lakes, rivers and reservoirs that supply fresh water for towns and cities as well as agriculture. As the temperature increases, there is less snow cover and therefore less fresh water - all when the global need for fresh water is already significant.

One of the more recently announced concerns of Arctic ice melt has to do with methane gas, of which enormous amounts are now stored in the Arctic, kept there by the sea ice sheet. In March 2010, Science reported the amount of methane trapped by Arctic ice is the equivalent of between 1,000 gigatons and 10,000 gigatons of carbon dioxide. For comparison, the total amount of carbon dioxide emitted by humans since 1850 is 1,475 gigatons.

This means that, according to a *Nature* July 2013 article, upwards of a "50 gigaton methane burp" is now "possible at any time". That means now. Such events would be catastrophic across the board. As well-respected climate researcher Paul Beckwith, at the University of Ottawa, put it, "It is my view that our climate system is in the early stages of abrupt climate change that, if left unchecked, will lead to a temperature rise of five to six degrees

---

[86] Luckman A and MIDAS team (2017) Larsen C Ice Shelf poised to calve http://www.projectmidas.org/blog/larsen-c-ice-shelf-poised-to-calve/

Celsius within a decade or two."[87] This would make virtually all farmland, and most ecosystems, unworkable. The last 'Great Dying' occurred from a six-degree Celsius increase, and killed 95 per cent of all life on earth. Humans would very likely be included. And this is a matter of a decade or two, not a century or two. It would be the death of humanity and the destruction of the human race via "prepotency overkill".

Increased disease

The knock-on effects of some of the other symptoms of climate change includes an increase in the spread of disease that can have a significant impact on human, plant and animal health. Warming climate, heavier and more frequent rain, more severe and long lasting droughts, and rising sea level are spreading a variety of pathogens around the world which could further impact our ability to create the food we need.

Malaria is moving to the highlands. Lyme disease is spreading across the U.S. northeast and eastern Canada. And outbreaks of cholera will increase as drinking water is contaminated. Director of the Global Health Institute at the University of Wisconsin, Madison, Jonathan Patz has expressed concern that many of the anti-poverty gains could be reversed because of the impacts of climate change – further polarising food inequality. For example, heavy flooding as a result of rising sea levels and more frequent storms has been scientifically linked to increased outbreaks of diseases such as hepatitis A, giardiasis, and norovirus infection occurring because of contaminated drinking water.

Diseases are also moving. For example, ciguatera is an illness that people get by eating fish that have a certain type of algae toxin; the disease causes nausea and vomiting and has negative neurological effects. Until recently it's never been found outside the Caribbean, but as global temperatures rise there have

---

[87] Quoted in Dahr Jamail, "The Methane Monster Roars," www.truth-out/ news, 13 Jan., 2015.

now been cases in the northern Gulf of Mexico. In 2013, there were 2,474 documented cases of West Nile virus in the US, characterised by symptoms like headache, high fever and joint pains and led to 114 deaths in 2012[88].

Changes to climate often change the way diseases behave and where they flourish. And this, of course, has far reaching consequences for our health and food system[89].

Lack or Loss of Cultivated Land

Climate change is already altering what we can do with the land we have and how much is going to be sustainable for food production in the future. While shifting weather patterns will favour some regions and potentially create food production opportunity in those areas the majority of climatic shifts will be negative and pose serious threats to our ability to meet global food demand. Current global land use can be seen in Figure 2.4.

Figure 2.4: **Global Land Use**

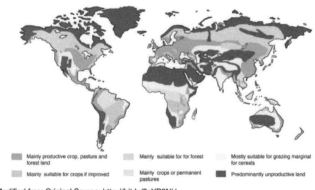

| | Mainly productive crop, pasture and forest land | | Mainly suitable for for forest | | Mostly suitable for grazing marginal for cereals |
| | Mainly suitable for crops if improved | | Mainly crops or permanent pastures | | Predominantly unproductive land |

Modified from Original Source: http://bit.ly/2nYB8NU

88 Lippman D (2014) How the Spreading Symptoms of Climate Change Can be Deadly Scientific American http://www.scientificamerican.com/article/how-the-spreading-symptoms-of-climate-change-can-be-deadly/

89 Watkins A and Wilber K (2015) Wicked & Wise: How to Solve the World's Toughest Problems Urbane Publications

In 2002, the Global Agro-Ecological Zone (GAEZ) conducted a study to look at the used and potentially usable land across the world. Combining a variety of factors, it is estimated that about 30 per cent of the world's land surface, or 4.2 billion hectares is suitable to some extent for rain-fed agriculture. Of this area, some 1.6 billion hectares are already under cultivation. Considering that food production must increase in developing or emerging countries to bring food equality to an end, reduce the numbers of people going hungry and improve levels of undernourishment it is interesting to note that 2.8 billion hectares is potentially capable of growing rain-fed crops at a yield above what is regarded as an acceptable minimum level. This is potentially good news for these regions. Of the 2.8 billion hectares, of varying land quality identified, 970 million hectares are already under cultivation which still affords considerable room for gain in these regions. Of the gross amount of land potentially usable in these areas it's estimated that the cultivation of at least 40 per cent would be relatively straightforward[90].

Unfortunately, we might need a lot more than that! In 2012 researchers attempted to comprehensively and realistically analyse a range of possible scenarios through to 2050, ranging from 'worst-case' (high-meat consumption: low production efficiency) to 'best case' (low-meat consumption: high production efficiency). In the former the total land use area under cultivation would require expansion to about 88 per cent of available productive land which represents a considerable threat to the world's ecosystems. The latter would see a contraction of about 15 per cent on current figures[91].

[90] Gardner B (2013) Global Food Futures Bloomsbury Academic

[91] Powell, T.W.R. and Lenton, T.M., Future carbon dioxide removal via biomass energy constrained by agricultural efficiency and dietary trends. Energy Environ. Sci. DOI: 10.1039/c2ee21592f (2012). https://www.researchgate.net/publication/264521914_Future_carbon_dioxide_removal_via_biomass_energy_constrained_by_agricultural_efficiency_and_dietary_trends

In these scenarios, high production efficiency considers a sustained annual yield growth of one per cent which seems plausible, especially with some of the new innovations on the horizon. It also assumes increased recycling of wastes and residues, together with adoption of a diet composed of a substantial amount of pork and poultry product which have less demanding land-use requirements. Given current trends in both dietary preferences and production efficiency, it is conceivable that we may move toward a high meat consumption/high production efficiency outcome which would require much the same land as we are using now. But our demand for land is not limited to food production, when we also consider the pressures on land from biomass production for energy sourcing, as well as increasingly urbanisation and the pressures created by climate change – this may not be a viable solution[92].

In addition, the rain-fed aspect of the GAEZ study is particularly important and acknowledges competing demands for land, water and energy. If we have to use colossal amounts of energy or divert huge volumes of water from the local area to create food, then not only does this massively increase the carbon footprint of the food produced but it is much less sustainable over the long term. Food is not the only wicked problem we face. It's therefore important that the solutions to one wicked problem (food supply) don't have negative knock-on effects on other wicked problems such as climate change or our continued demand for energy.

Of course, the GAEZ study was a global perspective and when we drill down into the detail it's clear that a great deal of the suitable land not yet in use is concentrated in several countries in Latin America, the Caribbean and sub-Saharan Africa, and not necessarily where it is most needed. China for example desperately need access to more land to grow more food for its burgeoning population but simply does not have the land necessary to meet

92 Global Food: Waste Not want Not (2013) http://www.imeche.org/docs/default-source/reports/Global_Food_Report.pdf?sfvrsn=0

likely future need. In addition, much of the identified land is only suitable for growing a few crops, not necessarily those for which there is highest demand. Bringing that land into usable farm land is not always easy. If it were then it's likely that it would have already been done! A great portion of the land not yet in use is not in use because it suffers from various constraints such as climatic unsuitability and a lack of infrastructure and these can't always be overcome easily or economically[93]. This was highlighted to one of us (MS) during a series of Harvard agribusiness seminars held in Boston, Shanghai and Cape Town. It was very interesting to observe the focus of the conversations in the three regions. The US talk was dominated by subsidies and price support mechanisms/ barriers to foreign competition, and everyone talked to the "African opportunity" viewing Africa as an important emerging market. In China/Australasia, the conversation was focused on growing demand from China and food safety (a big issue for China). In Africa, the discussion centred around risks of investing and doing business.

Increasing population is also going to put additional pressure on the available land. Ironically, however the pressure for more homes caused by urbanisation will not push into currently uncultivated or unused land – it is likely to push into highly productive, arable land that currently surrounds many of our existing towns and cities. This is also true in the developing world, and adds even greater pressure to the food supply chain. So, the wicked problem of food comes into conflict with the wicked problem of population management and city planning.

Land and Water Grabs

Another major challenge for developing and emerging countries, and an additional reason why our potential food scarcity will hit those nations harder, is the relatively new phenomenon of 'land

---

[93] Feeding the World Part 3 FOA http://www.fao.org/docrep/015/i2490e/ i2490e03a.pdf

and water grabs'. Following the 2007-2008 world food price crisis many wealthy countries, perhaps sensing their own vulnerability began buying up huge tracts of land in developing countries to meet their indigenous food needs. In 2008, South Korean firm Daewoo Logistics sought to increase the nation's prosperity by buying a ninety-nine-year lease on one million hectares of land in Madagascar. A company part-owned by a Japanese firm bought 100,000 hectares of farmland in Brazil[94]. Whether cultivated now or held for a future date the food grown or returns made from these land purchases will then be shipped back to the original country. Unsurprisingly, obtaining water resources is usually critical to these large-scale land acquisitions which has led to the additional trend of 'water grabbing'. Land without access to water is fairly useless – certainly for food production. This means countries and companies with the financial means can and are buying up critical water resources around the world, potentially leaving the countries own population vulnerable to drought and starvation[95]. One of the largest food businesses in the world has, for example, spent millions of dollars lobbying to prevent water being classed as a human right so they can buy up indigenous water supplies to create their products and sell a countries own water back to them in bottles!

If all of the 40 million hectares of land that were acquired in Africa in 2009 alone by foreign investors (predominantly China) came under cultivation, a staggering volume of water would be required for irrigation. The Oakland Institute estimates that 300 to 500 cubic kilometres (km3) of water per year would be used to produce crops on this land, approximately twice the volume of water (184.35 km3) that was used for agriculture in all of Africa in 2005[96].

---

[94] Stuart T (2009) Waste: Uncovering the Global Food Scandal Penguin, London

[95] The Oakland Institute (2011) Land Grabs leave Africa Thirsty https://www.oaklandinstitute.org/land-deal-brief-land-grabs-leave-africa-thirsty

[96] Food and Agriculture Organization, Irrigation in Africa in figures, Aquastat Survey – 2005, ftp://ftp.fao.org/agl/aglw/docs/wr29_eng_including_countries. pdf (accessed July 28, 2011); Oakland Institute calculations using the annual water requirements for seven of the most prevalent crops mentioned in available land deal agreements.

One cubic kilometre is equal to one billion cubic meters. One cubic meter equals 1,000 litres – that's a lot of water. In the event that the annual rate of land acquisition continues at 2009 levels, demand for fresh water from new land investments alone will overtake the existing supply of renewable fresh water on the continent by 2019[97]. There is a very real threat that in order for wealthy nations to secure food for their own populations they will leave the populations of those countries where they have secured land hungry and thirsty, further exacerbating the food inequality in developing and emerging areas.

Even more than food, we need water. As a species, we can survive about three weeks without food but only three days without water. And yet the availability of freshwater resources shows a very similar picture to that of land availability. Sufficient resources are unevenly distributed at the global level, and an increasing number of countries or parts of countries are reaching alarming levels of water scarcity, especially in the Near East, North Africa and in South Asia[98].

Since 1992, the FAO has calculated total renewable water resources available per capita. The data shows that increased human population, combined with shifting consumption patterns, has resulted in steadily increasing pressure on water resources. Nearly 50 countries experienced water stress or water scarcity in 2014, up from just over 30 in 1992. Africa has the highest proportion of countries experiencing water stress (41 per cent), but Asia has the highest proportion of countries experiencing absolute water scarcity (25 per cent)[99].

---

[97] The Oakland Institute (2011) Land Grabs leave Africa Thirsty https://www.oaklandinstitute.org/land-deal-brief-land-grabs-leave-africa-thirsty

[98] Feeding the World Part 3 FOA http://www.fao.org/docrep/015/i2490e/i2490e03a.pdf

[99] FAO. 2016b. AQUASTAT. Main Database, Food and Agriculture Organization of the United Nations. www.fao.org/nr/water/aquastat/data/query/index.html?lang=en

This is especially concerning because we need drinking water to survive never mind the amounts required to meet our escalating need for food.

Yield Issues

As mentioned earlier most of the increase in food production over the last 50 years has originated from increases in yield and higher crop intensity. Given the limited opportunities for expanding agricultural land and competing demands on the available land this pattern is expected to continue although the rate of yield growth for most crops has been decelerating in the past few decades – globally. For cereals, which account for over half the harvested area in the world, the slowdown in yield growth has been pronounced: down from three per cent per year in the 1960s to just over half that the 1990s, before rising to 1.8 per cent in the last decade. For other staples, such as pulses and root crops, growth in global yields have been much smaller – well under one per cent per year over the previous five decades[100].

This is understandable when you consider that yield gains originate from improved cropping techniques, fertilisation and irrigation. A great deal can and has been achieved by narrowing the gap between average farm yields and the yields obtained in experimental fields, and by reducing wastage and post-harvest losses. China's major rice-producing provinces, for example, have reached a point where the average yield is about 80 per cent of that obtained in experimental fields. This is very encouraging, especially when you consider that it will probably never be possible to replicate yields experienced under experimental conditions and real world crops. There are too many variables in real world harvest, not least local corruption or lack of investment that can throw a potential spanner in the productivity works so 80 per cent is very positive. The gap between experimental yield

---

[100] Feeding the World Part 3 FOA http://www.fao.org/docrep/015/i2490e/i2490e03a.pdf

and real world cultivation of corn in sub-Saharan Africa are, for example, still significant offering even more room for productivity improvements[101].

We know how to increase yields in many crops and have already made a lot of the possible gains as evidenced by the significant increase in productivity in half a century. While impressive it does mean that we are already at the outer edges of what can be done to increase yield with *current* technology, certainly in developed countries. What we fail to fully appreciate however is that there is still significant room for improvement in developing and emerging countries. Most of the developing world's farmers still use inefficient manual tools and their plants and domestic animals have benefited very little from improved breeding and selection. In addition, underequipped farmers, with their inefficient production methods, are exposed to increasingly fierce competition from better equipped and more productive farmers as well as to the strong decline in real agricultural prices. This continually condemns resource-poor farmers with low productivity to extreme poverty, making them vulnerable to hunger and prompting their migration to towns and cities that are themselves underequipped and under industrialised. The outcome is a real-world contradiction between the modern agricultural revolution, the green revolution, the expansion of irrigation, land clearing and the development of mixed farming systems on one hand and stagnation, lack of efficiency, waste and impoverishment on the other[102]. Making it possible for farmers in developing and less developed countries to access the very best of the improvements made possible by the agricultural revolution will have a profound effect on their ability to meet their own food needs and potentially supply into the global market too. And this is true with or without chemical inputs. Increased capital investment in supply chains all over the world would also help to increase efficiency and help us to protect and utilise the food we currently produce.

[101]   Feeding the World Part 3 FOA http://www.fao.org/docrep/015/i2490e/ i2490e03a.pdf

[102]   FAO The State of Food and Agriculture 200 http://www.fao.org/docrep/ x4400e/x4400e10.htm

Like access to greater food choices the perpetual drive for increases in yield can be a double-edged sword. Much of the gains, in the last twenty years, have come through increased mechanisation, crop management and the application of chemical fertiliser and pesticides. Of these, chemical interventions have undoubtedly increased yield but their continued use, and at times overuse, has affected nutrient level and soil quality.

In an attempt to optimise production farms have frequently switched from crop rotation to monoculture, but such production systems may not allow the soil to rejuvenate between growing cycles to the same degree as crop rotation. To compensate, chemical fertilisers are often used to reintroduce nutrients back into the topsoil but they usually only contain three main nutrients – nitrogen, phosphorous and potassium. Healthy soil contains about 15 nutrients and a shortage of any one of them can limit crop yield and nutritional value of whatever is produced. M.S Swaminathan, the Indian geneticist widely considered as the father of the Green Revolution said, "Soil anaemia also breed human anaemia. Micronutrient deficiencies in the soil result in micronutrient malnutrition in people, since crops grown on such soil tends to be deficient in the nutrients needed to fight hidden hunger.[103]"

But it's not just the nutrients in soil, healthy soil is a living, dynamic ecosystem, teeming with microscopic and larger organisms that perform many vital functions. These organisms convert dead and decaying matter as well as minerals into plant nutrients through nutrient cycling. They also control plant disease, insects, weeds and pests. In addition, they improve the soil structure with positive effects for soil water and nutrient holding capacity. All of this ultimately improves crop production. A healthy soil also contributes to mitigating climate change by maintaining or increasing its carbon content[104].

---

[103] Healthy soils are the basis for healthy food production FAO Factsheet http://www.fao.org/3/a-i4405e.pdf

[104] Healthy soils for a healthy life FOA http://www.fao.org/soils-2015/news/news-detail/en/c/277682/

Anyone who has spent time in the country, observing agricultural life will no doubt have noticed the disappearance of the birds. Thirty odd years ago, a farmer would plough his fields with a constant flock of birds diving at the worms and bugs that the ploughing would expose. Follow a plough on a monoculture farm today and there are no birds following the tractor because there is no free lunch anymore, the soil is no longer the dynamic ecosystem it once was and that is largely down to intensive farming and chemical fertilisers and pesticides.

In addition, although nitrogen based fertilisers have had a profound impact on yield, they are created using the Haber-Bosch process. This process uses natural gas. Putting aside the fact that natural gas is a fossil fuel and deeply detrimental to the planet as evidenced by climate scientists the world over – it's running out. Our ability to feed the population we have right now is going to be questionable in the years to come unless a substitute for nitrogen based fertilisers that don't use fossil fuel can be found[105]. On a global scale, fertiliser manufacturing consumes about three to five per cent of the world's annual natural gas supply so sourcing a sustainable alternative is going to be crucial[106].

The continued use and over use of chemical products are also raising question on food purity. For example, The International Agency for Research on Cancer (IARC) – the World Health Organisation cancer agency stated that glyphosate the main ingredient in Roundup is probably carcinogenic[107].

Roundup is the most widely used pesticide in the world. In late 2016, unsafe levels of glyphosate were found in a range of US

---

[105] Fossil fuel – fertilizing our food (2009) https://www.greenlivingtips.com/articles/Fuel-and-food.html

[106] Global Food: Waste Not want Not (2013) http://www.imeche.org/docs/default-source/reports/Global_Food_Report.pdf?sfvrsn=0

[107] (2015) Roundup weedkiller 'probably' causes cancer, says WHO study The Guardian https://www.theguardian.com/environment/2015/mar/21/roundup-cancer-who-glyphosate-

based food from breakfast cereal to snacks and biscuits[108]. It's worth pointing out however that in 2016, two days before an EU vote to relicense Roundup, the UN's Joint Meeting on Pesticides Residues (JMPR) found that the chemical was "unlikely to pose a carcinogenic risk to humans from exposure through the diet"[109]. Both sides are arguing about the validity and independence of both studies. Either way, amongst consumer groups there is definitely growing concern about the impact the chemicals we currently use to enhance yield are having on our long-term health. That said, eating more fresh fruit and vegetables is something that should still be encouraged because of the vital nutrients they provide.

With growing concerns about the efficacy and safety of chemical inputs, we will need to ensure we achieve increased yields in the developing world through investment in infrastructure, supply chain improvements and production efficiency rather than relying on the same chemical inputs that are now causing so much concern in the developed world. Chemical fertilisers, herbicides and pesticides may provide much needed yield gains that could certainly help reduce the food inequality that currently exists but if we even suspect that these chemicals are potentially dangerous to human health and detrimental to the food chain we may need to consider the long-term implications of their use. Especially when the developed world is already sourcing new, cleaner and more sustainable solutions. As we will discuss in chapter five, new technologies and innovations are likely to help solve these challenges and reduce food inequality while providing the yield that we will need. Ideally the developing world will be able to 'leapfrog' the traditional chemical inputs in a similar way that

---

[108] Glyphosate: Unsafe on any plate. Alarming levels of Monsanto's glyphosate found in popular American Foods. https://s3.amazonaws.com/media.fooddemocracynow.org/images/FDN_Glyphosate_FoodTesting_Report_p2016.pdf

[109] Nelson A (2016) Glyphosate unlikely to pose risk to humans, UN/WHO study says The Guardian https://www.theguardian.com/environment/2016/may/16/glyphosate-unlikely-to-pose-risk-to-humans-unwho-study-says

countries such as Africa have leapfrogged landline infrastructure in communications and gone straight to digital communications and smart phone technologies. Of course, feeding the expanding population will probably also require more cultivable land and that too poses more challenges for the developed world.

It is clearly in all our interests to help these less developed countries to improve productivity, storage and distribution of the food they currently make, as well as offering technology and bringing forward innovative solutions to improve food production. Forget for a moment that this is morally the right thing to do, if we don't support these regions to address their food security issues, they will fail, which will mean either mass starvation that we will need to collectively address or mass migration as people leave their home in search of food. The failure in these areas is also very likely to lead to even less global food supply which will increase food prices as everyone fights over limited imports and exports.

Food Price Volatility

Volatility is inherent in agricultural markets. While demand for various food commodities may increase, or decrease, demand remains relatively stable at a macro level. The same, however is not true of supply. Supply can be very spikey, difficult to predict and challenging to react to immediately. With food, this volatility has a big impact on consumers and producers in particular, and can lead to economic and political instability. Once again, the most severe impacts falling on the poor.

In June 2008 food commodity prices reached their highest levels since the oil crisis of the 70s, pushing an additional 115 million people into chronic hunger[110]. Soaring food prices came as

---

[110] FAO (2009) The State of Agricultural Commodity Markets http://www.fao.org/docrep/012/i0854e/i0854e00.htm

a shock because consumers had become accustomed to the notion of 'cheap food'. (see Figure 2.5)

Figure 2.5: IMF Food & Energy Commodity Indices

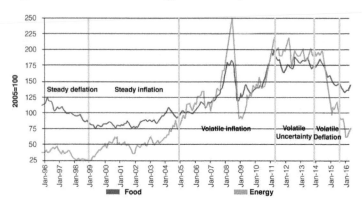

The real cost of the global food basket had fallen by almost half in 30 years and the newspapers were full of stories blaming different stakeholders in the supply chain for the "problem" of all this cheap food! The subsequent spike in food prices was also laid at the door of various groups, most notably commodity speculators, seeking to switch from less volatile, more traditional investments.

However, the real drivers behind the advent of cheaper food was yield improving advances, and the implementation of government policies. For example, subsidies in OECD countries entrenched the role of a few countries in supplying the world with food while others became more dependent on food imports. The net effect during this time had been to reduce stock levels. When production shortages then occurred, because of a poor harvest or bad weather, supply was no longer able to cope with the increasing demands created by the growing, increasingly wealthy population. That elevated demand included increased demand for animal protein (and associated pressure on grain as an animal feed), as well as the new demand for biofuels that had come about as a result of increasing oil prices and concerns around environmental impacts and US energy security.

Unfortunately, although the high prices were acutely felt by many struggling to access basic food at affordable prices, farmers in developing countries were not able to capitalise on the opportunity rising prices represented. The high prices did not filter down to producers, they were not encouraged or enabled to invest in production and productivity as a way to counter the rising prices and develop greater local food security.

Farmers in developing countries continued to struggle with limited access to affordable inputs, such as energy and fertilisers, had little access to useful technology and had to work within a poor or degraded infrastructure. But instead of addressing these issues and supporting producers to improve yield and efficiency, many governments simply enacted reactive policies in response to growing civil unrest over escalating food prices. For example, governments, bending to political pressure, imposed export restrictions to try to curb domestic prices, rather than address the real issues. Collectively these failings actively reduced the incentive to produce for farmers[111].

From the second half of 2008, food commodity prices started to decline due to recession, oil prices and an appreciating US dollar, but the structural vulnerability of developing countries to volatility and price inflation remains today. The need to balance the acute, short-term protection of consumers from higher food prices with the incentives for productivity raising investment over the longer term still exists. Many developing countries need international support with this. Developed countries also need to consider the impacts of our agricultural systems, trade and energy policies on international food prices and availability. There are many ways that we can collectively reduce and manage some

---

[111]   FAO (2009) The State of Agricultural Commodity Markets ftp://ftp.fao. org/docrep/fao/012/i0854e/i0854e.pdf

of the risk of volatility so that the poorest can continue to access a healthy and adequate diet, but lessons need to be learned from the shock in 2007/8. More widespread international trade in food would dampen volatility, so that shocks can be compensated by adjustments in other regions, but this is a very wicked challenge for governments tasked to act in the short-term interests of their electorate.

In addition to managing the risks of volatile food supplies, as outlined above, crop protection and biotechnology will also help to increase resistance to pests, disease and some elements of the weather; education and awareness of the various ways we can improve risk management; and targeted food reserves through the World Food Programme for vulnerable countries (though counterproductive for more developed countries) all provide a safety net for emergency food resources.

Early 2017 saw another upswing in commodity prices, following the post 2008 'correction'. Many of the underlying structural supply and demand factors, such as population growth, the development of diets and the availability of the crops that feed them, are still at play. What can be seen from the graph (see Figure 2.3), is that following the period of relative stability, we are now in an environment where volatility has become the norm. Leaders and many organisations talk of the VUCA world, where volatility, uncertainty, complexity and ambiguity are now facts of life. In a transactional world, where stakeholders withhold information and compete for returns and resources rather than work together to reduce uncertainties and to manage risk, this becomes even more of a critical dimension for our wise solution to resolve.

Changing Diets and Food Inequality

Food consumption is governed by Engel's law: As people become richer, they spend a decreasing proportion of their income on food (even if what they actually spend on food increases). In the UK, the wealthiest 10 per cent of the population spend only seven per cent of their household income on food, people in the poorest households spend 15 – 17 per cent of their total income on food[112]. In the least developed countries of the world the proportion of household income spent on food can range from 30 to 90 per cent[113]. Again, this points to food inequality.

In broad terms, there is a two stage change in the consumption pattern as countries or indeed individuals become wealthier. First comes increased calories and more grains. Second comes a move towards proteins, and specifically a greater demand for animal protein, grains and fresh produce. (The increased demand for meat also creates a further demand for grain as animal feed.)

At a certain point as income increases the total amount of food should stop increasing but the range of foods consumed will switch away from carbohydrate staples toward meat, dairy products, fruits and vegetables. This is usually extremely beneficial as it provides access to better quality nutrition and a stable supply of vital macro and micronutrients. It's also more interesting and enjoyable to eat from a diverse range of food and product types.

Of course, one of the responses to increasing demand for food is to drive for efficiency of food production. This makes sense and this drive for efficiency has led to the emergence of a handful of truly global food companies. These companies have helped to make food available to more people but this has also led to increasing similarity in food delivery and consumption around the world. This phenomenon is known as 'convergence'. It means that more and more people are getting access to more and more of the same types of food[114].

---

[112] UK Government, Cabinet Office, The Strategy Unit, Food: An Analysis of the Issues. Report to Government (London: Cabinet Office, January 2008; updated and reissued August 2008)

[113] Gardner B (2013) Global Food Futures Bloomsbury Academic

[114] Gardner B (2013) Global Food Futures Bloomsbury Academic

But convergence is a double-edged sword. Along with greater access to high quality protein, carbohydrate and fresh fruits and vegetables consumers in developing nations are also getting greater access to more highly processed foods including unhealthy options that are high in fat, sugar, salt, additives and preservatives. Cost of living changes affect the poor and hungry in any country. When food prices rise, consumers in developing countries are just as likely to switch to cheaper less-nutritious foods leading to the same health problems that are now plaguing the Western world.

The impact of the global advance of the 'Western diet' has already been observed over the last ten or twenty years in many emerging economies of the Middle East, North Africa, Latin America and East Asia. Per capita consumption in these regions has approached 3000 calories per person per day[115]. Younger generations in these emerging countries want ready meals, fast food, snacks and many of the unhealthy processed food options we take for granted in Western economies. But the consequences of an excess of many of these unhealthy food options associated with a 'Western diet' are already acutely evident - it's fairly obvious that something is going wrong with the food we are using to fuel our bodies.

Hippocrates, the Greek physician and namesake of the Hippocratic Oath who believed that all doctors should "First Do No Harm" also stated that we should "Let medicine be thy food and food be thy medicine". And yet, certainly within the much lauded 'Western diet' this connection between health and what we put into our bodies through the food and drink we consume has been lost or at least trivialised. The west's over indulgence in poor quality nutritionally devoid but tasty or convenient food is having a knock-on impact on our health and the spread of our diet into developing economies is already spreading the

---

[115] Feeding the World Part 3 FOA http://www.fao.org/docrep/015/i2490e/i2490e03a.pdf

associated problems. Take diabetes as a case in point. It used to be considered a relatively wealthy Western disease. Not anymore. As mentioned in chapter one, changing diets, greater affluence and greater access to different types of food are fueling obesity and diabetes in countries not normally associated with these conditions. There are now an estimated 65 million adults with diabetes in India, nearly seven million in Pakistan and nine million in Indonesia[116].

Changing consumption to a more western diet will almost certainly include a higher intake of fats (especially saturated fat), sugar and salt, more meat and less fish. At the same time, urbanisation and the reduction of physical activities associated with more sedentary lifestyles are also contributing to the problem. Increased weight and the greater consumption of the wrong food types are likely to combine and spawn an increase in diet-related diseases. This will produce a significant increase in associated social and health costs[117]. Hence the double-edged sword.

In the rush to embrace a western diet are emerging countries improving their food or opening their gates to an influx of cheap products that are going to make consumers fat, ill and unhealthy? Who can forget the 2004 documentary *Super-Size Me* starring Morgan Spurlock who, for 30 days only ate McDonalds fast food. The film then documented the drastic effects this had on his physical and mental well-being while exploring the fast food industry's corporate influence. There is little doubt the documentary was influential in changing corporate policy within McDonalds and has led to the introduction of many more healthy options. In fact, it could be argued that this, along with other negative publicity was instrumental in provoking corporate reinvention. So much so that McDonalds is now leading the way

---

[116] Lipska K (2104) The Global Diabetes Epidemic The New York Times http://www.nytimes.com/2014/04/26/opinion/sunday/the-global-diabetes-epidemic.html?_r=0

[117] Feeding the World Part 3 FOA http://www.fao.org/docrep/015/i2490e/i2490e03a.pdf

amongst the fast food chains in offering healthier alternatives which is an extremely positive outcome for both the company and their consumers. McDonalds are seldom given credit for their industry leading food quality, safety and environmental sustainability standards. As a huge global brand that is reliant on such a small number of products (chicken, beef and potatoes) they go to great lengths to encourage and build robust, high welfare, agricultural systems and long-term supplier partnerships to protect them from potential brand risk. These standards apply, in the case of chicken for example, from the production of animal feed all the way to restaurant delivery, and will include policies specifically designed to improve and address issues relating to quality, ethics, environment and economic viability in the supply chain. Many point to the iconic burgers as the symbol of "evil fast food", but the main ingredients - the grilled chicken breasts or lean beef patties - are actually of a very high standard relative to many competing propositions. The dietary 'evils' tend to be in what accompanies the burger - highly calorific, sugar-laden milkshakes, special sauces and mayonnaise! It's also worth pointing out that, even allowing for the old menu on which the documentary was based, the program itself was pretty unfair. Ubiquitous fast-food chains such as McDonalds are an easy target but no one is supposed to consume any type of fast food or take away meal every day for 30 days. Apart from maybe fruit and vegetables, too much of any type of food will have negative health consequences.

It is clear that emerging markets represent significant opportunity to food manufacturers, distributors and retailers. They are the next great frontier in the hunt for double digit growth. Much of what these companies will do will be beneficial to the people in those countries – bringing consistent and more affordable access to good quality nutritious food. It would however, be naïve to imagine that the good food will not also be accompanied by other, less nutritious choices as well. And that's the challenge. Millions of cash strapped families currently living in affluent countries routinely eat cheap poor quality food. Remember obesity is usually a poverty problem not an affluence problem. The risk therefore is that these new consumers, many of whom are already poor will be equally mesmerised by the marketing and allure of the same products that are contributing to the health challenges in the developed world. Convergence may bring better food to those who need it but if the better food is more expensive than the junk food, the poor of the developing nations are going to be drawn to that food in the same way their counterparts are drawn to it in the developed world and that is a humanitarian disaster waiting to happen. One of the additional dangers in emerging economies that will further contribute to the food inequality is that if those nations get the food balance wrong the consequences are likely to be much more severe due to the lack of widespread health care. The problem with food will be amplified by the wicked problem of healthcare which will be amplified by the wicked problems that always arise in an emerging economy (corruption and power grabs for example). One of the lessons that is clear from our experience of the evolution of a Western diet is that when we reduce the quality of the food we buy when our income drops, or we consume too many calories, too much fat, sugar, salt and additives we increase obesity, ill health and malnutrition. It is almost guaranteed that the same will happen in developing or emerging nations unless we can help their population leap-frog those painful lessons and move more seamlessly to a better, balanced and healthy diet.

Obviously, access to higher quality, safer meat, good quality fruits and vegetables and quality carbohydrate are going to improve diets but a balance will need to be struck between education, nutrition and profit so that people gain the benefits of a more stable food source wherever they live in the world without the potential pitfalls.

At the same time, we also need to address the obesity crisis in the developed world. As mentioned earlier, many of the food challenges we face could easily be considered a 'first world problem'. The vocal, often media friendly cries for 'real food', 'wholefood' or the drive toward organics make great headlines and there may very well be health benefits from eating this type of food but it's almost always more expensive – often considerably more expensive. It is therefore not a viable option for low income families who are also more likely to be struggling with obesity. Demonising all processed or fast food as bad is clearly too simplistic and often doesn't help the many people who are struggling to find the time or energy to cook when they get home from work. Like all wicked problems, it's just not as black and white as that. We eat what we are used to, like and can afford and that is true regardless of where we live in the world.

In his very enlightening article 'How Junk Food Can End Obesity' which featured in *The Atlantic*, author David H. Freedman discusses some of the snobbery in food and how this, together with misinformation and disinformation, is simply exacerbating the problem – certainly when it comes to obesity.

Experts who work with the obese readily acknowledge that bringing about real change is a tough transition and is not simply about telling people to eat more broccoli. Kelli Drenner, an obesity researcher at Stephen F Austin State University in Nacogdoches, Texas states, "They won't eat broccoli instead of French Fries. You try to make even a small change to school lunches, and parents and kids revolt."

Driving away from the wholesome-food-happy, affluent, and mostly trim communities of the northwestern part of L.A. Freedman drove to East L.A to witness the comparison of options and messages. The population in this part of town was largely Hispanic, clearly not affluent and visibly plagued by obesity. The area had its fair share of commercial food outlets but it was dominated by bodegas - considered part of the convenience store, low-income 'food desert' landscape we mentioned earlier.

Freedman went into several of these bodegas and saw pretty much the same thing in every one – "A prominent display of extremely fatty-looking beef and pork, most of it fresh, although gigantic strips of fried pork skin often got pride of place. A lot of canned and boxed foods. Up front, shelves of candy and heavily processed snacks. A large set of display cases filled mostly with highly sugared beverages. And a small refrigerator case somewhere in the back sparsely populated with not-especially-fresh-looking fruits and vegetables."

Freedman also visited a bodega that had been recently redesigned to emphasise healthier choices – "A large produce case was near the entrance, brimming with an impressive selection of fresh-looking produce. The candy and other junky snack foods were relegated to a small set of shelves closer to the more dimly lit rear of the store." But, unlike the other bodega's Freedman visited this one was empty. And this is the rub. People are not simply going to change their ingrained food choices because someone suggests they eat a banana instead of a bag of crisps and can of soda - especially if the good stuff is hard to get, not terribly fresh or expensive. Food inequality for low income families is therefore likely to continue, especially in the food deserts[118].

Those Hardest Hit

It is clear that we need significant improvements in efficiency and productivity of water and land use. Technologies can help us to reduce the environmental pressure and carbon emissions from agriculture but these initiatives alone will not necessarily close the yield gaps or reduce wastage and post-harvest losses (more on that in the next chapter). In addition, less developed countries don't tend to invest in agriculture or the technology that's required to improve it. Over the last thirty years the proportion of foreign

---

[118] Freedman DH (2013) How Junk Food Can End Obesity: Demonizing processed food may be dooming many to obesity and disease. Could embracing the drive-thru make us all healthier? The Atlantic http://www.theatlantic.com/magazine/archive/2013/07/how-junk-food-can-end-obesity/309396/

aid going into agriculture has dropped from 17 per cent in 1980 to three per cent in 2006[119]. Total aid spending on agriculture fell 58 per cent in real terms over the same period. More money is needed and yet in these areas more money is often not available.

The investment required to get us to a better place is not just about technology and mechanisation. Investment will also be required to create well-functioning input and output markets, better infrastructure, as well as better finance and risk management tools. The same applies to the reduction of wastage and post-harvest losses, which require better-functioning, more efficient supply chains which will invariably come from big business investment. Clearly, finding a way to harness that predominantly foreign investment while also assisting local economic and social development and long-term sustainability is key. There is clear opportunity, especially in developing countries, to leapfrog the early developmental stages and go straight to the latest disruptive technologies, innovations and efficiency improvements. These types of improvements are certainly possible in food production and supply and global business is likely to play a key role.

In the end, we all must all come together to solve the food problem. Ensuring that the right crops are grown in the right places to maximise yield while minimising the constant use of chemical fertilisers and pesticides, better plant breeding, and more efficient use of natural resources are all going to be part of the solution. This may involve moving away from nationalistic tendencies where each country looks after themselves and lets everyone else do the same. Taking a more enlightened trans-national approach may be challenging, especially as many countries are collapsing backwards toward a more ethnocentric, nationalistic stance rather than finding truly collaborative global solutions. There is a balance to be struck between national sustainability and self-sufficiency and proper utilisation of global

---

[119] Evans A (2010) The Feeding of the Nine Billion: Global Food Security for the 21st Century Chatham House, London

resources for the betterment of all. And this is going to become increasingly important as global temperatures rise – adding more and more pressure, often to the very places that are already struggling to meet their own food needs.

The challenges facing us, regardless of where we live, are considerable and they can feel overwhelming because it's difficult to know what we can do – at least individually. But we can all make a difference to the topic of the next chapter… waste.

Chapter 3:

What a Colossal Waste

Despite the fact that we currently produce enough food to feed the global population of about 7.5 billion, half to a third of all people are still suffering from malnutrition – either too little food or too much of the wrong type of food leading to obesity[120]. If we are to feed the 9.7 billion people who are likely to inhabit the Earth come 2050 we will need to increase food production considerably. The degree to which we will need to increase food production will depend significantly on our willingness and ability to tackle food waste.

It is estimated that at least 30 per cent of all the food grown and produced worldwide is wasted before or after it reaches the consumer. Some estimates put this figure as high as 50 per cent[121]. This is equivalent to anywhere between 1.2 and two billion tonnes of food currently being squandered every year[122].

---

[120] Global Nutrition Report 2016: From Promise to Impact, Ending Malnutrition by 2030 http://ebrary.ifpri.org/utils/getfile/collection/p15738coll2/id/130354/filename/130565.pdf

[121] Foresight. The Future of Food and Farming (2011) Final Project Report. The Government Office for Science, London. https://www.gov.uk/government/uploads/system/uploads/attachment_data/file/288329/11-546-future-of-food-and-farming-report.pdf

[122] Global Food: Waste Not want Not (2013) http://www.imeche.org/docs/default-source/reports/Global_Food_Report.pdf?sfvrsn=0

The direct economic consequences of food wastage (excluding fish and seafood) run to $750 billion annually[123].

This is a staggering amount of food waste. When millions of people across the planet are still hungry and undernourished these figures are also morally reprehensible. Ironically however these food waste statistics also represent a huge opportunity. When searching for food chain solutions preventing or minimising waste is surely one of the most obvious and doable avenues to explore. And frankly, if we were not currently so wasteful and there wasn't room for such huge improvement in this area then we really could be facing a humanitarian crisis.

In order to prevent food waste, we must understand the details of what is wasted as well as where and how the waste occurs in the food supply chain. The Food and Agriculture Organization of the United Nations (FAO) considers 'food waste' to be an important part of 'food loss' and refers to "the removal from the food supply chain of food which is fit for consumption, or which has spoiled or expired, mainly caused by economic behaviour, poor stock management or neglect[124]." Food is still considered waste even if it is redirected to non-human food such as animal feed.

Waste will occur at every stage from the provider's field, yard or fishing net through to post-harvest handling and storage, primary and secondary processing, transportation, onward preparation, presentation and sale to consumers to storage, preparation and consumption in the home. Needless to say, there are significant challenges in accurately measuring the different elements of food waste. For example, the capture and subsequent discard of fish stocks not intended for consumption are not currently measured

---

[123] Food and Agriculture Organization of the United Nations (FAO) Food Wastage Key Facts and Figures http://www.fao.org/news/story/en/item/196402/icode/

[124] Global Initiative on Food Loss and Waste Reduction (2015) Definitional Framework of Food Loss http://www.thinkeatsave.org/docs/FLW-Definition-and-Scope-version-2015.pdf

by the fisherman and will therefore not likely be included in any subsequent post-harvest accounting of food waste[125].

Getting an accurate account of this data at each stage for each country or region is almost a wicked problem in its own right. If those involved in the food supply chain even collect the data in the first place, each stakeholder group is likely to be focused on the implications of waste or loss to their own financial position, rather than the waste of the food itself.

Of course, the data itself could be commercially sensitive, or even very difficult or costly to capture, audit and report (as we can see in the case of the fisherman). A collaborative, industry-wide, global exploration of this problem is critical, and companies need to demonstrate leadership if they are to fully engage with their customers and employees' concerns. In 2013, the UK's biggest food retailer Tesco started sharing detailed waste data from their own operations, seeking to set an example and stimulate other supermarkets and food businesses to follow suit. In consultation with Tesco, leading UK food waste expert Tristram Stuart had successfully outlined how symbolic such a move would be for the industry, and how important it was to ensure that the data was independently audited. Tesco's data for example is audited by KPMG.

In 2016, Sainsbury's shared their data, by which time significant public awareness had been raised around food waste and a lot of proactive work was taking place within supermarkets' own operations, and in their broader supply chains. Initially the Sainsbury's waste definition was slightly different to Tesco's, who had opted for the broadest measurement (including all surplus bakery products that were sent on for animal feed, for example). Subsequently the conversation then moved on to how Tesco and Sainsbury's could help to influence their key supplier partners to

---

[125] Foresight. The Future of Food and Farming (2011) Final Project Report. The Government Office for Science, London. https://www.gov.uk/government/uploads/system/uploads/attachment_data/file/288329/11-546-future-of-food-and-farming-report.pdf

publicly share their data. Those actively involved, including one of us (MS), hope that the balance of time invested by all food industry stakeholders will shift from how data might be defined, measured and reported, to what action needs to be taken to further improve the situation.

However, much of the public debate in the UK is still focused on whose problem food waste is, rather than what can be done about it. When one of the authors (MS) gave evidence to the House of Lords EU sub-committee on food waste in Dec 2013, a huge amount of ground was covered and anyone interested can read the transcript on Hansard[126]. What the *Daily Mail* pulled from all the evidence presented across 27 pages of open and broad discussion was a front page spread under the headline, "Supermarket boss blames customers for food waste"[127]. This type of flagrant distortion and massive over simplification in the hunt for a headline can be brand damaging and can only serve to make companies think twice about sharing their data. The media will argue that the public have the right to know and that they are 'naming and shaming' companies that need to improve, but when they cherry pick statements, take them out of context or present them as 'facts' to suit their argument, then such media outlets are actually part of the problem and not part of the solution. Sooner or later we need to come together to solve the food waste issue and that is going to mean transparency and open sharing of information for the greater good without fear of media repercussion.

Whether food waste is 30 per cent, or more, and exactly which combination of factors in each supply chain are the main drivers, it's still way too much waste.

---

[126] http://www.parliament.uk/documents/lords-committees/eu-sub-com-d/food-waste-prevention/unrevised-transcript-101213-ev15.pdf

[127] Groves J (2013) Tesco blast at 'fussy' shoppers: Supermarket boss blames customers for food waste http://www.dailymail.co.uk/news/article-2521625/Tesco-boss-blames-customers-food-waste.html

As we collectively wake up to the size and scale of this problem many companies and governments are getting much better at gathering, reporting and sharing data. In the UK for example government funded NGOs such as WRAP (the Waste and Resources Action Programme) have been instrumental in gathering data and helping reduce waste.

According to WRAP over half the food waste in the UK occurs in the food industry. Their 2007 figures estimated that 8.3 million tonnes of food waste come from consumers (41.5 per cent), 1.6 million tonnes from retailers (8 per cent), 4.1 million tonnes from food manufacturers (20.5 per cent), three million tonnes from restaurants (15 per cent), and three million tonnes from other groups including agriculture, horticulture and commercial waste from hospitals and schools etc. (15 per cent)[128].

Since the original study, food and drink waste has received much more attention around the world. Governments, international agencies, businesses, local authorities, community groups and many others have worked with consumers to change the way we use food. Figure 3.1 illustrates the reduction in food waste across the sectors updated for 2012. WRAP estimate that 7.0 million tonnes of food waste come from consumers (46 per cent), 0.2 million tonnes from retailers and wholesalers (1.3 per cent), 3.9 million tonnes from food manufacturers (26 per cent), 0.9 million tonnes from food services (6 per cent), 0.1 million tonnes from food waste in litter (0.7 per cent) and three million tonnes from pre-farm gate (20 per cent)[129]. While some of these figures increased as a percentage of total waste, the actual amount of waste generated in each area reduced.

---

[128] Published by the Department for Environment, Food and Rural Affairs (January 2010) Food 2030 http://appg-agscience.org.uk/linkedfiles/ Defra%20food2030strategy.pdf

[129] Estimates of Food and Packaging Waste in the UK Grocery Retail and Hospitality Supply Chains WRAP http://www.wrap.org.uk/sites/files/ wrap/UK%20Estimates%20October%2015%20%28FINAL%29_0.pdf

Figure 3.1: Amounts of Food Waste Arising in the UK by Sector 2012 Report

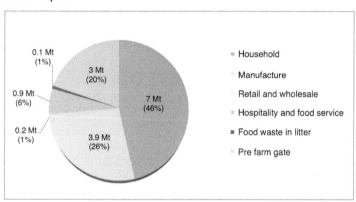

0.1 Mt
(1%)

3 Mt
(20%)

0.9 Mt
(6%)

7 Mt
(46%)

0.2 Mt
(1%)

3.9 Mt
(26%)

- Household
- Manufacture
- Retail and wholesale
- Hospitality and food service
- Food waste in litter
- Pre farm gate

Modified from Original Source: http://bit.ly/2ojLRys

Improvements across the board have been achieved. Major retailers, food brands and other manufacturers have helped through innovations in products, packaging and labelling. Although very difficult to prove, it is also thought that the financial crash of 2007 and subsequent economic uncertainty made consumers more frugal helping to reduce food waste. No doubt, a combination of factors led to the 15 per cent reduction, despite an increase of four per cent in the number of households in the UK[130] (see Figure 3.2 for breakdown).

It's worth pointing out however, seven million tonnes of food waste are enough to completely fill Wembley Stadium nine times over! The 4.2 million tonnes of avoidable waste alone is worth a staggering £12.5 billion and is the equivalent of the average household throwing away six meals per week costing £470 per year. This figure goes up to £700 per year for families with children[131].

---

[130] Household Food and Drink Waste in the United Kingdom 2012 WRAP
http://www.wrap.org.uk/sites/files/wrap/hhfdw-2012-summary.pdf

[131] Household Food and Drink Waste in the United Kingdom 2012 WRAP
http://www.wrap.org.uk/sites/files/wrap/hhfdw-2012-summary.pdf

Figure 3.2: WRAP Infographic on Waste in the UK 2011 (2012 Report)

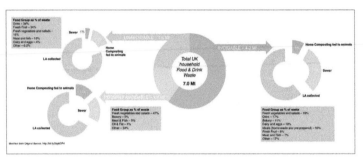

Modified from Original Source: http://bit.ly/2op0OP4

In the UK, every day, consumers waste:

- 1.4 million bananas
- 1.5 million tomatoes
- 1.2 million yoghurts
- 1.5 million home-made meals
- 24 million slices of bread[132].

Clearly, we need to do better, and this was driven home with the publication of the 2015 WRAP data for household food waste that showed food waste was on the rise again – up 4.4 per cent from seven million tonnes in 2012 to 7.3 million tonnes in 2015[133]. Avoidable waste increased 5.1 per cent from 4.2 million tonnes to 4.4 million[134]. Although statistically insignificant it's troubling

---

[132] Household Food and Drink Waste in the United Kingdom 2012 WRAP http://www.wrap.org.uk/sites/files/wrap/hhfdw-2012-summary.pdf

[133] WRAP (2017) Estimates of Food Surplus and Waste Arisings in the UK http://www.wrap.org.uk/sites/files/wrap/Estimates_%20in_the_UK_Jan17.pdf

[134] Quested T and Parry A (2017) Household Food Waste in the UK, 2015 WRAP http://www.wrap.org.uk/sites/files/wrap/Household_food_waste_in_the_UK_2015_Report.pdf

that we are heading in the wrong direction again, despite much greater public awareness of the issue.

While the latest UK research shows a discouraging increase in food waste, gathering this data is still a crucial first step toward change. At least if we know the scale of the problem we can start to strategically address the issues across the whole food supply chain, stakeholders can better appreciate the impact their actions have on others when it comes to food waste so that collectively we can make real headway in reducing it.

If we stand any chance of feeding a population of 9.7 billion come 2050 we need to look at the challenge from multiple perspectives and that means seeking improvements in yield and production efficiencies while also radically reducing waste.

Where is the Food Wasted and Why?

Like the quantity of waste itself, where that waste is being created is fairly hard to pin down and reliable data is not always available across different countries.

Some sources suggest that the split is 1/3 producers/supply chain, 1/3 retail and 1/3 households[135]. However, the UK's WRAP research repeatedly shows that households make the single largest contribution to waste across all sectors in the UK. Whatever the source or split it's clear we have a serious food waste problem. As such it's safe to say improvements can and must be made – at every level of the food supply chain and it's also worth taking some time to go through the supply chain to unpack where the waste is happening and why. This enables us to 'size the prize' and identify where some of the greatest gains can be made and how quickly savings can be achieved.

---

[135] Food Waste Statistics Food Aware http://www.foodawarecic.org.uk/stats-2/

Farmers and Growers

How and where the waste occurs pre-farm gate depends on where the farmers and growers are located.

In low or middle income countries, much of the post-harvest waste occurs because of a lack of infrastructure. Growing urbanisation means that the food must travel longer distances without adequate transport or storage facilities and limited temperature controls. In 2007, in parts of Africa for example, substantial areas experienced losses of the maize (corn) crop often reaching as high as 30 - 35 per cent of yield. In South-East Asia, China experiences rice losses of about 45 per cent despite being a significantly developed country[136]. In less developed Vietnam, rice losses between the field and the table can reach a staggering 80 per cent of production[137]. One Indian study showed that at least 40 per cent of all its fruits and vegetables are lost between grower and consumer due to lack of refrigerated transport and inadequate chill-chains as well as poor roads, inclement weather and corruption[138]. In addition, India loses about 21 million tonnes of wheat annually because of inadequate storage and distribution – equivalent to the entire wheat production of Australia[139]! In countries already struggling to create enough food for their population this type of avoidable waste is tragic.

To add to the challenges in less developed countries, most agricultural operations, including harvesting, are done by hand. This is slow and increases the manual handling of the produce leading to higher spoilage. If the crop is ready for harvest but

---

[136] FAO, Estimated post-harvest losses of rice in South-east Asia. (Food and Agriculture Organization of the United Nations, Rome, 2011

[137] World Resources Institute. Disappearing food: How big are post harvest losses? World Resources 1998–99. (World Resource Institute, Washington).

[138] Global Food: Waste Not want Not (2013) http://www.imeche.org/docs/default-source/reports/Global_Food_Report.pdf?sfvrsn=0

[139] Global Food: Waste Not want Not (2013) http://www.imeche.org/docs/default-source/reports/Global_Food_Report.pdf?sfvrsn=0

the grower or farmer can't source sufficient labour to harvest the crop in time, then waste can occur. Pests and weather patterns can also play a part in reducing the quantity and quality of the crop – often destroying it altogether.

Desperate for food or cash, poor farmers can also sometimes harvest crops too early. As a result, the food can lose nutritional and economic value, and may get wasted if it is not suitable for consumption. Poor communication and cooperation among farmers leads to waste as they rarely work together to manage overproduction or underproduction[140]. This insular inward looking behaviour creates multiple operational silos which can increase waste. Buyers often use surplus to drive prices down while sellers seek to minimise surplus so they can achieve a premium price. It would however be more beneficial if buyers and sellers work together for mutual benefit to better match expected demand with supply and so minimise waste. Unfortunately, the silo mentality, which is widespread in the developing world is also prevalent in most developed countries amongst farmers and growers. This is, at least in part, due to years of excessively combative commercial negotiations where one stakeholder group, usually the more powerful one, sought to win at the expense of the other which made stakeholder groups suspicious of each other and cause them to simply fight their own corner rather than collaborate.

When it comes to reducing waste with farmers and growers in the developing world the widespread adoption of innovation and advances in harvest, transportation and storage technologies right along the food supply chain could deliver significant benefits to these countries. This alone would help reduce waste substantially.

---

[140] Causes and prevention of food losses and waste http://www.fao.org/docrep/014/mb060e/mb060e03.pdf

Thankfully, there are already many examples of simple techniques that can reduce post-harvest losses in developing countries. The FAO have provided sealed storage drums for grain farmers in Afghanistan[141]. Other relatively low-cost interventions to prevent food waste are basic packaging for transport of fresh produce; innovation in low technology storage to reduce grain losses on small farms; and simple, non-fuel intensive, cool chain development for perishable foods and fish[142]. Inward investment from large multinational retailers, FMCG brands and global agribusiness can also make a huge difference to under-developed infrastructures. Commercial input of this type can help to usher in 'best practice' up and down the supply chain by improving production efficiencies; risk management; storage and distribution through effective chill chains across temperature regimes, including refrigerated trucks, distribution centres, store backrooms and cabinets at point of sale and the imposition of health and hygiene standards in food production and handling.

Use of modern scientific advances to produce crop varieties that are less susceptible to pests and spoilage are also likely to increase yield and reduce waste. Greater understanding around storage could also minimise spoilage, although these innovations may be more prohibitive because of their financial and environmental cost. However, there are still several low-cost technologies such as mini combine harvesters, grain-drying equipment, mechanical rice threshers/winnowers, or better fish-smoking kilns that reduce losses and demand less fuel.

Infrastructure improvements including communications could also help to manage the supply chain more appropriately and

[141] FAO 2008. Information sheet—household metal silos: key allies in FAO's fight against hunger. Rome: FAO.

[142] FAO 2003. Ministerial round table on the role of water and infrastructure in ensuring sustainable food security. Rome: FAO.
KADER, A. 2005. Increasing food availability by reducing postharvest losses of fresh produce. *Proceedings of the 5th International Postharvest Symposium, Vols 1-3, 2169-2175.*

reduce waste. Mobile phones and internet connectivity could provide much needed market information that could in turn help producers to work together to make better supply decisions. Better storage would also give producers options. When the season has been plentiful they could safely store the produce instead of having to sell when prices are at their lowest, or waste it. Better information about fisheries stocks could also help suppliers and improve sustainability[143].

Growers and farmers in the developing world have perhaps the greatest room for manoeuvre in terms of reducing food waste relatively inexpensively. That's not to say it will be easy but with foreign investment together with local consumer and government support, growers and farmers can hopefully access and implement the best of existing technology and innovation so they can significantly reduce waste in the food supply chain.

As countries develop, food wastage tends to move further up the supply chain although there are still significant regional and national variations.

In wealthier nations, pre-farm gate losses tend to be caused by insect damage or crop infestation or loss through animal death or disease. Discarded fish would also come into this category although the volume of waste from discarded fish is not currently measured. We do know the waste in commercial fishing is significant. Unwanted fish that are either too small or the wrong species are thrown back into the sea and an estimated 70 – 80 per cent of these fish die in the process. Greenpeace suggest that of the 186 million fish caught by European fleets, 117 million are thrown back. In the North Atlantic, an estimated 1.3 million tonnes a year are thrown overboard. The market value of the cod, haddock and whiting thrown away by UK trawlers alone comes

---

[143] Foresight. The Future of Food and Farming (2011) Final Project Report. The Government Office for Science, London. https://www.gov.uk/government/uploads/system/uploads/attachment_data/file/288329/11-546-future-of-food-and-farming-report.pdf

to €75 million – equivalent to 42 per cent of what fishing fleets actually bring ashore. This colossal waste of a finite and valuable resource is largely down to poorly considered regulation in the form of the European common fisheries policy which allocates a quota to member states that specifies how much of each kind of commercial fish they are allowed to bring ashore. If a fishing vessel catches more than its allotted quota, it's illegal to land those fish so they must be thrown away otherwise the owner of the vessel will be fined[144]. This is an example where regulation has clearly created unintended yet extremely harmful and costly consequences and reform in this area is desperately needed.

Preserving food through chilling and freezing, instead of canning or drying, places significant demands on the integrity of the infrastructure. Clearly, maintaining a cold chain for fresh or chilled food is significantly more demanding than transporting and storing a relatively robust product such as a can. We frequently talk of 'farm to fork' but few of us have any idea of the complexity of the logistical supply chain that makes that possible, safe and effective.

More efficient farming practices, better transportation, storage and processing facilities ensure a larger proportion of the food produced reaches markets and consumers but there is still significant waste in the farmer, grower end of the supply chain – even in developed countries.

Food businesses of all types are usually more focused on preventing financial loss, rather than considering the volume of waste. The waste that's created right along the food chain represents lost revenue so often their internal measures will be driven by the need to improve financial returns from yield. For example, producers would concentrate on winning and defending stable contracts for their highest-grade products, and

---

[144] Stuart T (2009) Waste: Uncovering the Global Food Scandal Penguin, London

then run operations to sell on any lower-class grades that fall out of the specification of the core customer. In this way, most of the crop would typically find a home, but the return to the producer would diminish as his selling became more distressed.

Although there are strong signs of improvement in this area the nature of commercial contracts between growers or producers and wholesalers or retailers has also resulted in significant waste.

In his book, *Waste: Uncovering the Global Food Scandal,* author and UK food waste activist Tristram Stuart visited several British farms to better understand this issue. Among them, Stuart visited M.H. Poskitt Carrots in Yorkshire, a major supplier to one of the UKs largest supermarket chains. At the farm, the author was shown large quantities of 'out-graded' carrots. These were considered not straight enough for consumers and sent off as animal feed. In the packing house, the straight carrots were then passed through photographic sensor machines, searching for aesthetic defects. Carrots that were not considered orange enough, had a blemish or were broken were also swept off into a livestock feed container. In total, 25-30 per cent of all carrots handled by Poskitt's were out-graded[145]. Not only does this represent a huge waste of a perfectly edible product but a sizable financial loss for the grower who must accept less for the out-graded product.

This type of situation has been a significant and common contributor to pre-farm waste up to this point. In their quest to meet consumer expectations buyers will often reject perfectly edible fruit and vegetables at the farm because they don't meet a standard based on their physical appearance. Up to 30 per cent of the UK's vegetable crop is never harvested as a result of this issue[146].

---

[145] Stuart T (2009) Waste: Uncovering the Global Food Scandal Penguin, London

[146] Global Food: Waste Not want Not (2013) http://www.imeche.org/docs/default-source/reports/Global_Food_Report.pdf?sfvrsn=0

There is little doubt that when consumers visit a shop to buy their food groceries they will inevitably self-select the produce that looks the nicest. As such the supermarkets are simply seeking a uniformity of delivery that would appeal to the customer and reduce waste in their own operations. We as customers, will usually select the roundest, freshest, reddest tomatoes, the apples without a bruise or the parsnips without the blemish. This means that as the shops receive fresh deliveries the cosmetically imperfect produce is systematically de-selected in favour of 'better, fresher' produce and ultimately goes to waste. But uniform specifications have certainly increased total system waste – albeit unintentionally.

Commercial arrangements also often specify how much of a certain product a buyer would purchase. This makes sense, but Stuart makes the case that large scale buyers such as retailers, large wholesalers or manufacturers don't enter into supply contracts with farmers but instead opt for 'supply agreements'. This may sound like semantics but it means that the buyer will only buy a certain amount not the entire crop. Only the farmer never knows exactly what the crop will be because yield is impacted by weather conditions during the growing season. If the weather is favourable and the yield is higher than the agreement the farmer is left with surplus produce they may struggle to sell or may be prevented from selling as part of an exclusivity clause in the supply agreement. In this case, the excess crop is often simply ploughed back into the field.

Alternatively, if the yield is too low due to poor weather or pests then the buyers may impose a financial penalty for failure to deliver the agreed quantities or terminate the contract with that grower all together. To avoid either scenario the grower will often then purchase any shortfall on the open market which can chew into profits. In one example, M.H. Poskitt Carrots, who also supply parsnips, had to purchase a thousand trays of parsnips at £18 a tray to add to their own order so as to meet targets only he was selling his parsnips for £12.50 a tray.

Poskitt's therefore took a £5,500 hit so as not to disappoint their customer[147].

The consequences of these types of commercial arrangements can therefore incentivise the farmers to grow much more of a crop than they know they may sell as a form of insurance against unfavourable weather and other factors that may reduce the yield. This tactic also tries to ensure that as much of the crop as possible is sold for the maximum price. Produce is graded on a particular standard of quality. Obviously, the grower will receive the most money for the produce that meets the highest standard. While different buyers may purchase second or third grade produce for other reasons, the grower gets less money for this produce which can make a difference to their annual income. This is on top of the fact that part of the crop or even all of the crop could be rejected because of its physical appearance. It is easy to see why there may be significant waste pre-farm gate.

It's worth pointing out that many of the quality standards are informed by government regulation. In the UK, the Department of Agriculture and Rural Affairs (DEFRA) decide how EU regulation will be applied in the UK. It is European classification for example that determines what 'Extra', 'Class I' and 'Class II' produce is and buyers are obliged to adopt these interpretations. In 2008, one British wholesaler was forced to throw away 5,000 kiwi fruits for being four grams lighter than the required EU standard to 62 grams minimum weight. That's equivalent to being one millimetre too thin – a difference impossible to detect with the human eye. As a result, perfectly good kiwi fruits were dumped. If the grower took them back from the wholesalers he could have been fined several thousand pounds even if he'd given them away[148]!

---

[147] Stuart T (2009) Waste: Uncovering the Global Food Scandal Penguin, London

[148] Stuart T (2009) Waste: Uncovering the Global Food Scandal Penguin, London

While some regulation, say on limiting pesticide use or preventing the use of growth hormone in beef production, is beneficial to the end consumer, others like the cosmetic appearance of an apple can be profoundly detrimental. The unintended consequence of excessively stringent rules around appearance go way beyond just waste – which is bad enough. They also encourage growers to concentrate on varieties that produce more uniform fruit and vegetables rather than focusing on taste and nutritional content. It also means, rather ironically, that farmers are forced to use even more pesticides and fungicides than they would otherwise to prevent superficial blemishes[149]. This is a classic example of the duplication and contradictory nature of too much regulation – one government department is seeking to limit use of pesticides while another is creating arbitrary cosmetic standards that actually demand elevated pesticide use!

There is a real 'chicken and egg' quality about the argument regarding this type of waste. Did we as customers start demanding straight carrots and perfect tomatoes or did we simply get used to buying straight carrots and perfect tomatoes? Buyers, certainly in the UK, may point to EU regulation as the source of standards and while regulation definitely informs buyer specifications, the resulting specification used by buyers to source their produce is often even more stringent than those imposed by the EU – this is especially true for high-end retailers. We would argue that finding who is to blame is secondary to finding a way to change the practise to minimise waste and improve variety and nutritional content.

Thankfully these types of commercial arrangement and business practices are being replaced with strategies that minimise food waste and use as much of the crop as possible. For example, Tesco have value 'farm brands', helping to broaden the specifications set by their own brand products, and a "Perfectly

---

[149] Stuart T (2009) Waste: Uncovering the Global Food Scandal Penguin, London

Imperfect" brand where the less physically attractive fruit and vegetables such as knobbly parsnips or small strawberries are bagged separately and sold at a discount. Sainsbury's have a 'basics' range that does the same. This makes sense – the produce is every bit as edible and nutritious as the rest, just not quite as cosmetically perfect and uniform. Alternatively, collaborations are established between the growers and food manufacturers who then take excess production or the produce that is too large, too small or oddly shaped to convert into ready-meals of other value added products. Our quest for convenience for example has created opportunities to use previously rejected produce to create products such as pre-sliced carrots, spiralised courgettes or diced onion.

Produce production doesn't need to be inefficient and wasteful though. In the pursuit of finding a return for production that will not make the higher value grades, most larger scale growers and suppliers will endeavour to find markets for nearly everything they grow. Looking at carrots as an example, anything a retailer doesn't want, might go into manufacturing, foodservice, or to wholesalers that supply smaller independent shops that don't mind bends or cracks in their carrot. Broken carrots that are still not wanted might be chiselled down to make 'baby carrots', or if unsuitable for any other use turned into juice or condensed to make natural sweetener to be added to other foods. Once all these options have been exhausted, what's left goes to animal feed.

It is easy to see the wicked nature of the challenge with food. We need a system that is perfectly balanced in terms of supply and demand at all times, irrespective of external fluctuations, like the weather! That balance needs to be across multiple stakeholders, across multiple producing and selling geographies, across multiple supply chains, and catering for multiple consumer requirements, that change frequently and dynamically. This is not easy, but we do believe it's possible.

Retail

Food retailers around the world, in developed and developing countries are generally very single-minded about waste and stock loss as it represents a major financial cost. Not only is waste a loss of potential income but it also costs resources to manage and money to dispose of.

With the exception of the centrally controlled product and overhead costs of a retail business, the biggest and most controllable costs of any retailer are labour and stock loss (waste, or 'known' loss; and shrink, or 'unknown' loss). For a broad range food supermarket, its labour costs may run at around 10 per cent of sales, and the costs attributed to stock loss would be one to two per cent of sales. This relates to the cash value of sales that has either been reduced to clear, damaged, out of date and therefore unfit for sale, or simply stolen or missing versus the stock record of what had been delivered to the store.

Retailers employ different methods of controlling both waste and shrinkage. For the purposes of understanding food waste, we will ignore stock loss and theft, and focus on 'wastage' through the eyes of a retailer. Traditionally, food retail stores behave like clearing houses. Products are delivered, and ideally will be sold before the store incurs the cost of marking down products reaching their date codes. All stores operate to very tight budgets, and will have to balance often conflicting KPIs that report the availability of products that customers want to buy, and also the wastage that is incurred. To avoid as much waste as possible, products that are not moving quickly enough will be marked down, or 'reduced to clear'. In this sense, the retailing of food is no different to the retailing of fashionable clothing, for example. All products have a shelf life, and as a product approaches the end of its season, interest and relevance to customers, it must be discounted to improve its perceived value to trigger a consumer's marginal purchase decision.

In simplistic terms, therefore, a lot of effort goes in to having the right products on sale at the right time for the customers that frequent the store, and to try to increase the 'life' and freshness, particularly of perishable products, so that the store has a chance of clearing the stock through normal, full price, sales.

Forecasting and sophisticated supply chain management are therefore crucial to ensure that just enough of any product, with optimum shelf life, are ordered to meet customer demand but not too much to leave the store with excess that it then must get rid of. On the forecasting side the key variables include the weather, seasonal events and product promotions, all of which significantly change the demand for products directly, or indirectly. On the supply side, the better the capability and relationship with supplier partners and service providers, and the better the communication of the underlying requirements and the variations, the more likely the retailer is to receive the right quality and quantity with the right shelf life.

Of course, it doesn't always go to plan, which means that products lose their shelf life and can't be sold or the discounted produce isn't all sold. This together with product damage in store results in physical food waste. Most supermarkets in the UK do not send any of this waste to landfill, but it may be collected for animal feed, anaerobic digestion or incineration. There has also been a lot of work, often with the help of WRAP, to simplify date coding on packaging, as consumer confusion around date labels and storage guidance was found to be a major contributing factor of in-home food waste. WRAP research showed that when packaging also included a visible 'display until' date, a largely internal date code to assist retail staff with stock rotation, alongside 'use by' or 'best before', consumers became even more confused. Consumers incorrectly interpreting the additional 'use by' date as a quality indicator rose from 25 per cent to 32 per cent when positioned alongside a 'display until' date. The proportion interpreting 'best before' as a safety date increased from 14 per cent to 20 per cent when positioned alongside a 'display until' date. WRAP recommended the removal of 'display until' dates and instead only using 'use by' dates when they are required for food safety, or "best before" dates to give guidance on optimal food quality.

Increasingly, supermarkets are also forging links with local charities in order to ensure that wherever possible, no food that is safe for human consumption is wasted in their stores and is instead distributed to those in need. For example, Tesco have made the commitment that no food safe for human consumption will be wasted in their UK retail operations by the end of 2017.

Smaller retail chains or individual shops are also creators of food waste. The sophisticated ordering and forecasting systems of the large supermarkets together with streamlined and highly efficient supply chains means they waste far less, as a percentage, than smaller retail chains or individual shops. According to Dr Timothy Jones, a specialist on food waste in the US, the best managed supermarket chains in America have reduced their waste to less than one per cent, whereas food waste in convenience stores can be as high as 26 per cent. This is in part because convenience stores tend to attract drop-in, top-up shoppers. This type of purchase is very hard to predict which can lead to greater waste. Although often more engaged because it is their store, sometimes owners simply don't have the time or expertise to reduce waste. Given that the majority of waste risk for a retailer is in the management of short life fresh, perishable food, and this food often needs to be transported, stored and merchandised in expensive chilled equipment, it is easy to see why most smaller, convenience stores stock more ambient or processed products with longer shelf life. Even shops we would imagine would be red hot on food waste such as organic wholefood stores are falling short, largely because of their focus on fresher goods[150].

---

[150] Stuart T (2009) Waste: Uncovering the Global Food Scandal Penguin, London

Waste costs money, it therefore makes commercial sense as well as ethical sense for all retailers, regardless of size, to do everything they can to reduce food waste in their business.

Food Service

In the UK, we spend £50 billion a year eating out. We order on average 10 take-aways a month[151]. Eating out or ordering take-away are now seen as a normal part of weekly life in the UK and many other developed nations. Where once these activities were seen as an occasional treat or something we did on a special occasion this is no longer the case. Consumers want convenience and choice and are prepared to pay for that outside the home in increasing numbers.

Again, data on this type of food waste is hard to come by globally. In the UK where WRAP have been doing a fantastic job gathering data on waste across many channels for many years we are able to get a clearer picture of what's going on. In the UK Hospitality and Food Services sector (HaFS):

- 920,000 tonnes of food is wasted at food outlets each year, 75 per cent of which is avoidable and could have been eaten!

- In addition to this a further 130,000 tonnes of food waste is generated from the preparation of ready to serve food items and meals for the HaFS sector, at food manufacturing sites.

- The amount of food that is wasted each year is equivalent to 1.3 billion meals, or one in six of the eight billion meals served each year.

- The total cost of food wasted in 2011 is estimated at over £2.5 billion; three subsectors (restaurants, pubs and hotels) account for 54 per cent of this financial cost. Quick service restaurants, leisure outlets, staff catering, education, healthcare and services make up the rest.

---

[151] Channel 4 (2016) Tricks of the Restaurant Trade Series 2 Episode 4

- On average:
  - – 21 per cent of food waste arises from spoilage;
  - – 45 per cent from food preparation and
  - – 34 per cent from consumer plates.

- 40 per cent of food that is wasted is carbohydrate, including potato, bread, pasta and rice[152].

This is a heart-breaking amount of wasted food – made all the worse because it is ready to eat and could have been consumed by a human being. Part of the problem in this sector is portion size. In 1988, the UK government published a book called *Food Portion Sizes*, probably not a bestseller but the bible for nutritionists.

The book was updated in 2002 by the Food Standards Agency and contains typical UK portion sizes from that time. The 2002 recommended portion size for steak was four to seven ounces[153]. Go out for a steak today and you will likely be offered a steak anywhere between seven and 23 ounces. Order a huge steak and that's three or almost four times the recommended portion size! Of course, we as consumers have come to expect generous portions and will complain or feel short changed if the portion is considered too small – even if it is perfectly adequate for our needs. This raises commercial challenges for food service outlets. On one hand, they want happy, repeat customers but they also don't want too much food waste, not only because of the cost of the ingredients that were never sold, but also the labour costs used in preparation, in addition to costs of disposal.

Take restaurants as an example, in the UK they create 199,000 tonnes of food waste every year at a cost of £682 million. What

---

[152] Overview of waste in the hospitality and food service sector WRAP http://www.wrap.org.uk/content/overview-waste-hospitality-and-food-service-sector The True Cost of Food waste within Hospitality and Food Service WRAP http://www.wrap.org.uk/sites/files/wrap/The%20 True%20Cost%20of%20Food%20Waste%20within%20Hospitality%20 and%20Food%20Service%20Sector%20FINAL.pdf

[153] Channel 4 (2016) Tricks of the Restaurant Trade Series 2 Episode 4

we, as consumers rarely realise however is that it is us that are paying for that waste as it's factored into our bill. So not only is it morally and ethically questionable that we as a society are wasting so much food but the end consumer is usually the one picking up the tab.

The good news is that most food service outlets are taking waste much more seriously. There are even some shining lights in the industry. Wahaca, the Mexican food chain for example is one of the few food service chains in the UK with a zero-landfill policy. Co-founder Mark Selby said that they initially analysed what customers were leaving on their plates to see how they could reduce the waste. Initially they provided individual salsa pots to each customer, but a huge amount was wasted so the salsa was put in bottles on the table so customers could just help themselves if they wanted it or leave it if they didn't. When you consider that 34 per cent of restaurant waste is coming from food left on customers plates it makes sense to focus on this issue. To this end Wahaca have also trained their waiters to be upfront with customers about how many portions is enough and not to deliberately oversell. This may seem counterintuitive because it could reduce sales but as consumers become more conscious of this issue and how wasteful it is, this is a potential point of difference for any company taking this route. If customers still don't manage to eat everything the leftovers are then boxed up with a note that includes some tips and suggestions about what they could do with the leftovers – such as taco leftovers make great fillings for omelettes[154].

It could be argued that all the restaurant is doing is moving the waste further down the food chain to consumers. They may know or not care that the consumer then dumps the left-overs in the nearest bin. But as we've said many times we have all contributed to this situation and we must all do our bit to solve it. It may be true that Wahaca gets rid of the waste, can promote

[154] Channel 4 (2016) Tricks of the Restaurant Trade Series 2 Episode 4

a zero-landfill policy and doesn't have the additional food waste disposal cost but these types of efforts are absolutely critical if we are to solve the problem, and it is also up to us as consumers to do the right thing too – including monitoring our portion sizes. If we can't eat it all – don't order it all!

The idea of taking left-overs home in a doggy-bad used to be quite popular in more frugal decades. It is still very much expected in the US and is fast becoming law in mainland Europe but in the UK a quarter of us wouldn't even consider it. This is a cultural issue as much as anything else and there is also a social stigma attached to asking for a doggy-bag. People feel cheap. Perhaps it's time we shifted our thinking and took our left overs home, or simply ordered a little less. Of course, there are establishments that will refuse to allow consumers to take their left overs home. In the Channel 4 food show *Tricks of the Restaurant Trade* the presenter went undercover to eat at a variety of London restaurants and asked for a doggy-bag to take home anything he didn't finish. Most places agreed, but one exclusive Chinese restaurant refused on potential health grounds. This too, throws up another challenge in the food service industry – no one wants to be sued so they can err, perhaps too much, on the side of caution.

There are also innovative start-ups looking at this issue in food service. For example, Too Good To Go (TGTG). This is an App that's been developed as an environmental social enterprise to reduce food waste in this sector. At the end of the day or end of service food outlets often have left over food that they would normally have to throw out. The TGTG app allows restaurants, cafes, bakeries etc. to list what they have left, the customer then chooses what they want to eat, pays for the left-overs at a deep discount and collects the food. Prices in the UK are as little as £2 with a maximum of £3.80 per meal and it's a win/win/win for everyone. The food service outlet wins because they are paid for what they would have had to pay to get rid of, plus it feels better not to waste delicious food. The customer benefits from tasty meals at a fraction of their normal cost and gets plenty of variety. And finally, the environment wins as that food doesn't end up in landfill[155].

There is also promise in the development and use of cheap, mass-produced sensor technology that could detect spoilage in certain perishable foods. This would allow more sophisticated food management by consumers than reliance on estimated 'best before' dates in retail or food service food labelling, and has the potential to ensure food quality as well as reduce waste[156].

Food Manufacturers

Food manufacture is also a significant contributor to food waste globally. Manufacturing involves multiple stages in the process of turning ingredients into products that are in demand from customers in the food value chain. Starting with basic primary processing such as milling or animal slaughter through to multiple complex processes and logistic stages in the preparation of ready meals for example. Each stage presents a new opportunity for waste in a largely mechanised food chain and poses significant challenges as a result[157].

Manufacturers are also impacted by the need to produce to a specification, for the brands or product ranges that they are supplying. While 'Lean' (efficient) practices are employed by most good manufacturers to ensure that waste is minimised and customers are kept happy, waste does still occur. For

---

[155] Too Good To Go website http://toogoodtogo.co.uk/about/

[156] Foresight. The Future of Food and Farming (2011) Final Project Report. The Government Office for Science, London. https://www.gov.uk/government/uploads/system/uploads/attachment_data/file/288329/11-546-future-of-food-and-farming-report.pdf

[157] Bond, M., Meacham, T., Bhunnoo, R. and Benton, T.G. (2013) Food waste within global food systems. A Global Food Security report http://www.foodsecurity.ac.uk/assets/pdfs/food-waste-report.pdf

example, to ensure consistent delivery of the sandwiches that consumers have come to expect, the manufacturer supplying one of the high-end retailers in the UK loses four slices of bread from every loaf used – the ends and the first slices in from either end of the loaf. In total that's about 17 per cent of every loaf wasted (or sold on) or 13,000 slices from a single factory every day[158].

When it comes to data on global food waste in manufacturing it's challenging to collect, not least because the definitions of food waste can be quite fluid which makes getting a handle on the problem even more difficult. As mentioned, this data is often sensitive or not recorded so it's completely understandable that it's not always available or reluctantly shared but it's also clear that collectively the food industry need to grasp the nettle and embrace a more transparent exchange of data and information so we can reduce the problem and meet the demands of a growing population.

In Figure 3.1 (2012 WRAP data) it was estimated that food waste in manufacture was 3.9 million tonnes. The most recent 2016 data indicates that in manufacture (including third-party logistics) there was 2.4 million tonnes of food surplus and waste, the equivalent of 4.2 per cent of UK production. 42,000 tonnes was redistributed to people, 635,000 tonnes used to produce animal feed and 1.7 million tonnes was food waste. Of food not sold as intended, 28 per cent was either redistributed or sent for the production of animal feed.

The near 40 per cent reduction in measured food waste has largely been the result of a better understanding of the nature of the surpluses and wastes arising in the sector. For example, food manufacturers produce a lot of waste product but only 50 per cent is food waste, the balance may be dirty water

---

[158] Stuart T (2009) Waste: Uncovering the Global Food Scandal Penguin, London

from site cleaning processes and other materials such as soil or stones. The improvement in the WRAP figures since those published in 2012 also includes a 10 per cent improvement in food waste prevention (1.7 million tonnes vs 3.9 million tonnes for 2012) as well as of a genuine reduction of waste in food manufacturing.

To help reduce waste in manufacture and retail still further, WRAP established a 'Manufacturing and Retail Working Group' in early 2015 to develop resources aimed at maximising the effectiveness of actions to reduce this problem. This information will be important for those developing strategies to achieve international, national or organisational targets to prevent food waste and will inform delivery of Courtauld 2025.

Courtauld 2025 is an ambitious voluntary agreement that brings together organisations across the food system – from producer to consumer – to make food and drink production and consumption more sustainable. At its heart, is a ten-year commitment to identify priorities, develop solutions and implement changes at scale – both within signatory organisations and by spreading new best practice across the UK.

So far, the analysis suggests that:

- Of the current food surplus and food ending up as waste, 270,000 tonnes may be suitable for redistribution, including 37,000 tonnes currently being used to produce animal feed, 190,000 tonnes going to waste (where on average around 40 per cent goes to anaerobic digestion and other recycling options, 40 per cent for energy recovery and 20 per cent to land spreading) and the 47,000 tonnes already being redistributed. This suggests therefore that 18 per cent of what may have been suitable for redistribution was actually redistributed in 2015; and

- 860,000 tonnes of food surplus and material now going to waste could be suitable for use in animal feed, compared to the 660,000 tonnes currently being used for this purpose[159].

Of course, the animal feed issue also raises concerns. Feeding excess food to animals has been an environmentally friendly and sustainable way of feeding animals for centuries. Pigs were frequently fed food waste and would thrive on it. It was a win/win for everyone. But over the years what was considered edible or useable in the food chain shifted, sometimes with disastrous results. Animal by-product waste including bone, which would never or could never be considered as human food entered the animal food supply chain. And it was this waste product converted into animal feed that is largely attributed to UK BSE 'Mad Cow' outbreak of the late 1980s, early 1990s[160]. The BSE outbreak led to it becoming illegal to feed food waste to animals in the UK although what really should have been illegal was feeding other animal by-product waste to animals. The lack of distinction in this area almost certainly increased food waste for many years.

The law and the systems about food waste is now changing again so that more food waste can be used in this way, although there are still, quite rightly, tight restrictions around animal by-product and meat of any type being fed to other animals.

Feeding food waste to animals, especially fruit, vegetables or even bakery products is unquestionably a good idea and part of the solution for reducing food waste.

---

[159] Quantification of food surplus, waste and related materials in the grocery supply chain WRAP Final Report (2016) http://www.wrap.org.uk/system/files/private/WRAP%20Quantification%20of%20food%20surplus%20and%20waste%20-%20May%202016%20Final%20Report%20Summary%20v2.pdf

[160] Meikle J (2012) Mad cow disease – a very British response to an international crisis https://www.theguardian.com/uk/2012/apr/25/mad-cow-disease-british-crisis

Although the data in this section and indeed this chapter is largely focused on the UK, it is likely that the same drivers and trends are apparent in the US and the rest of Europe. The main point however is that food manufacture across the board, just like all other stakeholders produce a significant amount of food waste and we need to work together to reduce it.

Households

Consumers have a huge part to play in food waste. Like all the other stakeholders their impact on food waste depends on where they are in the world.

In less developed countries, for example, patterns of domestic wastage vary dramatically between rural and urban areas. Much of this is common sense. Rural households, who perhaps don't have ready access to shops are obligated to store staple crops from their annual harvest right through the year. These households unsurprisingly tend to be more frugal and losses are kept to a minimum. While the will to minimise waste is strong, often from a simple survival perspective, the storage facilities are likely to be fairly basic, often unchanged for generations. Spoilage either through rodents, insects or mould is therefore common.

In urban areas of the developing world, wastage is often reduced still further because consumers are able to purchase only what they need for that day, or even the next meal. Small shops and market stalls purchase foods from a farmer or processor and dispense tiny quantities from bulk bags or cans. It is not unusual for families to buy food twice or even three times daily.

Look at developed countries however and the picture is often reversed. In affluent, 'advanced' countries the food chain may be significantly more sophisticated, safe and efficient but huge amounts of food is being wasted at the end of the supply chain by consumers. In the UK, for example the 7 million tonnes of food wasted by households in 2012 represents 19 per cent, by weight of the food and drink brought into the home[161]. Other high-income countries show similar patterns of household waste with the USA and Australia ranging from 15–25 per cent[162]. And, considering how difficult it is to measure household waste accurately it's probably underestimated.

In developed countries, there are fewer incentives to avoid waste. Being able to buy what consumers want is often a sign of their prosperity. This is a human behaviour issue and unfortunately, it's likely to be mirrored in emerging countries. As income increases they too will feel entitled to buy whatever food they want and waste what's left over without much regard for the profoundly negative consequences this attitude creates.

A small number of in-depth studies in the UK, USA and Australia have considered why high-income countries waste so much food in the home. The relatively low cost of food is clearly a primary driver. The amount spent on food as a proportion of household income is relatively low compared to the comparison in less developed countries. In the UK, an Office of National Statistics study suggested that, on average, food accounts for just 11 per cent of the household budget which certainly helps explain why we don't value food more highly[163]. In less developed countries the proportion of household income spent on food can be as high as 90 per cent[164]. Someone who spends almost all the

[161] Household Food and Drink Waste in the United Kingdom 2012 WRAP http://www.wrap.org.uk/sites/files/wrap/hhfdw-2012-summary.pdf

[162] Lundqvist J, De Fraiture C and Molden D (2008) Saving Water: From Field to Fork – Curbing Losses and Wastage in the Food Chain. SIWI Policy Brief. Stockholm: SIWI.
Griffin M, Sobal J and Lyson TA (2009) An analysis of a community food waste stream. *Agriculture and Human Values*, 26, 67-81.
Morgan E (2009) Fruit and vegetable consumption and waste in Australia. Victoria: State Government of Victoria, Victorian Health Promotion Foundation.

[163] ONS, Family spending survey 2011, Edited by Giles Horsfield (Office for National Statistics, 2010).

[164] Gardner B (2013) Global Food Futures Bloomsbury Academic

money they have on food is going to make sure they don't waste any. Human beings tend to value what is scarce. In developed economies, food is rarely scarce, if we want more we just got the shop and buy more. As a result, it's not real for us that food is actually a scarce commodity. We may not fully appreciate the connection between the cheap food we buy and so dismissively waste with the millions of people in the world who are going hungry or the escalating environmental damage caused by food production and waste. But it's time we did.

There is also a complex array of underlying consumer attitudes, values and behaviours that contribute to the problem as well as varying degrees of food knowledge which also affects our propensity to waste food. These studies attribute most of the avoidable waste to two factors:

- **Cooking too much** - Too much food being prepared and cooked in the home. Escalating portion sizes leads to more waste, plus our knowledge of how to use leftovers or willingness to use left overs has declined, or

- **Cooking badly** - Food was prepared badly and discarded. Food was discarded because it had visibly spoiled or smelled or tasted bad, but also because although it looked palatable, it had passed date marks[165].

While consumers are right to discard food that has passed dates relating to food safety such as 'use by' dates, consumers are also interpreting other date codes such as 'best before' as meaning food is unsafe to eat, rather than the actual meaning, which is to indicate the period during which food is of optimum quality[166].

---

[165] Foresight. The Future of Food and Farming (2011) Final Project Report. The Government Office for Science, London. https://www.gov.uk/government/uploads/system/uploads/attachment_data/file/288329/11-546-future-of-food-and-farming-report.pdf

[166] Foresight. The Future of Food and Farming (2011) Final Project Report. The Government Office for Science, London. https://www.gov.uk/government/uploads/system/uploads/attachment_data/file/288329/11-546-future-of-food-and-farming-report.pdf

Labelling of many foods, intended to improve food safety and avoid litigation are often very conservative – erring on the side of caution. In other words, 'use by' dates may actually be many days before the real 'use by' date of the product based on any real food safety threat. Often this might be because when considering food safety, food businesses are obliged to consider the 'real' supply chain, and not one that exists in perfect laboratory conditions. For example, even if products are delivered to stores under perfect temperature controlled conditions, they may sit on a cage for 20-40 minutes while other products are replenished. This eats into the real shelf life of a product and raises its temperature, meaning that it takes longer to come back down when sitting in the refrigerated display case. There is still too much confusion around labelling and the difference between 'best before' and 'use by' dates and consumers will frequently use the dates interchangeably. Throwing out a product that's past it's 'best before' date is not necessary. Especially if we are a little smart about it. For example, if bread has passed a 'best before' date it still makes perfectly good toast or breadcrumbs perfect for cooking or freezing.

As consumers, certainly in developed countries, we have become increasingly disconnected from the food we eat. We don't think about the time, energy, land, water and resources that have gone into creating that product when we select it for our shopping trolley. As a result, we don't really consider the damage we are causing when we then throw it away.

Multi-buy offers in retail outlets, promotional deals or attractive advertising can also encourage us to buy more than we need. Everyone loves a bargain so if we can get two loaves of bread for the price of one it's very hard not to put the second loaf in our trolley. Clearly, the retailers and branded manufacturers have some responsibility here as they have a huge influence on demand inside their stores and for their products. There are encouraging signs from some retailers who are moving away from this type of promotion for perishable items that can so often end up as food waste. For example, Tesco have not run any buy-one-get-one-free promotions on fresh produce since 2014. Instead they offer discounts on single purchases therefore providing a bargain without requiring customers to buy a quantity that they may not otherwise have chosen.

Many supermarkets are also now taking the initiative to educate customers about how they can keep their produce fresher for longer and avoid waste. Considering that we as consumers are the single biggest stakeholder contributor to food waste there is still significant room for improvement and scope for innovation in this space. As customers become more aware of the problem, one would hope that more entrepreneurs will lead the way for more sustainable solutions for consumers that meet their needs, but also create less waste, or utilise more of the imbalances we have mentioned.

As consumer's we all have a responsibility to minimise food waste – regardless of where we live in the world (see Figure 3.3 for some easy suggestions). If we don't it's very likely that market forces will do that for us through rising food prices. Like our friends in developing countries, we may re-learn the true value of food and treat it with the respect it deserves.

Figure 3.3: Ideas for Minimising Waste

137

As part of the push toward prevention, productive recycling of surplus food is also making a positive contribution to reducing food waste. Good-quality surplus food is often redistributed to consumers via schemes such as FareShare in the UK. FareShare is an independent UK charity that promotes the message that 'No Good Food Should Be Wasted'. It provides surplus 'fit for purpose' products from the food and drink industry to organisations working with disadvantaged people in the community. In 2015 FareShare reached over 995 towns and cities in the UK, providing enough food, mainly fruit, vegetables, meat and dairy products, to create 21.9 million meals and support 499,140 people every week. By ensuring good food is not wasted FareShare turn an environmental problem into a social solution[167].

If the food is no longer fit for human consumption, then it is redistributed as animal feed or a source of energy through processes such as anaerobic digestion. Waste food used in this way would then make a positive contribution to the global food and energy balance, rather than producing greenhouse gases from landfill.

Wasting Food to Create Biofuel

Many of us are now familiar with the need to find alternative energy sources to fossil fuel. Our survival depends on it. One of the 'solutions' is biomass, where food is produced for energy rather than food.

Although the production of biomass often uses crops that can be grown on marginal or relatively unproductive land, bioethanol and biodiesel require prime arable land to be diverted from food production. As a result, biomass is controversial. Certainly, it

---

[167] About FareShare http://www.fareshare.org.uk/wp-content/uploads/2016/10/FareShare-Media-Information-November-2016.pdf

seems questionable that we produce food to effectively burn for energy when people in the world are still going hungry. In 2008, the UN special rapporteur on the right to food, Jean Ziegler, called biofuel 'a crime against humanity'[168].

It is however easy to see why biomass was so attractive. When oil was $100 dollars a barrel the commercial drive to find an alternative to fossil fuel was acute and sadly, much more relevant than even the undisputed damage fossil fuel does to the planet. Fortunately, or unfortunately, whatever way you want to look at it, innovation only tends to take hold and gather traction when there is a financial imperative or sufficiently big 'prize' to motivate that innovation. Biomass was certainly an answer to rising oil prices but as we've said before when solutions are sought without a complete, integrated and wise appreciation of the problem all it does is create new problems.

In 2007/2008, up to 95 million tonnes of cereal went to biofuel instead of human consumption. The World Bank and International Monetary Fund estimated that this was responsible for most of the spike in global food prices which pushed tens of millions more people into poverty and malnourishment[169].

As the global population grows biofuel is likely to become increasingly unacceptable. It's also not sustainable. Take ethanol as an example, at one time US members of Congress and environmental groups touted ethanol as a home-grown and environmentally friendly alternative to oil and a further step toward energy security – but that didn't pan out[170].

---

[168] Stuart T (2009) Waste: Uncovering the Global Food Scandal Penguin, London

[169] Stuart T (2009) Waste: Uncovering the Global Food Scandal Penguin, London

[170] Hanlon P et al (2013) Food, Water and Energy: Know the Nexus Grace Communications Foundation http://www.gracelinks.org/media/pdf/knowthenexus_final_051513.pdf

Ethanol derived from corn is the most widely used biofuel in the United States, but the mandated amount of ethanol exceeds the supply, which is helping to drive up the price of corn. In 2010, nearly 40 per cent of U.S. corn was converted into ethanol[171]. Greater demand for corn for biofuel increases production but this increased demand can have detrimental environmental impact that far outstrips any expected environmental benefit.

When grown for biomass it's all about volume and yield so even more fertiliser is used on the crop, this can create toxic run-off which pollutes waterways and causes overgrowth of algae in rivers and lakes. Algae blooms can consume much of the oxygen in the water creating 'dead zones'. Within the Gulf of Mexico, the combined farm run-off emanating from the Mississippi River has resulted in the formation of a seasonal 'dead zone' that averages 5,200 square miles[172].

Different studies have produced different figures, but corn-based ethanol has been shown to be less effective at lowering greenhouse gas emissions than other biofuels. For example, one complete life-cycle analysis calculated that corn-based ethanol reduces greenhouse gas emissions by only about 12 per cent relative to gasoline[173]. Corn-based ethanol production also takes a toll on already scarce water, energy and food resources and is therefore not an environmentally friendly alternative to oil. One of us (MS) has visited one of the largest processors of sugarcane ethanol in Brazil. The plant is viewed as a policy model for this type

---

[171] Amber waves of ethanol, (2011, January 11). Wall Street Journal. http://online.wsj.com/article/SB10001424052748703396604576088010481315914.html

[172] Rabalais, N. N. & Turner, R. E. (n.d.) 2011 Forecast: Summer Hypoxic Zone Size, Northern Gulf of Mexico. Louisiana Universities Marine Consortium. Gulfhypoxia.net. http://www.gulfhypoxia.net/Research/Shelfwide%20Cruises/2011/HypoxiaForecast2011.pdf

[173] Hill, J., Nelson, E., Tilman, D., Polasky, S. & Tiffany, D. (2006). Environmental, economic, and energetic costs and benefits of biodiesel and ethanol biofuels. Proceedings of the National Academy of Sciences USA 103: 11206–11210. http://www.cedarcreek.umn.edu/hilletal2006.pdf

of production, in part, because they make marginal production decisions dynamically between sugar or ethanol. The sugar is grown for human consumption but whether it ends up as sugar or ethanol will depending on the prevailing commodity prices of both. Although not perfect, and certainly not the solution it was hoped it might be, ethanol production is still considered one of the most successful alternative fuels to date.

We rarely think about food production in terms of energy supply and demand but they are inextricably linked. When the price of oil goes up, the price of food will also go up because it becomes even more scarce as more food is diverted to biofuel. Conversely when the price of oil goes down, people will just use oil for their energy needs and so demand for food for biofuel will go down and the price of food may drop.

It's worth pointing out however that regardless of how morally offended we might be that food is being used for energy instead of eaten, the amount of food going to biofuel is still less than half of the food wasted unnecessarily in the world[174].

It Gets Worse – Wasted Resources

The amount of food we waste globally is shocking but food wastage is just the visible tip of colossal waste iceberg. Underneath is a massive waste of resources – specifically all the land, water and energy that is therefore wasted making food we don't even eat.

When we go to the supermarket or local shops we don't think about all the resources that have been used to make the products we buy. When we pick up a smoked salmon for Christmas breakfast very few of us appreciate that the salmon we are about to enjoy actually took three years to mature. It almost definitely

---

[174] Stuart T (2009) Waste: Uncovering the Global Food Scandal Penguin, London

started its life in temperature controlled trays, transported to fresh water fisheries after hatching and eventually on to salt water fisheries before ending up on the top of our Christmas blini. Or perhaps we opt for prawn cocktail – again most of us have no idea that it takes two kilograms of fresh fish to create one kilogram of prawns[175]. We may add some broccoli to our weekly shop but we don't understand that people harvested that broccoli by hand placing each floret into a mechanised transporter where someone else would immediately pack it, box it ready for transportation to our local store. We don't appreciate the time and energy required to grow and harvest green bananas in the plantations of Central America or the two week journey they make in polyethylene bags at 13 degrees Celsius in temperature controlled reefer ships before arriving at the ripening houses in the UK that ensure that they hit the stores with the minimum human contact and the exact colour profile to ensure that they achieve the un-blemished, ready to eat, quality that customers are looking for - only to end up in the bin.

We can no longer see food in isolation of land, water and energy – they are all inextricably linked. Producing all the food we eat involves a significant amount of land, water and energy. Not to mention the increasing proportion of edible food being diverted to produce energy as well as water quality and access which is directly impacted by food production. The waste behind the food is every bit as tragic as the waste of the food itself. Especially when it puts even more pressure on already scarce resources.

Land

The FAO estimate that 1.4 billion hectares of land – 28 per cent of the world's agricultural area is used annually to produce food that is lost or wasted[176]. This is hugely significant. Remember that 2012 research in chapter two that sought to anticipate

---

[175] Stuart T (2009) Waste: Uncovering the Global Food Scandal Penguin, London

[176] Food and Agriculture Organization of the United Nations (FAO) Food Wastage Key Facts and Figures http://www.fao.org/news/story/en/item/196402/icode/

possible scenarios through to 2050. While the best case (low-meat and higher efficiency) would see a contraction of land use by 15 per cent of current figures[177], it's still unclear whether the global population will embrace a lower meat strategy. What's probably more likely is a move toward a high meat consumption/high production efficiency outcome which would require much the same land as we are using now. But, if we already know we are currently wasting 28 per cent of the land we use now, then theoretically at least, if we stop wasting so much food that land could be repurposed.

We must consider the opportunity cost of that wasted land. It could be used in many different ways – from housing and recreation for us to the many different plants and animal species we share the planet with. Sure, we could move further into the Amazon rainforest to cultivate soy to feed cattle or graze cattle for our table but at what cost to the indigenous people of the region? What cost to the water supply that is diverted to cultivate that food? What cost to the ecology and biodiversity of the region and ultimately to the planet?

Biodiversity of life on Earth is fundamental to the multiple, complex life systems that underpin it. Life supports life itself and we are all part of that same equation. If we do nothing to support and restore this rich biodiversity then the natural world and the life support systems, as we know them today, will collapse. We may not always appreciate it, but we are completely dependent on nature, for the quality of the air we breathe and water we drink to climate stability, the food and materials we use and the economy we rely on. And yet, wildlife populations have already shown a concerning decline. On average the planet has experienced a 58

[177] Powell, T.W.R. and Lenton, T.M., Future carbon dioxide removal via biomass energy constrained by agricultural efficiency and dietary trends. Energy Environ. Sci. DOI: 10.1039/c2ee21592f (2012). https://www.researchgate.net/publication/264521914_Future_carbon_dioxide_removal_via_biomass_energy_constrained_by_agricultural_efficiency_and_dietary_trends

per cent decline in biodiversity since 1970 and is likely to reach 67 per cent by the end of the decade[178].

Wasting the food that the land produces has profound ecological consequences that we simply can't ignore indefinitely. If we did a better job at utilising and distributing the food we produce globally a significant amount of land conversion from forests, grasslands and wetlands to agriculture might be avoided. This would also significantly reduce the negative impact we are having on the natural world. A more efficient and less wasteful food supply chain could for example decrease pesticide and fertiliser runoff that can be so devastating to local ecology and water quality. Intensive agriculture which relies heavily on chemical inputs have made agriculture one of the leading causes of water pollution in the United States[179]. Contaminated runoff can kill fish, degrade aquatic habitats and threaten drinking water supplies.

In addition, food wastage's carbon footprint is estimated at 3.3 billion tonnes of CO_2 equivalent of GHG released into the atmosphere per year. The vast majority of global food waste still ends up in landfill. There it decomposes and releases methane, a greenhouse gas that traps 21 times more heat than carbon dioxide[180]. Methane emissions of this type represents one of the largest sources of GHG from the waste sector[181]. When considered in these terms the fact that we waste so much food from the land we already have is utterly abhorrent.

[178] WWF. 2016. Living Planet Report 2016. Risk and resilience in a new era. WWF International, Gland, Switzerland

[179] The National Water Quality Inventory: Report to Congress for the 2004 Reporting Cycle – A Profile. (2009, January). U.S. Environmental Protection Agency, EPA 841-F-08-003. http://water.epa.gov/lawsregs/guidance/cwa/305b/upload/2009_01_22_305b_2004report_factsheet2004305b.pdf

[180] Basic Information about Food Waste. (2012, July 24). U. S. Environmental Protection Agency. http://www.epa.gov/osw/conserve/materials/organics/food/fd-basic.htm

[181] Food and Agriculture Organization of the United Nations (FAO) Food Wastage Key Facts and Figures http://www.fao.org/news/story/en/item/196402/icode/

Water

Freshwater accounts for only 0.01 per cent of the world's water and covers approximately 0.8 per cent of the Earth's surface[182]. It's an incredibly scarce and valuable resource and yet the FAO estimate that the total volume of water used each year to produce food that is lost or wasted (250km3) is equivalent to the annual flow of Russia's Volga River, or three times the volume of Lake Geneva[183]. Remember this water isn't the water used to create the food we eat this is just the water used to create the food we waste! Again, this seems criminal when freshwater and access to freshwater is a problem for millions of people around the world.

Food production uses an immense amount of water. Crop irrigation accounts for about 30 per cent of all the water used in the United States and these statistics are from 2005 so it's likely to be significantly higher now[184]. In the UK, the water used to produce food and drink that is then wasted, represents six per cent of the UK's water requirements. In per capita terms, this is 243 litres per person per day, approximately one and a half times the daily average household water use in the UK. A quarter of this water footprint represents water used to grow and process food in the UK and accounts for water taken from the UK's rivers, lakes and aquifers[185].

---

[182] Dudgeon, D., Arthington, A.H., Gessner, M.O., Kawabata, Z., Knowler, D.J., Lévêque, C., Naiman, R.J., Prieur-Richard, A., Soto, D., Stiassny, M.L.J. and C.A. Sullivan. 2006. Freshwater biodiversity: importance, threats, status and conservation challenges. Biological reviews 81 (2): 163-182. Doi: 10.1017/S1464793105006950.

[183] Food and Agriculture Organization of the United Nations (FAO) Food Wastage Key Facts and Figures http://www.fao.org/news/story/en/item/196402/icode/

[184] Barber, Nancy L. (2009). Summary of estimated water use in the United States in 2005: U.S. Geological Survey Fact Sheet 2009–3098. U.S. Geological Survey. http://pubs.usgs.gov/fs/2009/3098/

[185] WRAP (2011). The water and carbon footprint of household food and drink waste in the UK. http://www.wrap.org.uk/sites/files/wrap/Water%20and%20Carbon%20Footprint%20report%20Final,%20Nov%202011_0.pdf

All branches of agriculture and horticulture from 'field to fork' depend on a reliable supply of water delivered by natural rainfall, watercourses such as springs, ponds, rivers and streams, or by engineered means including irrigation, hydroponics and others. Over the past century, human appropriation of fresh water has historically expanded at more than twice the rate of population increase. An estimated 3.8 trillion cubic metres (m3) of water are now withdrawn for human use each year[186], equivalent to the contents of 1.5 billion Olympic-sized swimming pools[187]. The bulk of this extracted water, about 70 per cent, is taken by the agricultural sector[188].

It takes significant quantities of water to grow, harvest and process our food prior to consumption, from washing produce on arrival in processing or packing plants to preparation systems such as steaming, cutting and blanching. There is also waste water in cleaning the machinery and facilities themselves. This is on top of the water used to create the raw ingredients in the first place. Assuming that the food supply for an average person is 3,000kcal per day by 2050 and is derived 80 per cent from plants and 20 per cent from animals, the water needed to produce that quantity of food will be around 1,300 m3 per capita per year[189] (half the contents of an Olympic-sized swimming pool per person each year). Depending on how food is produced in the future and how accurate current assumptions are regarding future population trends and diet, it has been estimated that water requirements to meet food demand in 2050 might be between 10 and 13.5 trillion m3 per year, or about triple what is currently used

---

[186] UNDP, Human Development Report 2006–Beyond Scarcity, Power, poverty and the global water crisis. (UN Development Programme, New York, 2006).

[187] Global Food: Waste Not want Not (2013) http://www.imeche.org/docs/default-source/reports/Global_Food_Report.pdf?sfvrsn=0

[188] IMechE, Population: One Planet, Too many People? (Institution of Mechanical Engineers, London, 2010)

[189] Falkenmark M. and Rockström J., Balancing water for humans and nature: the new approach in ecohydrology (Earthscan, Routledge, London, 2004).

in total for human use[190]. Clearly that's a problem – especially as rainfall becomes more erratic with climate change.

Generally, we as consumers have no concept of the water that is used to create our food and drink. There is little doubt that is going to have to change as we educate ourselves on the challenges we face. The Water Footprint Network (WFN) have broken down a number of common food and drink products to figure out how much water is takes to create them. The results are genuinely mind-boggling. Like many people, you might enjoy a cup of coffee during the day. Next time you reach for one you might like to know that it takes 18,900 litres of water to produce one kilogram of roasted coffee. Considering a small cup of coffee requires about seven grams of roasted coffee in a 125ml cup – that's 130 litres of water! If you enjoy a chocolate treat with your coffee - 100 grams of chocolate takes 1,700 litres to water to make[191].

Over the last seven years there has been a sharp rise in the number of coffee shops in the UK alone (see Figure 3.4). Recent estimates suggest that there are now more than 5,000 outlets. Costa, a subsidiary of Whitbread leads the way with more than 1,500 shops, more than twice as many as the 658 it had in 2010. Wild Bean Cafe, which is found at BP service stations, has grown from just 11 stores five years ago to 288 today. There are a similar number of Pret A Manger locations, an increase of around 50 per cent from 2010, while Caffe Nero has boosted its presence by 44 per cent to 508 branches and Starbucks has grown by a fifth to 719 locations[192]. That's an awful lot of water.

---

[190] De Fraiture, C., Wichelns, D., Rockstrom, J. and Kemp-Benedict, E., 2007. Looking ahead to 2050: scenarios of alternative investment approaches. In: Molden, D. (Ed.), Water for Food, Water for Life: A Comprehensive Assessment of Water management in Agriculture. Earthscan and International Water Management Institute, London and Colombo (2007).

[191] Water Footprint Product Gallery: http://www.waterfootprint.org/?page=files/productgallery

[192] Davidson L (2015) Mapped: the spread of coffee shops across the UK The Guardian http://www.telegraph.co.uk/finance/newsbysector/retailandconsumer/12033580/Mapped-the-spread-of-coffee-shops-across-the-UK.html

Figure 3.4: The Rise in the Number of Coffee Shops in the UK

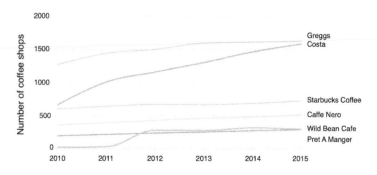

Modified from Original Source: http://bit.ly/2pd2LmA

Like all scarce resources, water needed for food production also competes with countless other demands including drinking water for us. The amount we use in the home varies considerably from country to country (see Figure 3.5). Considering that we each need a minimum of two litres of drinking water per day to survive, which is less than one cubic meter per year, some countries are clearly more wasteful than others.

Other demands include fossil fuel production and cooling of power plants. Nearly half of all the water withdrawals in the United States are used for thermoelectric power plant cooling[193]. Hundreds of US power-plants withdraw 58 billion gallons of water from the ocean and 143 billion gallons of freshwater every day – more than any other water use category including

---

[193] Barber, Nancy L. (2009). Summary of estimated water use in the United States in 2005: U.S. Geological Survey Fact Sheet 2009–3098. U.S. Geological Survey. http://pubs.usgs.gov/fs/2009/3098/pdf/2009-3098.pdf

Figure 3.5: Domestic Water Use By Country

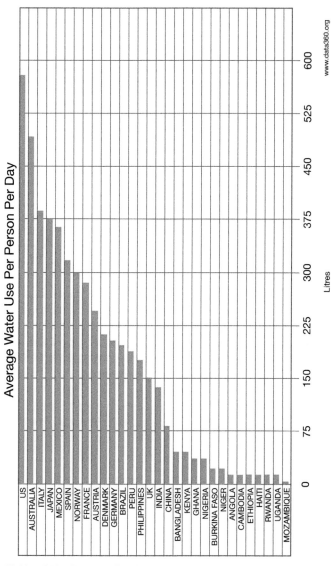

www.data360.org

Modified from Original Source http://bit.ly/2olbmum

crop irrigation and public water supplies[194]. And while water withdrawal uses the water and returns it to its source, the use of the water can, at least theoretically, contaminate the water adding to the challenge.

But water availability is not the only problem. Rising global temperatures and climatic irregularities are likely to put even greater strain on existing water supply. Periods of drought around these power plants can heat up the water they use so it is no longer effective at cooling the plant which can lead to plant shut down. In an Electric Power Research Institute survey two-thirds of utility executives polled reported "great" or "very great" concern about water and expected that concern to escalate in the next decade[195].

Water may be a renewable resource but it's not inexhaustible and it's clear we are going to have to find more efficient ways to utilise the freshwater supplies we have globally.

In the UK, The Federation House Commitment aims to reduce overall water usage across the Food and Drink sector by 20 per cent by the year 2020[196]. According to the 2012 progress report, since its launch in 2007, 70 of the UK's leading food and drink manufacturers have signed the FHC, pledging to improve their water efficiency and thereby reduce water use.

Together, these signatories represent an estimated 24 per cent of UK food and drink manufacturing. Between 2007 and 2011 signatories collectively made a 14.4 per cent reduction

[194] Kenny, J. F., Barber, N. L., Hutson, S. S., Linsey, K. S., Lovelace, J. K., & Maupin, M. A. (2009). Estimated use of water in the United States in 2005: U.S. Geological Survey Circular 1344. U.S. Geological Survey. https://pubs.usgs.gov/circ/1344/

[195] Boutacoff, D. (2011). Water pressure: Meeting the sustainability challenge. EPRI Journal,11. http://my.epri.com/portal/server.pt?Product_id=000000000001023458

[196] FHC (2013). FHC2020. (www.fhc2020.co.uk/fhc/cms/)

in their water use (excluding that in product). This reduction is equivalent to 5.9 million cubic metres or around 2,400 Olympic-size swimming pools.

There has also been a significant reduction in water use (excluding that in product) per tonne of product; 22.7 per cent compared to the 2007 baseline – a reduction of 0.58 cubic metres per tonne of product. This is a significant achievement given that production for these sites increased by 10.7 per cent over the same reporting period.

Between April 2011 and December 2011, 50 site visits were undertaken by FHC technical advisors, with around 1.3 million cubic metres of water saving opportunities identified in addition to the water already saved. This represents an average of 10 per cent of total water used by these sites[197].

In addition, the British Retail Consortium (BRC) has established a set of climate goals, which respond to the threat of climate change in both the operations of their members and those of their suppliers and customers[198]. As of their progress report for 2015 the consortium members have increased the measurement of water use by 28 per cent, reduced the amount of water used in stores by 23 per cent as well as several other environmental improvements[199].

Energy

If the quantity of food currently wasted in the UK alone was not wasted, the saving in energy consumed in its production,

---

[197] The Federation House Commitment: Helping the food & drink industry improve water efficiency, Progress Report: 2012 https://www.fdf.org.uk/industry/FHC_2012_annual_report_web.pdf

[198] BRC (2007). A Better Retailing Climate.

[199] Better Retailing Climate: Progress Report 2015 http://www.rebnews.com/pdfs/news/brc_betterretailclimate_report.pdf

packaging and transport, would be the equivalent of taking seven million cars off UK roads[200].

A study in the US calculated that the energy embedded in wasted food represents approximately two per cent of annual energy consumption in the US[201]. One of the authors of the study, Michael Webber, suggested that was equivalent to hundreds of millions of barrels of oil; more energy than the country of Switzerland uses in an entire year for all purposes; is more energy than we save by switching to compact fluorescent light bulbs; or more energy than we produce from all the corn ethanol we make in a year as a nation[202].

Whatever way you slice that – it's a staggering amount of wasted energy to create something we need and yet throw away.

We use energy to produce food all along the food supply chain, from the energy used to create feed or grow produce, to the fossil fuel inputs to create chemical fertiliser, to the energy used to run irrigation systems, to the fuel in the tractors and machinery, to the energy used in processing, packaging and transportation of the food. Some foods are more water and energy dependant than others. Industrially produced beef raised in 'concentrated animal feeding operations' (CAFOs), can require 35 units of fossil fuel based energy to create one calorie of beef. Clearly, this isn't sustainable – not least because fossil-fuel isn't sustainable.

The core of the challenge is found in the fact that in terms of land-use, agricultural food production based on livestock is far less efficient than crops, largely because only about three

[200] WRAP & WWF (2011) The water and carbon footprint of household food and drink waste in the UK http://www.wrap.org.uk/sites/files/wrap/Water%20and%20Carbon%20Footprint%20report%20Final,%20Nov%202011_0.pdf

[201] Cuellar AD and Webber ME (2010) Wasted Food, Wasted Energy: The Embedded Energy in Food Waste in the United States http://pubs.acs.org/doi/pdf/10.1021/es100310d

[202] Wasted Food Energy Science Update transcript http://sciencenetlinks.com/science-news/science-updates/wasted-food-energy/

per cent of the feed energy consumed by livestock remains in edible animal tissue[203]. Thus, animal-based agriculture needs considerably greater areas of land to output product of equivalent energy value. For example, while one hectare of land is needed to produce sufficient rice or potatoes to feed 19 to 22 people per year, the same area would produce enough lamb or beef to supply only one or two people per year. For this reason, 78 – 80 per cent of current agricultural land is already used for livestock production, either for direct grazing or feed crops[204].

Like water, energy is a key resource across all food production stages from growing or rearing to harvest, processing, packaging and transportation. It has been estimated that, if the contribution consumed in processing and transporting food is included, it takes an average input of seven to ten calories of energy to produce one calorie of edible food[205].

How we supply the world with the energy we demand is already a separate wicked problem in its own right. The idea therefore that we use so much energy on food we don't even eat is mind boggling but again most of us simply don't connect the dots.

A Stark Reminder of the Need for Change

By now you may feel a little overwhelmed. The waste issue, in all its forms is a serious problem and if we don't do anything about

---

[203] Powell, T.W.R. and Lenton, T.M., Future carbon dioxide removal via biomass energy constrained by agricultural efficiency and dietary trends. Energy Environ. Sci. DOI: 10.1039/c2ee21592f (2012). https://www.researchgate.net/publication/264521914_Future_carbon_dioxide_removal_via_biomass_energy_constrained_by_agricultural_efficiency_and_dietary_trends

[204] Global Food: Waste Not want Not (2013) http://www.imeche.org/docs/default-source/reports/Global_Food_Report.pdf?sfvrsn=0

[205] Fossil Fuel and Energy Use – Serving up healthy food choices, www.sustainabletable.org

it, it's almost certainly going to get worse. We as consumers can be unsure what to do and we certainly don't think that our actions are impacting others. It's not like our waste it actually taking food from the hungry somewhere else – right?

In his book, *Waste: Uncovering the Global Food Scandal*, author and respected food waste activist Tristram Stuart explores this question. By calculating the nutritional value of the food that is wasted it's possible to quantify the number of people that could theoretically have been fed on that food. When we talk about millions of tonnes of food waste it's easy to shake our heads in dismay. After all, it sounds like a lot of waste but it's very abstract. As such, it's also easy to dismiss it or ignore it or decide we might do something about it tomorrow.

Stuart makes this very hard for us to do…

Together with environmentalist Laura Yates they created a database of figures listing every type of food wasted by UK households from tomatoes to rice to poultry, pork, bread, cakes and beyond. Each item was assigned its established calorific value. This was multiplied by the amount of food waste according to detailed studies. The same exercise was repeated for American households using data from the United States Department of Agriculture.

According to the UN, in 2007 there were 923 million undernourished people in world, 907 million of which lived in developing nations. Ricardo Sibrián, Senior Statistician at the FAO has calculated how much extra food these people would need to satisfy their hunger and lift them out of malnourishment. It's surprisingly little – 250 calories per day. In other words, if someone was malnourished and received just 250 more calories a day on top of what they are already ate it would allow them to attain a minimum acceptable body weight and perform light activity. Malnourishment damages the immune system, retards brain development in children and causes stunted growth and yet an extra 250 calories a day could prevent all that.

We might like to believe that our excess or indifference to food waste is not connected to hunger and poverty in other parts of the world but this is naïve and just plain wrong. Ever since the food crisis of 2007-08, largely caused by global shortages of cereals it has been abundantly clear that fluctuations in consumption in rich countries affect the availability of food everywhere else. Academics, policy analysts and journalists tended to focus on new pressures that triggered soaring prices such as the diversion of cereals to biofuel, the increase in meat consumption which requires cereals as animal feed all compounded by drought conditions in Australia – normally a major grain exporter, high oil prices and the much-debated impact of financial speculation.

As discussed in the last chapter, these pressures had a direct impact on the price of cereals (some grains and oilseed doubled in the two years to July 2008). But there was also an indirect impact on other food prices too.

When all food prices increase, the poor in developed and developing countries are particularly vulnerable to those increases. It is this group that will change their purchasing habits to buy food that has higher calories but low cost. Not all calories are equal and invariably this means a move away from fresh fruit, vegetables and meat to a more carbohydrate based diet. Of course, carbohydrate is made with cereals which pushes those prices up even more. This squeeze on global cereal supplies caused average food prices around the world to increase by 23 per cent in 2007 and by 54 per cent in 2008[206]. As a result, an estimated 115 million were pushed into chronic hunger[207],

---

[206] FAO (2008) The State of Food and Agriculture 2008 Rome ftp://ftp.fao.org/docrep/fao/011/i0100e/i0100e.pdf

[207] FAO (2009) The State of Agricultural Commodity Markets ftp://ftp.fao.org/docrep/fao/012/i0854e/i0854e.pdf

increasing child mortality rates in some countries by as much as five to 25 per cent[208].

With cereal crops, it is perhaps easier to see the connection between our waste and the impact that waste has on others. Cereals, mainly wheat, rice and maize (corn) have global prices which affect the cost of food in markets all over the world. If crops are reduced due to weather events, or some is diverted for biofuel or animal feed there is less on the market. Supply constricts and the price goes up. In the developed world, we divert millions of tonnes of food, which has directly or indirectly utilised cereal crops in its production – and then we waste it. As such we are effectively taking that additional cereal off the market and out of the mouths of the hungry.

In the UK alone, consumers throw enough grain based products into the bin, mainly in the form of bread to alleviate the hunger of more than 30 *million* people. That food could supply 30 million people with the vital 250 extra calories a day that could lift them out of malnourishment.

In the US consumers, food service and retailers throw away about a third of all the cereal based foods they buy – enough to lift another 194 million people out of malnourishment. And that doesn't include the industrial food waste, pre-farm gate waste, manufacturing or processing food waste! Stuart points out that if we include arable crops used as animal feed then it comes to 1.5 billion people – more than all the malnourished people in the world right now. If we in the developed world had not out-bid the poor for those crops, they could have stayed on the world market, other people could have bought it and eaten it. Instead our excess prevents that.

Stuart makes a very sobering point... "Imagine living in a closed

---

[208] FAO (2008) The State of Food Insecurity in the World 2008 http://www. fao.org/3/a-i0291e.pdf

room with five other people. One of them is much richer and more powerful than everyone else. The rich person eats more than everyone else, and keeps aside enough surplus food to fatten his pigs and cattle. He is also very negligent with his food, hoarding it in his corner, and sometimes forgetting to eat it before it goes mouldy. He throws away more food than the hungry person needs to regain his health and strength. We do live in a closed room – the Earth[209]."

We may not see the other people in the room, we may not appreciate that our actions impact them and we may feel suitably removed from them to consider it 'not my problem'. But as we've said many times, these wicked problems are not 'your problem' or 'my problem' they are collectively 'our problem' and we must come together to solve them.

---

[209] Stuart T (2009) Waste: Uncovering the Global Food Scandal Penguin, London

Chapter 4:

Waste of Time and Human Potential

Amongst all this food waste perhaps the greatest tragedy and also one of the greatest opportunities is the human waste. Thus, if the entire 'food system' sets farmer against retailer, manufacturer against distributor, scientist against scientist then there is an enormous amount of time, energy and ultimately money wasted battling against each other rather than coming together to resolve the wicked problem of food. The extent of *this* wastage is not measured at all but it probably completely eclipses the cost of all other wastage since it is so deeply entrenched in the way complex systems work. For example, when problems involve multiple stakeholders an enormous amount of time is spent in these stakeholders meeting with each other to address disputes of various sorts. Most stakeholders tend to operate from an "I'm right you're wrong" perspective so tensions frequently erupt as each side attempts to "win the battle". Of course, once the other side loses they often redouble their efforts to regain ground on the next battle. Disputes of this nature can waste years. Thus, in the time it has taken the British Government to sanction a third runway at Heathrow China has built seven new international airports from scratch while the British haven't even put a spade in the ground yet.

We are not suggesting that China's way of governing is perfect, it's not. But, it does facilitate greater long-term planning because the Chinese don't have to engage in the party-political beauty contest every few years, instead they can focus on the problems they need to solve[210]. Another good example of this is the supply and demand of energy, goods and commodities internationally in the "one belt, one road" initiative physically connecting China, Asia and Europe. While European politicians row with each other and get stuck in unproductive inward-facing negotiations about how to share the existing cake, China has invested nearly one trillion dollars of government money into developing and merging a land-based modern Silk Road from China via Central Asia to Turkey and the EU, and a maritime route via the Indian Ocean, Africa and Europe[211]. Both of these routes were created to develop transport infrastructure, facilitate economic development and increase trade. In this way, Beijing intends to be more proactive in protecting its national interests and action explicit policies in line with concepts such as the Harmonious Society by former President Hu Jintao, and President Xi Jinping's "new type of major power relations". Not only will this investment change the physical landscape, but some hold the view that its explicit focus on the wide definition of inclusiveness and the right to development will ultimately change the current Western principles of global governance[212].

A great deal of the wastage we are highlighting in this chapter is driven by sub-optimal human relationships. Often such interpersonal tensions are themselves driven by individuals not reaching their own potential. Thus, many people involved in the food system are operating from a basic survival level. This is particularly true in developing nations, where many

---

[210] Watkins A and Stratenus I (2016) Crowdocracy: The End of Politics Urbane Publications, Kent

[211] Bruce-Lockhart A (2016) Why is China building a New Silk Road? World Economic Forum https://www.weforum.org/agenda/2016/06/why-china-is-building-a-new-silk-road/

[212] Loesekrug-Pietri A (2015) Why Europe can't afford to ignore China's New Silk Road World Economic Forum https://www.weforum.org/agenda/2015/11/europe-china-new-silk-road/

farmers, suppliers, manufacturers and retailers, not to mention consumers, are living a hand to mouth existence. Millions are simply trying to survive each day. They are not in a position to plan their own futures and tend to take the view that tomorrow is not their problem. They will deal with tomorrow when it comes. Thus, most human beings are operating well short of what neurologist and psychiatrist Kurt Goldstein, described as a state of 'self-actualisation'. Self-actualisation is the drive to realise our full potential. The expression of all that we are, our creativity, our quest for enlightenment, pursuit of knowledge and a desire to give to or positively transform society in some way. Carl Rogers talked of something similar when he spoke of our tendency to actualise ourselves, to become our potentialities... to express and activate all of what we are capable of.

You may remember the idea from chapter one in Maslow's hierarchy of needs – a framework that brought the concept of self-actualisation to the public domain (see Figure 4.1).

Self-actualisation is however very difficult to reach when we are struggling to feed ourselves properly or we simply don't know we have such capabilities. So far, this book has focused on the

Figure 4.1: Maslow's Hierarchy of Needs

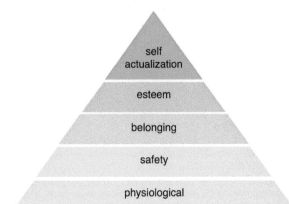

first two levels of Maslow's hierarchy. We all need food to survive and we also need that food to be safe so it doesn't poison us. If we have to fight each other for our food supplies, then we have not yet achieved the second level of Maslow's hierarchy of needs. There is a real risk, as the global population grows and climate change starts to impact crop production, that wars will erupt over scarce food or water supplies. If, however, we come together more effectively to address the wicked problem of food then we can start to build more sustainable communities where we can belong, develop self-esteem and ultimately self-actualise.

In order to access the top three levels of Maslow's hierarchy of needs we need to ensure that we all have access to good quality, safe and nutritious food. This creates a platform from which we at least have the possibility of developing our potential.

This chapter is an exploration of how we avoid squandering or wasting our human potential. In fact, we will argue that we must, tap into this potential if we are to truly resolve the wicked problem of food.

When we strip back the complexity and interdependency of any wicked problem, human beings are at the epicentre. Wicked problems are human problems. They may be very large, very complex and highly interconnected human problems, but they are human problems none the less. Climate change is a wicked problem exacerbated by too many human beings on the planet and our love affair with fossil fuel. Solving climate change will require widespread human behavioural change. Poverty is a wicked problem exacerbated by over-population and exploitation of resources from the hands of the many into the hands of the few. It is also further amplified by other human issues such as poor education and socio-economic problems. Solving poverty will also require widespread human change. What we do or don't do, what we think, believe and value has a profound impact on all wicked problems. And what we do or don't do, think, believe and value is largely down to our level of development. Wicked problems, including the food supply chain and the future of food are therefore often human development problems. As a result, it makes sense that individually and collectively we recognise this wasted potential and do something about it.

In short if we want to solve the wicked problem of food or any wicked problem it's time to wake up and grow up!

Wake Up and Grow Up

US philosopher Ken Wilber suggests that there are two key processes in human development 'waking up' and 'growing up'. First, we must 'wake up' to the delusions of power and control. The world may not be as it appears. In order to 'grow up' properly it is necessary to 'own up' to those parts of our nature that we dislike so we can re-integrate them. If we 'wake up' and 'grow up' this alone can make a dramatic difference to how we 'show up' in the world as consumers and members of other stakeholder groups.

Although this terminology may be new, we all move through very well defined levels of development. Everyone understands that children go through key stages of development - physically, emotionally, cognitively and morally. These stages are often visible, vocal and obvious. Most of us, as parents or aunts or uncles have witnessed this development first hand. Infants wake up to the world around them and figure out their place in that world as they physically grow up. When most human beings reach the level of development of the average 14-year-old they have most of the necessary skills and capabilities they require to function in an adult world. In most cases, there is no strong need for them to develop further. A few years later, they leave school or university and believe they've finished growing up because they look in the mirror and see a 'grown up'.

But, just because someone looks "all grown up" on the outside doesn't mean they are "all grown up" on the inside. Of course, there are some very obvious physical transformations that occur, most notably going through puberty and becoming taller. But there are also some internal physical changes that occur in the brains of children. Most of these occur before the teenage years as children go through extremely well described levels of development, not just physically but cognitively, emotionally, socially, morally and in terms of their sense of identity or ego. In addition to all of this development there is a great deal of learning that happens. In fact, schools are predominantly focused on helping a child to learn. The child's development is not really attended to other than how it inadvertently affects a child's ability to learn. Thus, schools and educational systems largely privilege learning and focus on the acquisition of skills, knowledge and experience. This change has been described as a 'horizontal' process to contrast it to a child's development which can be seen as a 'vertical' process. Of course, learning is absolutely critical to our evolution as human beings but it is just the beginning – it gets us to the starting line not the finish line. Learning, skills and the accumulation of experience allows as to function in the world at varying degrees of efficiency but it doesn't step change capability.

Vertical development is where the real magic happens. It is this internal, invisible change in capability that holds the key to unlocking the vast reservoir of human potential. It is what enables us to become more, not just physically but energetically, emotionally and cognitively. It is what facilitates the emergence of a deeper more mature perspective, one that is capable of embracing an increasing number of challenges with grace and agility. When we expand our awareness and unlock our potential in this way it can radically alter behaviour and the results we are capable of achieving. This vertical development is the real frontier of human evolution and allows us to 'grow up' far beyond the physical evolution from child to adult.

When it comes to adult development there have been many significant contributions from the early days of Piaget[213], Kohlberg and Loevinger[214] to luminaries such as Ken Wilber, Susanne Cook-Greuter, William Torbert and Clare Graves. Each describes the vertical evolution of some dimension of the Self. Each academic makes a contribution to our understanding of the magnificent potential of who we are from a slightly different perspective. Cook-Greuter has explored the evolution of ego maturity. Torbert's Action Logic's look at how those levels of identity play out in business. Graves' model, which we will unpack in this chapter, describes how the value sets of an individual or a group of individuals evolves in a never-ending spiral of increased sophistication. Different cultures can be studied and it is possible to determine whether any one culture is more or less sophisticated than the next. Wilber offers us a model for understanding all these vertical developmental models and provides us with a map for making sense of the entire human landscape.

Each of these models offer us clear and elegant frameworks for understanding some profound truths and insights into how our life works. Or as Graves puts it, their purpose is to illustrate, "that the psychology of the mature human being is [an] unfolding, emergent, oscillating spiralling process marked by progressive subordination of older, lower-order behaviour systems to newer, higher-order systems as an individual's existential problems change. Each successive stage, wave, or level of existence is a stage through which people pass on their way to other states of being. When the human is centralised in one stage of existence, he or she has a psychology which is particular to that state. His or her feelings, motivations, ethics and values, biochemistry, degree of neurological activation, learning systems... conceptions of and preferences for management,

[213] Piaget J (1972) *The Psychology of the Child* Basic Books, New York

[214] L-Xufn Hy, Loevinger J, Le Xuan Hy (1996) *Measuring Ego Development (Personality & Clinical Psychology)* Psychology Press

education, economics, and political theory and practice are all appropriate to that state.[215]"

Wilber's 'growing up' requires us to become aware of which level of development we are operating from at any given time. Whatever level we are operating from may feel very real to us yet they simply represent an evolutionary pit-stop toward the next evolutionary level and the next after that. One level is no better than the other in the same way that a molecule is no better than a wristwatch. They operate at different levels of sophistication and complexity. But with each new level we reach across various critical lines of adult development, the more potential we unlock. As a species, we need access to that potential if we stand any chance of solving the many problems we have created. Those problems have often been created by us all when we were operating from a less sophisticated level of being.

Unfortunately, most people are completely unaware that their development has stopped and they are looking at the world from a fixed level, through a single lens that is set by their individual level of adult development. Until we 'wake up' to this fact we can't truly 'grow up' or 'show up' in a way that facilitates a solution. Without this awakening we are likely to remain part of the problem.

Think of it like a fish swimming in water. The fish has no idea it's even in water and yet its entire life is determined by and viewed through that water. Human beings are the same in that we are swimming around in our own fish bowl, we operate from a certain perspective and interpret the world around us from that vantage point. We assume that everyone else is doing the same; seeing the world around them in the same way we do, thinking in the same way and making sense of the world in the same way but they are not. They are in their own fish bowl looking at life through their own level of development.

---

[215] C Graves (1981) Summary Statement: The Emergent, Cyclical, Double-Helix Model of Adult Human Biopsychosocial Systems presented in Boston

What we experience and think about and the depth and breadth of those thoughts is entirely dependent on what pool we are swimming in. As a result, it can be extremely helpful to understand what pool we are in or what level of evolutionary awareness we are currently operating from so we can understand where we are and appreciate the next step of our evolutionary journey of vertical development.

What makes this progression especially pressing is that a little over half of all leaders (55 per cent) are currently operating at a level of sophistication that is not sufficient if we are going to solve the problems we collectively face[216].

Grow Up: Vertical Development

Professor Robert Kegan likens vertical adult development to filling a glass with water - horizontal learning is about filling the vessel while vertical development expands the glass itself[217]. Growing up is like unlocking several new levels on a computer game with a 'cheat sheet', and in those new levels your character is able to do things that they simply couldn't at previous levels. With these new-found abilities, we are better able to create complex solutions because we have deeper, more nuanced perspectives that can transform results and unlock potential across each of the dimensions of 'being' ('I'), 'doing' ('IT/s') and 'relating' ('WE'). Vertical development thus unlocks our 'superpowers' that can step change performance. Where learning is the equivalent of adding more 'Apps', vertical development upgrades our operating system.

One of the quickest ways to appreciate the real-world difference between horizontal learning and vertical development is to consider the life of a six-year-old child. If you ask a six-year-

---

216 Rooke, D and Torbert, W R (2005) Seven Transformations of Leadership *Harvard Business Review*

217 Petrie, N (2011) A White Paper: Future Trends in Leadership Development Centre of Creative Leadership

old the questions "4X=16 what does X equal" they don't even understand the question. This is because their frontal cortex is not fully developed and they are incapable of abstract thought. If you asked a 12-year-old child the same question however, they will probably be able to tell you that x = 4. The frontal cortex is much more fully developed at 12 and this development has massively increased cognitive capability, brain processing speed and facilitated abstract thought. As a result, the child's ability to understand algebra has come 'online'. The older child has a level of capability and sophistication that didn't exist at six. Vertical development offers that kind of quantum leap forward for adults. Unfortunately, as mentioned earlier too many of us believe our development is finished once we leave school or university. If we remain open to the possibility that we are not fully developed we can tap into the real competitive advantage that lies not in what we know but the way that we know[218].

To Unlock Potential, We First Have to Appreciate It's Dormant

If we were to ask people how smart, capable and productive they are as a percentage of their ultimate capability the modest would suggest around 65 per cent and average response might be 75 per cent and the more confident might think 85 per cent accurately reflects their current ability. And yet, 50 years of neuroscience concludes that most people are functioning at around nine per cent of their capability. Imagine what would be possible for us individually and collectively if more of us could access and utilise the remaining 91 per cent. So far in our evolution our 'growth' has been focused on physical growth and more recently our cognitive development. But even the cognitive growth we may have achieved or the advances in our 'intelligence' has largely been driven by the acquisition of skills, knowledge and experience or horizontal learning.

---

[218]   Watkins A (2016) 4D Leadership, Kogan Page, London

As a result, many people, especially smart, educated people already consider themselves close to their optimum. And in some ways, this is true. Consider the lid of the cylinder in figure 4.2 below. Once you have scaled the learning curve at school, university or in your job you have filled out the cylinder lid and maximised your skills (black segments of the lid), knowledge (white segments) and experience (grey segments). But the biggest change is to increase the height of the cylinder. Until we realise that our potential is defined more by the height of the cylinder than the size of the cylinder lid we will continue to underestimate our own potential. Each of the stacks within the cylinder represent different 'lines of development' and each disc within each stack can add a different degree of altitude to the cylinder.

Figure 4.2: Your *Real* Potential

Although there are many potential areas to focus on in order to unlock our untapped potential capability, over the last twenty years one of us (AW) has identified what are probably the eight most important *lines of development*, capable of making the biggest impact in the shortest time in most organisations (see Figure 4.3). Drawing on a very rich scientific literature on 'adult development' these eight separate but inter-connected and cumulative lines of development facilitate verticality across all three dimensions - 'I', 'WE' and 'IT/s'. They are effectively the different stacks seen in Figure 4.2 stood next to each other.

Figure 4.3: Lines of Development

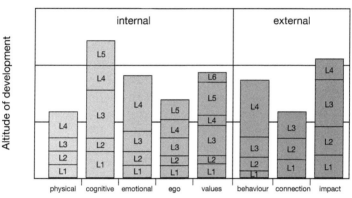

These lines of development also explain why so many people underestimate their own potential for improvement. If we have no frame of reference that separates the ingredients of consistent outstanding performance then we simply lump everything together and judge our current ability across one line of development, or if you like, out of 100. It is therefore easy to see why people routinely suggest they are already achieving 75 or 85 per cent on performance. When they realise that there are actually eight key lines of development they can see that their estimate which they based on 100 is actually based on a potential 800. Seventy-five as a percentage of 800 is 9.375 per cent which explains current output. Focusing on increasing our individual altitude across these lines of development can open up vast reservoirs of potential.

While it may be beneficial to increase our altitude or vertical development across all eight lines, certain lines can, at times, have more impact than others. For example, the values line of development can really help us to appreciate the complexity of the challenges we face, why relationships in particular are so tricky and illuminate what we need to do to create greater engagement and alignment across multiple stakeholders.

The Evolution of Value Systems

You will remember that one of the characteristics of a wicked problem that separates it from a tame or even complex problem is the involvement of multiple stakeholders. Each stakeholder group and often each individual stakeholder within each group will view the problem, causes, symptoms and potential solutions differently. It is this difference of opinion that can make finding solutions to anything so challenging.

And yet when we understand the evolution of value systems it's much easier to appreciate why these conflicts occur and more importantly what we can do about them.

Our understanding of how value systems evolve was significantly enhanced by the observations made by Clare Graves. When Graves was a psychology professor at Union College in New York he noticed that his students' responses to an essay assignment could be organised into four groups. He concluded that there were only four 'world views' and these determined the way students wrote their essays and what they thought was important or 'valued'. He realised that students were not representative of the entire population. So, over time, and based on observational data, his model developed. Initially he defined six and subsequently eight levels or value systems, each emerging to transcend and include the previous ones. Graves' work offers some profoundly useful insights when it comes to developing functional relationships.

What we value changes and evolves over time. What you valued as a 15-year-old is (hopefully) significantly different to what you value today. As we evolve up the spiral we don't lose access to the capabilities we had at lower levels of the value systems, we simply expand to transcend and include them into our new capabilities. In the same way as when you learn to run you don't lose the ability to walk. We become more sophisticated, more capable and more perceptive as we mature and evolve up the spiral because we understand the value of more things and are able to see situations from more sophisticated perspectives. That evolution doesn't mean we are 'better' than those who operate at the lower levels of the spiral and it certainly doesn't mean the higher levels will be happier or more successful. It is simply an expression of the depth of our perspective. The higher up the spiral we travel the more options we have in terms of how we behave, interact with others and the number of different things we can see value in.

Values are critically important in business because they provide direction and underpin corporate culture. There is however a great deal of very confused and frankly poor quality work done in most organisations on the issue of values and culture. Company values are not something to be decided upon in an off-site session involving senior executives and then rolled out across the business. This is an extremely widespread and pointless practice. It doesn't matter what the Vision or Mission Statement says in the front of the Annual Report if the business doesn't demonstrate that they really do value the things on that statement. Many companies claim to live their values but after 20 years of experience in this field it is apparent that most companies don't.

The classic example of this is Enron. Before its spectacular fall from grace Enron displayed their "Vision and Values" statement in their foyer proclaiming Respect, Integrity, Communication, and Excellence. Respect included the following detail, "We treat others as we would like to be treated ourselves. We do not tolerate abusive or disrespectful treatment. Ruthlessness, callousness, and arrogance don't belong here[219]." And yet, when forest fires shut down a major transmission line into California, cutting power supplies and raising prices, Enron energy traders celebrated and were caught on tape saying, "Burn, baby, burn. That's a beautiful thing"[220]. If you really want to know what someone values, regardless of what appears on the corporate posters – walk the floor, speak to the most junior person in the business and ask what does it really feel like to work here. Look at how they handle redundancy, look at how firms handle their suppliers. Look at how they talk to each other when no-one is watching. The mismatch between an organisation's stated values and their observable behaviour is sadly just as true for NGOs and governments as it is for most companies.

If an organisation is not brave enough to face the fact that they are not really living up to their espoused values, and most of them don't, they can never really develop their culture because they are not really being honest – even though honesty may, ironically, be one of their stated values. If they admit that there is a cultural issue, then they may attempt a cultural transformation programme. Most people who have worked in organisations for years will tell you stories of failed cultural transformations. People acknowledge that such change is incredibly difficult. In fact, most experts will tell you that the research is very clear that most cultural transformations fail. Most mergers or acquisitions fail to add the expected financial benefit that drove the merger simply because of cultural integration problems.

For most, cultural change programmes are a complete waste of time and money. One of the main reasons is the profound lack of understanding about values and how they evolve. Different values are not some 'flatland' variation of each other. If you have a

[219] Christensen, C M, Allworth, J and Dillon, K (2012) How Will You Measure Your Life? Finding Fulfilment Using Lessons From Some of the World's Greatest Businesses HarperCollins, London

[220] Elkind P and McLean B (2003) The Smartest Guys in the Room: The Amazing Rise and Scandalous Fall of Enron Penguin, New York

different value set to me, this does not mean we are simply living in different flatland locations. If our value sets were simply variations of each other what would be the point of shifting you to my value set or me to yours? This would risk creating a mono-culture.

Why try to change a corporate culture from value set X to value set Y? You are simply moving to a different static location. Such a move, at best, could deliver some advantages but the new location is just as likely to deliver some disadvantages too. When we appreciate however that values and therefore culture is not a static location but a vertical evolutionary spiral then the culture can evolve to embrace the best of each previous level while also mitigating the worst of each earlier value system. If we shift from the flatland dysfunction to a vertical evolutionary model, we can start to understand that there is in fact some implicit reason and momentum for change.

This shift in how we see values and organisational culture from flatland to vertical evolution is an absolute game changer in our ability to drive cultural change. This distinction is profoundly important especially for those leading cultural change. Thus, if you are a physics teacher and you mistakenly believe that electrons, molecules and cells are all the same level of phenomena then you will completely fail to run any effective experiments. In the same way, not all value systems are the same level of sophistication. So, 'cultural transformation' can never occur if the level we operate from doesn't change, and it will not if we consider all value systems at the same level but just different.

The evolution of an individual, team or organisation's' values is also not the same thing as the maturity of the ego or identity of an individual, team or organisation. Thus, at every level of the values spiral people can show up in a mature or less mature way. The mature individuals tend to be driven by and express the more positive characteristics of that levels value set whereas an immature individual is usually more driven by and therefore expresses the more negative characteristics of that value level.

This is important, because the stimulus for cultural or personal evolution is nearly always the problems that arise from the dysfunction, negative traits or dark side of the previous level. It is the dark side of the value system that triggers change – either a breakthrough or a breakdown. We either move up to the next values level and start the process again or we breakdown and regress to an earlier values level. Ken Wilber, sets out a very compelling argument that brilliantly describes the collapse of values and cultural regression that we are going through in the US and Europe right now[221]. We will unpack that in more detail in chapter eight. When the pain and suffering that flows from the downside of one value system's dysfunction becomes great enough it creates the energy for change and this pain can trigger a 'software upgrade'. We can therefore transcend the negative characteristic of the previous level and move up to a new level. It's the negative aspects of each level that ultimately create the burning platform for evolution and development. If that evolution fails, then we will end up with a regression or collapse to an earlier level.

Each level of the spiral has been given a colour which is relevant to that level and helps us remember where we are on the spiral (see Figure 4.4). As we progress up the levels the focus oscillates between the individual and the collective. What's especially interesting about the values spiral is that regardless of scale the model still holds true. Thus, we can predict the likely behaviour of an individual, a team, a division, a business, an industry, a nation, a region or the entire population of the planet based on where the gravity is on the spiral. Clearly none of us sits entirely at one level. We are a kaleidoscope with a balance between multiple levels and this changes depending on what we are paying attention to.

Beige: Survival (Individual Focus)

The journey up the evolving values spiral starts with our own evolutionary journey as a human being and what we need. At

---

[221] Wilber K (2017) Trump and a Post-Truth World: An Evolutionary Self-Correction Integral Life https://integrallife.com/trump-post-truth-world/

Figure 4.4: The Evolving Spiral of Value Systems

our most basic level we need food, water and shelter to survive the day. This corresponds with Maslow's hierarchy of needs and indeed Graves attempted to verify Maslow's work and ended up building on it significantly.

This value system can be witnessed amongst the poor and hungry of the world, whether in the developed or developing world. Their primary and only focus is daily survival. Sadly, as we approach the third decade of the 21st Century, there are still far too many people operating with this value system and living hand to mouth. People who have evolved beyond this value set can regress back to this level during times of economic hardship such as redundancy. We can witness this value system at work in disaster zones, refugee camps or areas of natural disaster or conflict. People suffering these circumstances have little concern for material possessions or the future, the goal is just to survive today.

In the food industry companies that are in financial distress may be in "survival mode". There is no future planning. Farmers in developing countries may be at this level, particularly if soil quality is marginal, their farm holding is small and weather conditions are not favourable. Farmers or small retailers at this level are almost entirely focused on the daily battle to keep going. The fight is so hard thinking about the future seems like a luxury. In this mind-set, they are just as likely, if they do manage a bumper harvest and generate a lot of cash, to blow all their money on a party than reinvest their profit back into their business or buy a vital new piece of equipment. As a result, people at the beige level often never really get out of the poverty trap[222].

The upside of the beige value system is that the individual survives. The downside is there is very little progress or forward movement. Beige can be a very lonely, scary and stressful place. The fight for survival provides the evolutionary impetus for individuals at beige to find or connect with others who are struggling. They recognise that it will be easier to survive as part of a group and it is this insight that pushes individuals up to the next level, to purple.

Purple: Belonging (Collective Focus)

Those operating from the purple value system have realised that survival is easier in groups. This requires people to start to learn the basic rules of social interaction and group conformity. Within the safety of a group individuals often start to wonder about who or what is controlling their future. Stories and mythologies emerge to explain what is happening. But such explanations are usually unsophisticated and confused. Unsure of how the world really works crop failure is as likely to be attributed to 'God's will' or some sort of 'voodoo magic'. In fact, any number of local cultural mythological narratives develop to explain what is happening. At this level of meaning making superstitions and rituals are

---

[222] Harrison P (1993) Inside the Third World: An Anatomy of Poverty Penguin Books, London

incredibly important. Individuals are likely to pray for rain, offer a sacrifice or food to the Gods for a blessing. Acts of ritualistic devotion are common as the group curries favour with the 'gods' or spirits who they believe are controlling the outcome. In the realisation that there is safety in numbers individuals are strongly motivated to follow tradition, respect the tribal hierarchy and not rock the boat.

The purple value system in the food industry is common and often leads to tribal behaviour in specific stakeholder groups. This can in turn create stakeholder silos. Siloed behaviour is a very widespread complaint in many modern organisations. Each stakeholder silo is busy looking out for everyone else in their own stakeholder silo but rarely considers their impact on the wider group of stakeholders. Little consideration is given to the bigger picture or the longer-term consequences of their siloed thinking. Protectionism and defensiveness is the norm. Walls and barriers are erected to defend 'territory'.

Such insular and simplistic thinking can make solving problems even harder than necessary as each stakeholder group, sub-group or tribe seeks to protect its own turf. Even if neighbours were minded to collaborate seeing great barriers of protectionism erected often collapses relationship dynamics into a tribal 'tit for tat' battle. Each silo, tribe or gang will be able to point to reasons and examples of why such turf wars and protection are necessary and whilst the injustice they feel often have some validity but protectionism doesn't solve the problem. Far from it such 'us versus them' thinking usually make matters worse.

People operating from this value system are often in a state of fear, defensive and armed ready to respond to any of the myriad of 'threats' they perceive. They remain hypervigilant. On the upside, they can often be super sensitive and perceptive to competitive challenges and can often 'read the market' and anticipate a change in behaviour earlier than most. This ability to anticipate threats can get wrapped up in its own mythology and people from the purple value system can come to be seen as a 'soothsayer' a 'mystic' or a 'seer'. In the food industry, this value system is very important in risk management and mitigation. Although this risk management is usually pretty simplistic and basic. We are not talking about nuanced management of market volatility. Rather at this level we see large scale threats to survival and trigger simplistic responses to such threats.

One of the main upsides of the purple value system is that there is often a very strong sense of belonging and community. People operating from this value system have understood the benefit of sticking together and see this as a way to survive more effectively.

However, there are downsides. One of the main issues at this level is reactivity. Decisions are often not that well thought through. There is little long-term thinking, what would be the point? The view is that the future is not controlled by me it is dictated by unseen forces that I do not know or understand. Again, they sense threats, but often don't comprehend them leading to unhelpful defensive manoeuvres. There is often no real sustained sense of direction. As a result, leadership is poor, absent or volatile and changeable. Decisions are often dictated by the latest surprise, of which there are many given the inability to understand why things happen, or the most recent set of conditions, numbers or the last person spoken to. This lack of clear sustained direction or leadership eventually spawns an evolutionary move up to the next level, to red.

Red: Power (Individual Focus)

Red is the first level where we see strong leadership. The pendulum swings back from the collective to the individual, and 'red leaders' step forward from the mass of the tribe to take charge. Red is the colour of power and passion and sooner or later a tribe needs a leader to 'take the reins' so that things can finally get done. The tribe needs to move beyond long debates with their unpredictable and lurching 'group think'. The tribe can no longer afford to make decisions driven by the latest 'fad', they need clear thinking and clear direction.

The military actively flush out red leaders by dropping recruits into ambiguous situations and waiting to see who steps forward to provide direction. Such individuals are then promoted. Military commanders know that the upside of purple (group bond) will soon give way to the downside of purple (lack of direction) and the latter will provoke someone to step up and take charge.

Red leaders are one of the two most common value systems we see in the upper echelons of all businesses from SMEs to global multi-nationals. Red leaders are often energetic, charismatic 'larger than life' individuals. Many of them have a good sense of humour, an ability to enjoy themselves. They like to move fast, keep it simple and make things fun or exciting.

However, on the downside, they can also lead by fear, intimidation or strength of will. They are great at clarifying the priorities which makes it easier to see what the next steps should be. Their clarity and sense of urgency injects pace into a business a fact that is further reinforced by their ambition to be the best or the number one in their market.

Because red leaders make things happen they are ideal if a business is opening up a new market or going into a new territory. Many of the emergent food companies are built by individuals with a strong sense of red values. Many of the large food retailers have been led by red autocratic leaders. They are restless, relentless and resilient. Generally red leaders have a low tolerance for detail. If that's not the case it's because another value set may also be at play. Red leaders ultimately want control and use their status, power or authority to dominate. They are good in a fight, an emergency or when a turnaround is needed and like to be seen as the hero.

There are clear benefits to the red value system individually and collectively. When red is driving the bus, stuff gets done. But a red leader can also create a bottleneck for decisions which can slow progress. The intoxicating nature of power can fuel a sense of omnipotence in the red leader and start to drive a wide range of unhelpful behaviours and ultimately egomania. The thirst for power can lead to narcissism and even solipsism. Such self-obsession is often the evolutionary trigger that causes the collective to get together to curb the excesses of the red leader. In short, the next level of values or blue 'order' emerges.

Blue/amber: Order (Collective Focus)

The emergence of the blue value system, although some authors have suggested 'amber' is a more appropriate colour[223], is often driven by the collective recognition that there needs to some order, structure and process in the system to diversify dependency on one or a few people's opinions. In the food industry, this is where quality and safety standards start to get implemented more widely. This is the value system that understands the importance of supply chain management. Whereas the red value system may have been driving production, establishing markets and distributing food the blue/amber value system starts to build an efficient infrastructure to enable this to happen on a wider scale. Someone operating from blue/amber is keen to 'do the right thing' and will involve others in determining what that right thing is. This may including a pricing policy. Thus, the red approach is to sell goods or services for the highest price whereas blue/amber would consider that there may be an 'appropriate' price. Principles and ethics within the supply chain or business become much more central to the business operation.

Blue/amber cultures are often much more prevalent within government departments, bureaucracies and public sector partnerships where order, rank and rules are imposed and adhered to. Most businesses often have to go through a blue/amber phase in order to really grow to scale. The red tendency to fly by the 'seat of the pants' is too chaotic to build an international business.

---

[223] LaLoux F (2014) Reinventing Organizations: A Guide to Creating Organizations Inspired by the Next Stage in Human Consciousness Nelson Parker, Brussels

The blue/amber value system establishes a stable platform for growth and high quality processes that can step change productivity. Most large retailers have incredibly sophisticated supply chain and logistics systems in place to deliver what the customer wants, with minimal waste. Trading standards, national and international regulations and tariffs are much more carefully constructed when organisations and countries reach this level of development. Corruption is increasingly weeded out. The rules, regulations and accuracy imposed by blue/amber can also bring some much-needed discipline and prevent red excesses from derailing the food industry.

One of the main benefits and upsides of the blue/amber value system is stability. But the benefit of the blue/amber value system can become an obsession with an individual or organisation becoming rigid and inflexible (think EU bureaucracy). Like all levels, it is the dysfunction of this blue/amber obstinacy that eventually creates the conditions for the evolutionary push up into the next level and orange emerges.

Orange: Wealth (Individual Focus)

The emergence of the orange value system illustrates a swing back to an individual focus. Most businesses are run by leaders from either a red or orange value system. Essentially the orange leader is a more mature version of the red leader because they've come to appreciate the importance of process, procedure and principle. They are also less likely to make unilateral decisions and will take more opinions into account.

The orange value system liberates itself from the stifling constraints of too many blue/amber rules. As a result, the orange leader looks to leverage the best parts of the blue/amber infrastructure and system and accelerate growth by being more flexible, competitive and results focused. The ultimate goal of orange is wealth creation. Orange leaders take a pragmatic no nonsense view of the world and they are happy to do whatever it takes to achieve their targets. This pragmatism has enabled many of the problems in the food industry to be solved through relentless trial and error experimentation or continuous improvement.

Individuals operating from an orange value system want to make money. They are highly competitive and want to win. This can be beneficial but it can also prompt big companies to bully smaller companies to maximise their own profits at the expense of others. When such behaviour is deeply entrenched, they can self-justify such excessive leverage because in this value set the ends always justifies the means. Smaller companies only response is to play a savvy game. If their profit margins have been cut, they must reduce their offering subtly to maintain their own margins. In the world of orange companies trying to work together many simply try to manipulate the situation to their own advantage.

The desire to win can lead such manipulations to extend to public perception and 'green washing' becomes very common as well as gaming the media - at times passing off isolated incidents of good behavior as common place, even though they might not be. For all the tremendous benefits that the orange value system has brought the food industry it is always necessary to look very carefully at what it being said and done because self-regulation is often not widespread, particularly if those companies have lost touch with their blue/amber ethics and principles in the pursuit of profit.

Whilst the upside of orange is wealth creation and increased prosperity it is often polluted by the excessive greed of the few which acts as the next evolutionary stimulus and green emerges.

Green: Social (Collective Focus)
The excess of orange triggers a swing back to a more collective orientation leading to green businesses or the emergence of green leaders. The green value system is borne out of a recognition that wealth is not just to be enjoyed by a tiny minority. The long-term ability of the system to thrive requires the wealth to be spread more evenly otherwise the people who are most disadvantaged

will destabilise the system because they have nothing to lose (illustrated by events in the US and Europe during 2016/17). The orange value system would take the view that so long as they individually have enough money such destabilisation will not affect them and so their greed is acceptable.

But the longer-term perspective of green means they are motivated to find a more inclusive way of achieving success that benefits the many not just the few. Green leaders understand deeply that the 'winners and losers' mindset is ultimately a zero-sum game. This more egalitarian approach is not just driven by an eye to longer term sustainability but there is a desire to take a more sensitive, people-centric approach. This care extends from profit to people and the planet. They are interested in their carbon footprint, fair trade, local produce, sustainability and the whole green agenda. They are also much more attuned to the needs of the collective. In fact, in many of the developed countries of the world most businesses operate from the orange value system and the green value system represents the cutting edge.

CEOs and leaders operating with green value systems are generally more emotionally intelligent, empathic and are driven by a desire to help. They attempt to include a wide section of opinion and have an intense dislike of hierarchies, particularly the dominator power hierarchies that exist in many businesses. Unfortunately, they often fail to distinguish such pathological dynamics from natural hierarchies, which can be helpful.

This distinction between dominator and natural hierarchies is so important in terms of the food industry and frankly many wicked problems that it is worth expanding on this for a moment. Hierarchies are not by definition bad. For example, molecules do not exist without atoms, which do not exist without electrons and protons. It would be ridiculous to suggest that atoms are better than protons. They are in a natural hierarchy with each other. If you get rid of protons you collapse everything above this level. Molecules need protons to exist. Just as a leader needs followers. One is not 'better' than the other but they play different roles and make different contributions.

The green value system is the developmental level that struggles the most with the idea of hierarchy and those operating from the green value system often want to bring everyone to the same level playing field. Their belief is that it is better to have a flatland than a hierarchy, and in so claiming, they accidentally advocate a hierarchy! The very thing they were trying to reject. Such blindness typifies the green contradiction. On the one hand, very caring and inclusive, and on the other hand myopic and judgemental.

The challenge with the green value system, as with all the previous levels is that they believe their perspective and approach is the right one and strongly defend their view. In fact, every leader in the first tier (beige to green) thinks they are right and everyone else is wrong. It is this mindset that is often at the very heart of wicked problems. Most of the world's big problems stem from this 'I'm right, you're wrong' duality. In business, this dynamic consumes a huge amount of time and effort as individuals or stakeholder silos defend their position, engage in organisational politics and slow initiatives because they don't agree with whatever value system determines the party line. And considering that everyone from beige to green is making the same fundamental error - struggling to step into someone else's shoes - then a huge amount of wasted energy goes into this unhelpful dance which wastes staggering amounts of time, energy, leadership and human potential.

In the food supply chain this unhelpful silo thinking takes many forms. Internal departmental silos in big food businesses such as procurement; operations; marketing; finance; corporate affairs; HR etc. Internal silos in farming across different agri-sectors. Internal silos in government and their often-conflicting priorities. As well as all the stakeholder silos, we've already identified in this book. Perspectives can too easily become entrenched which leads to too much wasted time and finger pointing rather than looking for solutions. A classic example of this is the phenomenal amount of time wasted globally by big food brands and big retailers – arguably the stakeholders with the most access to capability and opportunity to do something differently. The negotiations that occur are often-unnecessarily complex and time consuming with elaborate mechanisms for deciding pricing structures. Essentially, all big branded manufacturers operate a list price and conditional payments system, through which they try to enforce standard trading terms and exert influence on their customers' activities. The payments or "back margin" as they are known in the retail industry, are often very large, can create an industry of work in themselves and in many countries or commercial relationships the deals can literally take all year to negotiate or settle. This is an incredibly wasteful business practice not just in terms of lost management time, on both sides, that could be better deployed to innovate or drive collective efficiency but when viewed in the context of the real issues we face seems especially shallow and wasteful.

Green is the last level in the '1st tier'. And, according to Ken Wilber, it is the main stumbling block for widespread evolution and progress – in business, government and beyond[224]. Most leaders don't make it past the green consensual swamp and stay firmly rooted in the orange reality, or below. Most leaders have yet to make it to the 2nd tier value systems that could ignite major transformation and unlock our collective potential.

The upside of green is creative collaboration; the inclusion of diversity and care but unfortunately their drive for consensus and the ideal that all is equal stalls progress once again.

Yellow/Teal: Innovation (Individual Focus)

Since evolution gets stuck in the green swamp the yellow (or as some authors have suggested, 'teal') value system represents a

---

[224] Wilber, K (2003) Boomeritis: A novel that will set you free Shambhala Productions, Boston

genuine breakthrough opportunity[225]. With the emergence of the second tier the pendulum swings from the green collective back to the yellow/teal individual value system. Those operating at yellow/teal finally understand that it's not 'I'm right, you're wrong' but that all of the previous perspectives have some validity. They are all true but partial, incomplete descriptions of reality. By evolving past the 'consensual hell' and creative inclusivity of green, yellow/teal becomes disruptively innovative.

Yellow/teal is nuanced and sophisticated. Those that operate from yellow/teal can become innovation drivers, constantly coming up with better, brighter, more efficient solutions to the evolving challenges in the food industry. Yellow/teal businesses are usually small or if not they are organised into small, highly dynamic divisions – we can already see this innovation in the food sector as more and more small operators are bringing their innovative solutions to the market (more on that in chapter six).

Yellow/teal leaders know that the world is not binary and they are the first value system to really understand that they may be simultaneously part of the problem and part of the solution. Since they may be contributing to the problem themselves they feel a much greater responsibility for inventing a better future. Having largely freed themselves from the shackles of taking sides and transcended the world of 'I'm right' and 'you're wrong' they are much more adept at handling what others would consider to be conflicts of interest. When all problems are "our" problems they would consider that smart answers are in everyone's interest so taking sides doesn't really arise. They eschew answers that suit you or me in favour of wise answers that suit us. People operating from the yellow/teal value system are drawn to complex problems and see them as a challenge. They are excited by new ideas and want to have an impact beyond their own organisation.

---

[225] LaLoux F (2014) Reinventing Organizations: A Guide to Creating Organizations Inspired by the Next Stage in Human Consciousness Nelson Parker, Brussels

Although Wilber believes that only five per cent of the population are currently operating from this and the next level, this number increases to 10 per cent amongst the more developed population of 10,000 business leaders whose value systems one of us (AW) has assessed in the last few years. This growth in the second tier has the potential to bring about huge change in thinking and deliver genuinely innovative solutions to the world's problems.

This potential could certainly be unlocked more effectively if yellow/teal leaders start to use their innovative capabilities to not just focus on doing things but on transforming themselves and their relationships.

However, there are, as with all levels, downsides even in the second tier. People operating from this value set can get lost in the ideas and conceptual models they love so much. Lost in their own inner world of imagination and ideation they can come across as confusing or aloof. They can appear distracted or even detached. And it is this disconnection that often triggers the emergence of the turquoise value system.

Turquoise: System Balance (Collective focus)

People operating from the turquoise value system are extremely rare in business. In fact, individuals with this value set may not even be operating within traditional businesses. Their path is usually much less conventional. When moving from the yellow/teal to the turquoise value system the pendulum swings back to the collective again.

Often turquoise individuals tend to be more interested in initiating movements and creating large scale change or system change. Their perspective is on the long game and they are interested in the transformation of cultures and societies for the benefit of all people without falling into the trap of being too prescriptive or patronising. A turquoise leader is focused on what serves the greater good.

To many others who operate from an earlier value system turquoise leaders can appear distracted and don't appear to engage in the daily nitty gritty of what needs to happen to solve the current problems. This is actually an illusion - they are often very attentive to such details but they are not reacting to them in the way that most previous value systems do.

They have an ability to take in a huge amount of information, moving variables and different perspectives and are often reflecting on what is the best way forward for the long-term benefit of all concerned. This meta-perspective allows them to dynamically steer an organisation. But such lightness of touch can feel too free flowing and unnerving to those in the first-tier value system.

A turquoise leader can and will show up from many different value systems, since turquoise transcends and includes all previous levels. They can take the role of strong commercial leader, wealth generator or social missionary depending on what's needed. This can easily be misinterpreted by others as fickle but the turquoise leader is not playing a role they are just moving up and down the spiral depending on what the situation warrants. Such flexibility can be incredibly beneficial and it's why viewing culture change as a simple change of location rather than a vertical evolution is so detrimental to results. When we fully grasp the evolutionary nature of values and facilitate that upward advance we don't just swap locations we transcend and include all previous locations so we can use the advantages of all of the levels while avoiding the dangers. That can be genuinely game changing.

Using Value Systems to Better Understand Yourself and Others

Appreciating our own and others value systems can completely change all our relationships in the 'WE' dimension. Having a way of understanding the difference between our perspective and that of others, being able to see the upsides and downsides of both our view of the world and other people's view can enable us to better reconcile our differences, reduce any conflict and improve the quality of our communication.

So often disagreements between stakeholders and their advocates are misdiagnosed as a 'personality clash' but the conflict is usually nothing to do with personality. Rather it is to do with the different value systems we use to interpret the world. If we can recognise that both our different points of view have validity and are arising from our different value systems then we are much better placed to find a way to reconcile our differences. For example, say two people are having an argument where one wants to make a decision and get into action and the other wants to explore more options and find the consensus. When both individuals realise that most of what they are arguing about is actually a reflection of their value system then much of the heat is taken out of the situation. When the red individual realises they are operating from red and the green individual realises they are operating from green and both can appreciate the others value system then they can come to a compromise position that will facilitate a better, less fraught and more mutually agreeable way forward. This mutual understanding and value specific language alone can massively improve the quality and depth of relationships and a lot of the arm wrestling and power struggles simply disappear.

An understanding of value systems can also help improve performance and results because it allows us to work with and bring in the right people to get the various tasks done. For example, people who operate from the turquoise and yellow/teal values sets are particularly useful in strategy meetings because they can appreciate multiple perspectives and may come up with 'out the box' innovations. But these value systems play less of a driving role when it comes to implementation. Green individuals are great for ensuring everyone feels involved and part of the plan. The orange value set can add significant commercial nous:

the blue/amber values bring process and procedure to underpin the plan; while red can be invaluable for injecting energy and getting stuff done, particularly when the ignition is done at the right moment. If the red value set steps into a strategic debate too early it can be counterproductive.

In short, everyone has a role to play that allows the group to tap into the collective strength while mitigating the collective weaknesses. These insights allow us to appreciate that many of the stumbling blocks in business, government and beyond could actually be avoided when we effectively blend people who have different values. To be effective we need all the perspectives contributing to the decision.

Obviously, the more sophisticated the stakeholder the more options they have in dealing and working with their team. Remember we can move down and embrace earlier value systems at will in order to match the values of the people around us but we have to put the effort in to work our way up to the next level of vertical development. When we do we increase the sophistiction of the 'WE' dimension and unlock our potential.

Elevation in all the lines of development radically alters how we then show up.

Show Up

Einstein stated that we can't solve a problem with the same level of thinking that created it. We need access to more sophistication and cognitive flexibility and that means vertical development. When we wake up and truly understand what level of development we are currently operating from and what level of development those around us are operating from, much of the confusion so frequently associated with 'people management' disappears. When we invest in vertical development so we literally become more of who we are while also owning up to our failings and unhelpful behaviour patterns that have caused problems for us and those around us then we show up differently in the world.

If we are to solve these problems more of us have to show up differently in the world and hold ourselves and others to a higher standard. We need real leadership, bold individuals from all the stakeholder groups to come together to find collaborative solutions. Often that will mean owning up to the role we have all played in the food problems we now face. Acknowledging our culpability with a strong commitment for change.

If we look at the debate in the food industry there is still far too much 'I'm right, you're wrong' activity going on. Too few leaders are genuinely proactively collaborating and embracing multiple perspectives. Take food waste as the example. We are still debating how to measure food waste and whose measure is correct. The current crop of definitions of food waste can and do change depending on the stakeholder group you are talking to. This is partly because each one is seeking to find a definition that minimises their contribution to the problem. Whether from a tribal 'protect my company from too much exposure' purple perspective; or a 'compliance with all the rules and regulations' blue/amber perspective; or a 'game the rules to give my company a competitive advantage over the field' orange perspective; or a 'seek consensus' green perspective, we are wasting valuable time and energy in endless discussions about the nature and composition of the problem. When what we should be focused on is actually solving it.

If it literally takes years for us to collectively agree on what food waste actually is and align around that definition, it's going to be almost impossible to accurately quantify the scale of the problem at a global level. While agreed and universally used definitions of the problem are key to solving it, taking years to reach that point is a colossal waste of leadership time and energy and is all too frequently used as a 'cop out' to avoid or delay action.

We really need to break this deadlock and encourage whole industry cooperation instead of competition and create some real leadership around this issue.

At the heart of this deadlock is the fact that most stakeholders get stuck in a singular perspective and will often defend their view strongly. Most people are totally immersed in their own perspective, largely based on their value system and level of maturity and believe they are right and therefore all others must be wrong. They are wedded to their particular perspective with unshakable certainty. Understanding how to overcome such binary right/wrong thinking combined with the lack of awareness and sensitivity to the views of others is actually a crucial part of the solutions process. The problem is not that we have different views, it is that we are unyieldingly stuck in our own view with no awareness that we are stuck. Involving as many different views as possible from stakeholders at all levels of the values system is essential for a high-quality solution but this lack of awareness of perspective taking is seriously holding us back.

This lack of awareness of how to effectively explore a problem without it descending into an 'I'm right, you're wrong' impasse is worth expanding on here because without a more effective way of debating our differences we are very unlikely to ever solve the wicked problems we face.

Let's look at the anatomy of any discussion. When arguing about anything, a tame or a wicked problem, most individuals will take one of three stances – what is called 1st, 2nd or 3rd person perspective taking.

First person perspective is the personal subjective perspective. Stakeholders operating from the 1st person are focused on 'Me, My, I'. They enter discussions about how to grapple with and solve the problem believing they are right and everyone else is wrong. Their priority is to deliver on their own agenda and protect their own interests. When stakeholders communicate in the 1st person perspective, they are putting a stake in the ground about what they want, think or believe. As a result, they tend to be very attached to what they communicate. The 1st person perspective is very passionate, it is powerful and engaging, but it can also be dogmatic and unyielding. It is based on personal experiences in the world, things the stakeholder has witnessed and "knows" to be true because they have seen them with their own eyes.

Approaching all issues from the 1st person perspective is really about being stuck in the subjective view of the world. The first six value systems can all get stuck in the 1st person perspective. People operating from the red value system are convinced they are right because they are always right; people operating from the blue/amber value system are simply right because they have principle or a higher authority on their side; people operating from the orange value set believe they are right because they have evidence on their side; people operating from green often believe they are right because they believe they have considered others' views and embraced them. The lack of awareness of anything other than my subjective view can occur at all levels but it is most commonly and clearly seen in red leaders who tend to operate from the 1st person perspective – passionately advocating their opinion.

If a stakeholder does not get stuck in 1st person perspective, then they are most likely stuck in the 3rd person rational, objective perspective. Stakeholders operating from the 3rd person will helicopter up above the issue and present facts, figures and data to support their case. They believe the 'evidence' reveals 'the truth' and the answer must be evidence based. This is the approach of science and all data driven disciplines. These stakeholders will say things like, "the evidence states" or "the data don't lie". This perspective is very common in business. It is often claimed that the answer is "nothing personal". As such people taking the 3rd person perspective can inadvertently abdicate any personal responsibility for the outcome.

Again, every level can get stuck in the rational observer 3rd person perspective but it most commonly encountered in the orange value set. If leaders operating with red values take the 3rd person perspective, they tend to do so to try and control the outcome or force their facts on others. Leaders with blue/amber values will take the 3rd person perspective by pulling back to discover a higher order principle. But as we said the orange value system are the real masters of the objective stance. Most mature businesses operate from an orange value set. Leaders and teams that take the 3rd person perspective, while operating from the orange value system and simultaneously stuck at the 'expert level' of ego maturity are extremely difficult to change[226].

People operating with orange values often take a pragmatic or mechanistic view and like to consider all the options in order to determine what will work. They then take a dispassionate view based on 'the evidence' that they have sorted, being an 'expert' in their field. As a result, they take the view that there is absolutely no way they can be wrong. Occasionally they may contemplate, at least theoretically, the possibility that they could be wrong, but frankly they would consider it extremely unlikely because 'facts' and 'evidence' and their 'experience' as an expert prevents mistakes of judgement. Such leaders often create echo chambers around themselves that simply reinforce their views that they are right. If they inadvertently let someone in who has a dissenting view, they are likely to attack that view so they can 'win' the argument and prevail. Humility and reflection are uncommon visitors to their parlour. They do not like surprises and therefore they build organisations that minimises the risk of surprises. Consequently, they are not adept at dealing with outliers or data that doesn't fit their world view. When they encounter such data they are likely to reject it, thereby missing the real opportunity that is hidden behind such surprises. What such expert, pragmatic rationalists miss is the possibility of the world not being fully explained by their view of reality. There

---

[226] Watkins A (2016) 4D Leadership Kogan Page, London

is a developmental joke that you can always tell such expert rationalists operating from the 3rd person perspective - you just can't tell them much.

If stakeholders are not stuck in 1st or 3rd then they may flip between the two. At times, they will hold firm to the direct, passionate 1st person subject perspective, stating their case and hanging on to that position come hell or high water. If such passionate advocacy doesn't work, they may then flip into an objective rational 3rd person perspective and recruit 'evidence' that powerfully supports their 1st person argument. Thus, they co-opt 3rd person evidence to their 1st person belief to win their case on 'merit'. Similarly, when people who normally operate from a rational 3rd person perspective are struggling to make their case they will often become emotional, and may even throw their toys out of the pram in an attempt to force a conclusion in their favour.

To add to the complexity, these two perspectives (1st and 3rd) are often deeply intertwined. For example, stakeholders will often use the objective data to validate their own 1st person perspective while disguising themselves as dis-passionate rational observers. Alternatively, they may delude themselves that they are taking an evidence-based approach when they are selectively choosing only those pieces of evidence that they happen to believe are correct based on their 1st person values[227].

The great irony is that progress only ever tends to be made when stakeholders can access the gap between 1st and 3rd and get into genuine broad-based 2nd person perspective taking - this is why integration is so essential for wise solutions.

The essence of the 2nd person perspective is the ability to access common ground. This is the start point for real collaboration.

---

[227] Wilber K (1998) The Marriage of Sense and Soul: Integrating Science and Religion Random House New York

Unfortunately, very few people have developed the ability to operate from this perspective, or have any real-world experience of the difference it can make to successful collaboration. In fact, until we point this out to people most do not even recognise the difference between 1st, 2nd and 3rd person perspective taking.

Even after you have pointed out these perspectives to people they may still find it very difficult to access 2nd. When you have spent your life operating from the 1st or 3rd person perspective moving out of 1st person can feel like being asked to give up what you believe in and moving out of 3rd can feel like being asked to ignore 'the truth'. Of course, neither is the case but accessing 2nd person perspective and temporarily suspending 1st and 3rd can be very difficult for many, which is one of the reasons many people find genuine collaboration very challenging.

Early attempts to build a shared 2nd person perspective often result in a congealed version of 1st or 3rd person perspective taking. Thus, what actually happens is lip service is given to alignment when in reality what has occurred is forced capitulation when the most powerful player in the room brow beats the others into submission and then congratulates themselves that an agreement has been reached. But muscular submission is nothing like genuine engagement and such outcomes will inevitably unravel and cause problems in the medium term. When looking at any supply chain true partnership where real win/win relationships occur are always better commercially than expedient short-term price victories (in either direction). The difficulty is that many businesses are set up and lead with the short-term in mind. Longer term collaborative dynamics are uncommon even if leaders knew how to build them.

The ability to access the 2nd person perspective really begins to kick in when individuals are operating from the green value systems. Leaders operating from red values can often be very engaging but they largely come from a 1st person perspective. When the pendulum swings to the more collective orientation of the blue/amber value system the accompanying diplomacy and sensitivity to social rules can help those at this level to consider other people's opinions. Such an orientation helps individuals start to access 2nd person perspective taking but it can feel a little like relationship by numbers rather than the greater sensitivity that is available to people operating from the green value set. If individuals working from the orange value set understand the anatomy of perspective taking then they could engage from a 2nd person perspective but their preference is to pull back and operate from the 3rd person. The orange value set will have to work hard to set aside rationality to engage deeply in the more intimate 2nd person perspective.

At the emergence of the green value system the greater people sensitivity and the desire to be more inclusive boosts the 2nd person perspective taking capability and can vault individuals into the ability to go beyond the ability to take 1st, 2nd and 3rd person perspective taking and enable them to access 4th person perspective taking. The ability to access 4th person perspective taking is marked by the ability to step in or step out of 1st, 2nd and 3rd person perspective taking. Conscious awareness of which perspective you are taking at the exact moment you are taking it is the hallmark of 4th person capability.

When differences of opinion arise the ability to resolve differences requires common understanding and shared goals to be defined. Such sophistication does not mean forcing capitulation but genuinely understanding the nature of other person's view and being able to integrate the diverse points into a wiser more complete whole.

The complexity and inter-relatedness of perspective taking, value systems and maturity testify to how nuanced relationship dynamics really are and why it can be so difficult to resolve tension between two parties.

But as we have said the wicked problem of food involves many different stakeholders all with different opinions about the nature of the problem and how to solve it. The endless game-playing, manoeuvring, bickering and infighting that occurs in most 'negotiations' fuels the sense of futility around wicked problems, making them feel un-solvable. The good news is that when people develop the ability to consciously access and work with 2nd person perspective taking many of these obstacles fall away. An understanding of value systems and a knowledge of how ego maturity affects relationships provides us with a powerful ability to build extremely strong relationships with stakeholders, clients, customers, suppliers or anyone in the system that we need to. Such abilities can elevate us to a whole new level of 'WE' capability enabling real connections and genuine progress to be made.

This is what we need – vertically developed stakeholders determined to make real progress. Otherwise we are going to continue to squander much needed human potential.

Chapter 5:

Converging Forces of Hope

The scale of the problems we face around food are significant. It is a highly complex area with competing priorities and far reaching interdependencies. But there are converging forces of hope to suggest that we can solve this problem. They include, but are not limited to:

* Increased Global Will

* Greater Innovation

* Beyond Capitalism

* Increased Transparency and Corporate Visibility

Increased Global Will

There is growing acceptance amongst the global population as a whole and within key stakeholder groups within that population that we do not live in an infinite universe. Most informed human beings accept the validity of climate change science. The evidence is simply too comprehensive to do otherwise. It looks likely that a Trump Presidency will seek to obscure and question this science for a little longer in order to push forward the commercial agenda of fossil fuel and the claim that such short-sightedness will create additional jobs. As is so often the case, such a one-dimensional solution may deliver greater profits to the fossil fuel companies and may create much needed jobs for a few more years but if it accelerates our own demise as a species these short-term objectives seem somewhat ridiculous. Denying something is true just because we don't want to believe it doesn't make it any less true. And whilst we are all entitled to our own opinion we are absolutely not entitled to our own facts.

Encouragingly there is, however increased global will to tackle our diminishing resources and find ways to meet our needs sustainably. The United Nations have collectively created an agenda for transforming our world by 2030 through the Sustainable Development Goals (SDG) which include global aspirations to tackle our food problems as well as many others. Spearheaded by the UN, through a deliberative process involving its 193 Member States, as well as global civil society, the SDGs are a set of seventeen aspirational 'Global Goals' with 169 targets between them (see Figure 5.1). They are, to a large extent informed by the often-quoted assertion by United Nations Secretary-General Ban Ki-moon that "there can be no Plan B, because there is no Planet B."

Figure 5.1: Sustainable Development Goals

Modified from original Source: http://bit.ly/2ol2vsX

Solving any problem, especially a wicked one requires global recognition that there is a problem in the first place. The SDGs seek to do that and to push the need for change and new solutions to the top of the corporate and political agenda.

Many of these global goals relate to food supply and sustainability in some form or another but it's goal 12, 'Responsible Consumption and Production', that is the primary focus for many in the food industry. Under SDG 12 there are three primary objectives and eight separate sub-goals[228]

The sub-goals which are much more directly focused on food are summarised as:

1. Implement sustainable production and consumption.

2. Deliver efficient management and use of natural resources by 2030.

3. Halve food waste per head from field to fork by 2030.

4. Deliver sound chemical and waste management by 2020.

5. Reduce waste substantially by 2030.

6. Ensure companies report on sustainability.

7. Deliver sustainable government procurement.

8. Ensure everyone has awareness and information for sustainable development by 2030.

The fact that these goals even exist, and are widely known, is a reason for hope. There is no progress without awareness so the first step in changing anything for the better is to be aware

---

[228] https://sustainabledevelopment.un.org/sdg12

of what needs to change. The SDGs reveal that there is a global focus on these critical issues and a desire to find solutions. Progress so far on SDG 12 include:

- Basel Convention on the Control of Transboundary Movements of Hazardous Wastes and Their Disposal

- The Rotterdam Convention on the Prior Informed Consent Procedure for Certain Hazardous Chemicals and Pesticides in International Trade

- The Stockholm Convention on Persistent Organic Pollutants established international frameworks to achieve the environmentally sound management of hazardous wastes, chemicals and persistent organic pollutants.

With six exceptions, all Member States are party to at least one of those conventions. The number of parties to those conventions rose significantly from 2005 to 2015, particularly in Africa and Oceania. There are now 183 parties to the Basel Convention, 180 to the Stockholm Convention and 155 to the Rotterdam Convention[229].

One area of particular concern and a large focus in this book is 12.3 which seeks to halve per capita food waste and reduce food losses by 2030. In January 2016, at the World Economic Forum in Davos, a coalition of 30 leaders launched 'Champions 12.3' - a new effort to inspire and mobilise action to reduce food loss and waste globally[230]. The Champions include CEOs of major companies, government ministers, executives of research and intergovernmental institutions, foundations, farmer organisations, and civil society groups that are aware of the 'triple win' available by tackling this issue. Reducing food loss and waste can save money for farmers, companies, and consumers;

---

[229] https://sustainabledevelopment.un.org/sdg12

[230] https://champions123.org/the-champions/

feed more people; and alleviate pressure on water, energy and land resources.

Working together and each serving in a private capacity, these leaders will work to create political, business and social momentum to reduce food loss and waste around the world by:

- Leading by example on how to reduce food loss and waste;

- Motivating others to meet SDG Target 12.3;

- Communicating the importance of food loss and waste reduction;

- Showcasing successful food loss and waste reduction strategies; and

- Advocating for more innovation, greater investment, better information, and increased capacity to reduce food loss and waste[231]

Goal 12, in its entirety will also be reviewed and further progress assessed at the high level political forum on sustainable development in 2018. There is little doubt that these actions and interventions are encouraging and represent a strong force for hope although much more will need to be done, individually, culturally, economically, politically and societally if we are to reach this and the other 16 sustainable development goals.

Greater Innovation

Another reason for us to be hopeful of our ability to solve the

---

[231] World Economic Forum (2016) Press Release New "Champions 12.3" Coalition to Inspire Action to Reduce Food Loss & Waste https:// champs123blog.files.wordpress.com/2016/01/champions-12-3_press-release.pdf

food supply challenges that exist today and into the future is human ingenuity.

Futurist and inventor Buckminster Fuller proposed the 'knowledge doubling curve' in 1981 after he noticed that the more knowledge we accumulate the faster we create even more knowledge. For example, until 1900 human knowledge doubled every one hundred years or so. By 1945 the complete knowledge of mankind doubled every 25 years. Today on average knowledge doubles every 13 months[232].

Whatever the rate is today, it represents a very rapid, very large expansion of knowledge that is changing the world. What's even more startling is that when Fuller made his prediction the internet didn't even exist. There were no smart phones, no PCs or laptop computers, no satellite TV, no digital technology, no smart sensors, limited artificial intelligence and no social media. Considering the technological innovations of the last decade alone it's easy to see how this trend is such a powerful force for hope.

Remember the pessimists we discussed in chapter two - they believe we have already experienced the best of human innovations. Those inventions, improvements and inputs have cumulatively resulted in an increase in aggregate food production by 170 per cent over the last 50 years[233]. Their argument is that our best is therefore behind us and yet knowledge doubling and the speed and pace of innovation tells us we are only really getting started.

There are several elements to greater innovation that pour much needed optimism into the food challenges we face. First there is

---

[232] Schilling DR (2013) Knowledge doubling every 12 months, soon to be every 12 hours. Industry Tap http://www.industrytap.com/knowledge-doubling-every-12-months-soon-to-be-every-12-hours/3950

[233] Feeding the World Part 3 FOA http://www.fao.org/docrep/015/i2490e/i2490e03a.pdf

the innovation that is likely to come through greater access to data. Gadgets and sensors are engaged in a process of constant 'datafication'. Today, data is no longer just held as words, numbers or images and archived. It is being digitised and datafied for on-going collection and analysis. This analysis is sure to deliver more accurate, tailored and personalised information that will allow us to make better food production and consumption choices.

Everything is creating data. There are new types and forms of data that are accelerating the knowledge doubling still further. For example, sensors that collect data are now fitted to car and aircraft engines. Engine manufacturer Rolls Royce has transformed itself from a loss making British firm into the world's second-biggest maker of large jet engines by pursuing sensor technology[234]. Today Rolls Royce monitors the performance of more than 3,700 jet engines they manufactured via thousands of built-in sensors. The data allows the airlines to operate more efficiently and makes the skies safer. For example, lightning strikes are a common occurrence in air travel and they used to cause delays because they would automatically trigger a full engine inspection once the plane landed. This would slow down turn-around time, irritate customers and affect "On-Time Performance" (OTP) - a key performance indicator of air travel. The in-built sensors have stopped all that because if an engine so much as murmurs unexpectedly a torrent of data is automatically sent back to Rolls Royce HQ where screens jump into life, graphs are created and technicians assess the real-time impact of the data. In fact, very often the pilots will know if there is a problem to be fixed before they've even landed. This type of sensor technology will make a huge difference to food traceability and minimising waste. For example, there is currently a lot of development work being done in food supply chains around RFID (radio frequency identification technology), and/or expiry date encoded barcodes, that will give retailers and manufacturers the ability to track the life of

---

[234] The Economist (2009) Rolls Royce: Britain's Lonely High-Flier [Online] http://www.economist.com/node/12887368

products and have the right quantities in the right places at the right time, with, crucially, the right shelf life. By investing in this technology food companies will seek to lower stock levels and residency times, whilst also improving availability for customers and reduce waste. There is also some innovative work to extend these principles into consumers' homes. Sensors could provide a new level of 'fridge management' while also providing people with information and helpful tools to eat better, waste less and share more as part of a busier lifestyle.

There are now more objects and appliances collecting more types of data than people on the planet and they are increasingly being connected together by the Internet of Things (IoT) – a vast network connecting wired or wireless devices that exchange data to usher in a new level of automation, monitoring and management that will change the way we live.

This explosion in technological capability is described by Moore's Law. In the 1970s Gordon Moore, one of the inventors of integrated circuits noticed that it was possible to squeeze twice as many transistors on an integrated circuit every 24 months. Moore's law therefore explains this exponential growth rate in the advance in technology. And it is this exponential growth that has changed just about every business in every sector in every economy and it has made the Internet of Things possible. US inventor and futurist Ray Kurzweil points out that there will be 1000 times more technological change in the 21st century than there was in the 20th century[235]. According to Kurzweil even Moore's Law will be obsolete by 2019 because the rate of advancement will be even more rapid than the exponential growth it currently describes.

In his seminal essay *The Law of Accelerating Returns* Kurzweil states, "There's even exponential growth in the rate of exponential

---

[235] Kurzweil, Ray (2013). How to create a mind: The secret of human thought revealed. New York: Penguin Books

growth. Within a few decades, machine intelligence will surpass human intelligence, leading to The Singularity — technological change so rapid and profound it represents a rupture in the fabric of human history[236]. It's safe to assume we are living through that rupture in the fabric of human history and the technology that will emerge in the coming years will help us all to gain safe affordable access to good quality nutritious food.

Beyond Capitalism

Another potent force for hope in solving our food challenges will come as business – large and small - move beyond capitalism. Following a bruising few years after the global financial crisis (GFC) of 2007/08 business is starting to wake up to the fact that it can be a very powerful force for good that can shift the entire planet toward a new more sustainable and inclusive commercial environment. There is already evidence that business is beginning to embrace a broader, more expansive remit than quarterly results and maximising shareholder return.

When Milton Friedman's landmark article appeared in the *New York Times* in 1970 stating that the sole purpose of business was to make money for its shareholders, business took note. Friedman was a well-known economist – head of the Chicago School of Economics. He would even win a Nobel Prize for his 'contribution' and was described by *The Economist* as "the most influential economist of the second half of the 20th century... possibly of all of it"[237]. Suffice to say his opinion mattered and business liked his message. Friedman suggested business executives who pursued a goal other than making money were, in his words, "unwitting puppets of the intellectual forces that

---

[236]   Kurweil R (2001) The Law of Accelerating Returns [Online] http://www. kurzweilai.net/the-law-of-accelerating-returns

[237]   The Economist (2006) A heavyweight champ, at five foot two: The legacy of Milton Friedman, a giant among economists Online Extra [Online] http://www.economist.com/node/8313925

have been undermining the basis of a free society these past decades." They were guilty of "analytical looseness and lack of rigor." They had even turned themselves into "unelected government officials" who were illegally taxing employers and customers[238].

From this point forward business, especially publicly listed companies started to take a narrower view of themselves. According to Friedman business had no role to play in promoting desirable 'social' ends. Business didn't need a 'social conscience', there was no need for business to take all reasonable measures to eliminate discrimination, operate ethically, be a good employer, reduce pollution or support the community in which it operated. It's first and only priority was to serve the shareholders.

Several years later, in 1976, this idea was given wings by finance Professor Michael Jensen and Dean William Meckling of the Simon School of Business at the University of Rochester when they published a paper that would effectively provide a 'how to' guide to Freidman's initial ideas[239].

They identified what they referred to as the 'principal-agent problem' and created 'agency theory' to explain and propose a potential solution to this 'problem'. The authors suggested that the shareholders (principals) were often disadvantaged by the firm's senior executives (agents) because there is an incentive to optimise their own self-interest and not necessarily the interest of the shareholders. Although this idea sounded sensible and even fairly logical they provided no real-world evidence of the existence of the principal-agent problem. The assumption

238 Denning S (2013) The Origin Of 'The World's Dumbest Idea': Milton Friedman Forbes [Online] http://www.forbes.com/sites/ stevedenning/2013/06/26/the-origin-of-the-worlds-dumbest-idea- milton-friedman/

239 Jensen MC, Meckling WH (1976) Theory of the Firm: Managerial Behaviour, Agency Costs and Ownership Structure Journal of Financial Economics 3 no 4 305-360

however was that a CEO might, for example believe that his time and comfort was so important that he needed to fly first class to business meeting thus creating an 'agency cost' that diminished the return to investors.

The solution they proposed was to ensure that senior executive objectives were aligned with shareholder objectives. And, the best and simplest way to do that was to make senior executives shareholders themselves. What these academics suggested had some theoretical merit but the subsequent practical implementation of these ideas set off a chain of events in business that completely changed the corporate landscape. It provided senior executives and shareholders with a way to turn Freidman's earlier vision of what business should be all about into a commercial reality. In the 1970s stock based compensation packages accounted for less than one per cent of CEO remuneration. From 1976 onwards executive compensation became increasingly stock based. By 2009 stock based packages accounted for up to 97 per cent of leadership remuneration[240].

This is a radical shift that has undoubtedly fuelled the overly capitalist mindset and behaviour that was instrumental in creating the global financial crisis in the first place. The resulting preoccupation with shareholder return as demanded by 'the City' became a primary driver. This in turn shifted behaviour to shorter time horizons where greater emphasis was placed on what would positively impact quarterly results, sometimes at the expense of customers and the long-term sustainability of the company. When a business is driven in this manner, especially if that approach comes from the top it's almost impossible for the executives to do anything else. Even if they wanted to embrace a broader more expansive strategy that focused on long-term sustainability over short-term results it would be almost impossible to execute and they would be forced to focus on more tangible, shorter term deliverables.

---

[240] Martin, RL (2011) Fixing the Game: How Runaway Expectations Broke the Economy, and How to Get Back to Reality Harvard Business School Press, Boston

Clearly, shareholder return is an important goal of business not least because it supports many of our pension funds but this 'solution' didn't solve the hypothetical principal-agent problem it may have actually contributed to its acceleration and stimulated even greater inequality. In a report published to coincide with the World Economic Forum annual meeting in Davos, Oxfam said inequality was now "beyond grotesque" with the eight richest men in the world, worth an estimated £350 billion equivalent to the wealth of 3.6 billion people[241].

Most senior executives are remunerated through a combination of short term annual bonus and a longer term incentive plan (L-TIP). This often means that a significant part of their their annual take-home pay is based on a variety of annual financial performance metrics, and in addition to this there is often a longer-term dimension, usually awarded in deferred shares, that will only vest if certain stakeholder targets are achieved, designed to ensure executives are "tied in" for longer periods. This is not unreasonable and usually has the joint objective of securing the loyalty of key leaders whilst also binding their personal financial incentives with those of the principal, often institutional, owners of the company.

Even though their bonuses are determined by what is delivered across the year most senior executives are extremely aware of their very short term 'run rate' performance against their bonus targets, and in public companies will be acutely aware of the requirements to report progress on a fixed and formal quarterly basis. Many senior executives are personally involved in this quarterly reporting cycle to the City where they are likely to face a grilling from analysts and investors keen to have the most accurate assessments of forward discounted cash flows in their detailed models. Any variance from previous forecast expectations, or significant changes in sentiment picked up by

[241] Elliot L (2017) World's eight richest people have same wealth as poorest 50% The Guardian https://www.theguardian.com/global-development/2017/jan/16/worlds-eight-richest-people-have-same-wealth-as-poorest-50?CMP=twt_a-world_b-gdnworld

this highly tuned audience can and often does stimulate direct or indirect activity in the markets, with management often left perplexed as to why good news caused a fall in share price or bad news gave the price a lift, perhaps after previous falls (as it turns out that the bad news wasn't quite as bad as the models had initially predicted).

The way the City itself functions can be a significant contributor to the short-term focus in many companies. Whilst many equity stakes are held by long term investors who do have a long term interest in the company creating value (in the form of market capitalisation and dividends) over time with the lowest associated risk profile, these intentions are not shared by all in the money markets. For example, at the time of writing this book, three of the top 10 "most hated shares on the FTSE" are food retailers according to *Moneyweek*. Two of these retailers have 15-20 per cent of their stock currently being 'shorted'. In the last year 87 per cent of 'active' UK equity funds failed to beat the benchmark index, i.e. failed to beat what an automated tracker fund would achieve. The people who manage those funds are incentivised to make trades to generate commissions (irrespective of performance) and beat short-term peer performance, often judged over their own limited time horizons.

Occasionally a courageous leader like Unilever's CEO, Paul Polman will step forward and refuse to report quarterly. Polman believed the obsession was distorting behaviour in the company and that he and his senior team were spending too much time producing documents to satisfy the City instead of developing the business to satisfy the customers. Unfortunately, not enough leaders followed suit and so business is still engaged in the quarter by quarter battle[242]. Besides, if a private equity firm believe they can turn 15 per cent return into 22 per cent return even the most courageous leaders may have to park visions of

---

[242] Watkins A (2016) 4D Leadership: Competitive advantage through vertical leadership development Kogan Page, London

sustainability and long-term growth in favour of radical short-term behaviour to stave off the threat of a hostile takeover.

In fact, as we go to press Polman's Unilever is itself under attack from 3G, a private equity firm driven by three Brazilian corporate raiders. Although usually positioned in the media as just another corporate battle, it is actually much more - nothing short of a fight for the soul of global corporations[243]. And, the outcome could determine whether short-term asset leverage and high cash returns to a small group of investors or 'Conscious Capitalism' is the prevailing model for a generation. In the blue corner, Unilever, a global giant that prides itself on growing revenues and profits based on a sustainability model with a social purpose. In 2010 Unilever introduced the Unilever Sustainable Living Plan with dozens of metrics to measure progress. His advocacy of environmental sustainability even earned Polman the UN's 'Champion of the Earth Award'. In the red corner, 3G, advocating maximising short-term earnings to increase near-term valuation.

In February 2017 3G, through its ownership of Kraft Heinz, a business one third the size of Unilever, launched a hostile takeover bid. With Warren Buffet on board as part of the 3G attack team their unexpected approach shocked the markets[244]. If a company the size of Unilever could be 'taken out' by an aggressor then no company is safe. Such a move will also send a clear signal to the markets and beyond that pure profit still trumps profit and purpose. The raiders have honed their attack capabilities over ten years and have never lost a fight, creating $300billion for their backers in the process. They offered to buy shares above the market price at the time and planned to fund their takeover by restructuring Unilever's own balance sheet. The Twitterosphere

---

[243] George B (2017) The battle for the soul of capitalism explained in one hostile takeover bid CNBC http://www.cnbc.com/2017/03/24/kraft-heinz-unilever-battle-threat-to-capitalism-commentary.html

[244] Massoudi A Fontanella-Khan J (2017) The $143bn flop: How Warren Buffett and 3G lost Unilever Financial Times https://www.ft.com/content/d846766e-f81b-11e6-bd4e-68d53499ed71

erupted at the announcement of the attack. Polman and his board repelled the initial move in April 2017 announcing a strategic restructuring of their business including an intention to sell off their spreads business, massively reduce their cost base, alter the way they are listed on the stock exchange and the way they report to the markets[245].

The importance of this battle can't be underestimated. It is a 'predator-prey' fight. Unilever is cast in the role of the water buffalo, 3G is the lioness seeking to bring them down. If Unilever can become leaner and faster they may yet escape. The markets have initially looked favourably on Unilever's announcement of their structural and financial changes. But the fight is far from over. The future of food and whether the world allows private equity cash approaches to trump all other considerations will be defined by the outcome of this massive battle. The larger issue is not just the fate of a single, albeit global company but the fate of capitalism itself. Those of us, both authors included who believe capitalism is a great long-term value creator must care about the fate of great companies that are role models for the way capitalism should work. As such, it is surprising that there has not been more debate in the mainstream press about this fight. The lack of general coverage in the media is probably because too few people, even those in the 'Conscious Capitalism' movement, understand the implications of this particular battle.

Such takeover bids and the PE model itself is often driven by companies like 3G's ability to significantly reduce the corporate cost base. In practice this means massive job cuts and the imposition of often less experienced executives with a much harder financial focus. This drives up revenues and can make the company more efficient and sometimes will create a more sustainable platform but it can drift to the side of corporate cachexia or the deterioration of the corporate entity in the same

[245] Daneshkhu S (2017) Unilever chief now under pressure to deliver on reforms Financial Times https://www.ft.com/content/a2f1fe90-f792-11e6-bd4e-68d53499ed71

way that 'Conscious Capitalism' can drift to corporate obesity. Getting the balance right is not easy. It is not that lions should not hunt water buffalo. It is a matter of an ecological balance between both. We discuss this more in chapter eight.

Either way what is clear to everyone including business leaders and senior executives themselves is that Freidman, Jensen and Meckling were wrong or at best only partially right. Everything evolves through the different value systems we discussed in the previous chapter. What Freidman, Jensen and Meckling did was simply usher in the 'orange' wealth creation value level. Like all levels the orange level of thinking has significant merit and advantages. Business is an important engine for innovation and problems present opportunities for solutions and profit. However, like all levels there is also a dark-side. Many of us got to experience the dark-side of the orange value system post GFC. But let's not forget that it is always the dark-side that becomes the catalyst for forward movement and evolution to a better more inclusive paradigm. If Unilever manages to fight off 3G the corporate community may realise that aggressive asset leverage may generate great cash returns for a few in the short-term but our longer-term success requires us to embrace a more sophisticated view. That is not to say that Unilever does not need to undergo a strategic review of its business and indeed the 3G attack has triggered such a move. Rather it should cause us to consider how we determine the optimum balance between revenue, cash, profit and purpose or social contribution of any organisation.

Change is in the air. Increasingly leaders and senior executives, like Polman or John Mackie at Whole Foods[246] are seeking alternatives to a purely capitalist approach. Although a more inclusive, expansive measure of business success has been around for some time, it's often been more prevalent in the public

---

[246] Kowitt B (2015) John Mackey: The conscious capitalist Fortune Magazine http://fortune.com/2015/08/20/whole-foods-john-mackey/

sector. Concepts such as triple-bottom-line (TBL) which looks at people and planet as well as profit or more recently quadruple-bottom-line (QBL) which incorporates how well the business is taking a future orientated, sustainable approach allow a business or organisation to look beyond pure financial performance[247]. This is however easier in public sector organisations because while they have stakeholders they usually don't have shareholders in the traditional sense – at least not ones expecting a financial return on their investment. Increasingly however, post GFC more stakeholders including employees, customers and shareholders are demanding it.

In 2015, *The Harvard Business Review*, shifted how it assesses its "100 best-performing CEOs", including for the first time a variety of environmental, social, and governance (ESG) metrics. In the new reckoning, Jeff Bezos fell from first place to 87th, and Netflix's CEO didn't even make the list. The fact that even the HBR views performance beyond just profit is surely solid evidence that ideas such as TBL have finally entered the mainstream[248].

The man behind Triple-Bottom-Line (TBL), John Elkington has created a new initiative called Project Breakthrough with the aim of bringing together corporations with "next generation innovators and entrepreneurs" to spur more dynamic thinking about the world's sustainability challenges. Elkington has also called on companies to track their performance according to the Sustainable Development Goals, mentioned earlier and to take on an "exponential mindset" that matches the size of today's health, environmental, and food challenges. He argues we're now entering a sixth historical cycle where technology, including

---

247   Lawler EE (2014) The Quadruple Bottom Line: Its Time Has Come Forbes Magazine https://www.forbes.com/sites/edwardlawler/2014/05/07/the-quadruple-bottom-line-its-time-has-come/#38de3d596012

248   Schiller B (2016) It's Time For Exponential Thinking About Corporate Responsibility Fast Company http://www.fastcoexist.com/3064851/its-time-for-exponential-thinking-about-corporate-responsibility

artificial intelligence has the potential to create abundance rather than scarcity, and where businesses can meet unmet global needs, rather than simply measure their philanthropy and limit their harm[249].

Business is potentially facing a time defined by the rapid waning of legacy institutions, even though their replacements have not scaled up yet in this new emergent era. We are entering that messy, sometimes anxious and ambiguous space between the old and the new[250].

In the corporate sector these issues tend to be viewed through the lens of Corporate Social Responsibility (CSR) – a catch all phrase that denotes a commitment to transparent reporting about the business' material impact for good on the environment and people. More and more businesses are embracing the opportunity for differentiation, a more inclusive, sustainable approach can deliver. While little is ever achieved by going backwards, modern business is seeking to transcend and include the best of pre-Freidman business thinking which ironically, did see itself as having a social responsibility to its employees, suppliers, customers, environment and the community in which it operates, while continuing to deliver steady shareholder value. These outcomes are not mutually exclusive and a move toward this more enlightened outlook is going to be instrumental in solving our global challenges.

Business is a powerful force, if that force turns its attention to solving these problems while *also* delivering shareholder value and delivering sustainable growth then huge strides can be made, remarkably quickly. Far, far more quickly than disconnected

[249] Schiller B (2016) It's Time For Exponential Thinking About Corporate Responsibility Fast Company http://www.fastcoexist.com/3064851/its-time-for-exponential-thinking-about-corporate-responsibility

[250] Comstock B (2016) Welcome to The Emergent Era medium https://medium.com/emergent-era/welcome-to-the-emergent-era-d3d7afb81fca#.9q3tszm49

constellations of small businesses or isolated players tinkering at the edges.

We can see these positive steps already as big business embraces the relationship between brand value and market capitalisation.

The rising importance of CSR and sustainability are also key indicators of this converging force of hope. Although challenges still exist for business in how they integrate their CSR efforts with their day to day business activity and communicate those changes to an often-skeptical audience of employees, customers, investors and environmental or social activists the elevated importance in this area is extremely encouraging. In 2011, just under 20 per cent of S&P 500 companies published a sustainability or CSR report. Just two years later the number had grown to 72 per cent[251].

At the root of the skepticism is the conflict, whether real or perceived that has been created by years of overt capitalism and the tension between current CSR activities and cost or future cash flows.

Despite the two objectives appearing potentially contradictory, they don't need to be and indeed they shouldn't be. Part of the challenge is that shareholder value is very easy to measure and uses universally understood and agreed upon metrics. Those involved in this area tend to be male, start from an engineering, business administration, economics or accounting qualification. The most common route to CEO or CFO (those most responsible for shareholder value) is through finance, marketing and operations, while almost half of CFOs previously held accounting positions. This makes sense as all of these require a detailed and precise mind.

---

[251] Bliss RT (2015) Shareholder Value and CSR: Friends or Foes? CFO.com http://ww2.cfo.com/risk-management/2015/02/shareholder-value-csr-friends-foes/

CSR is a relatively new metric, it can contain multiple measures that cover a range of sustainability, environmental, social and governance (ESG) activities ranging from 'living wage' to carbon footprint to corporate philanthropy – each having multiple ways to measure across multiple jurisdictions. Interestingly, half the CSR positions are filled by women. Most in these roles, male and female, have less business focused backgrounds and tend to start with science, environmental or public policy qualifications rising through the company via marketing or HR.

The Finance executives may not be natural bedfellows with the CSR executives but this is changing as both parties come to appreciate that CSR activities create shareholder value when they increase future cash flows (profits) or reduce the risk of those cash flows. In today's environment, many CSR activities are directly improving financial performance by reducing costs, increasing revenues or reducing risks.

'Doing the right thing' is more than just a cliché on a CSR document. There is growing evidence that taking inclusive positions that assist multiple stakeholder groups and solve problems is developing brand value and trust. And that trust is delivering a very real payback in financial returns and corporate growth (see Figure 5.2).

Figure 5.2: Cumulative Return: FACTS® vs S&P 500

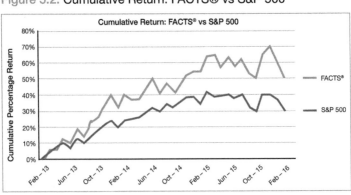

Modified from Original Source: http://bit.ly/2pNOx86

Working together to identify and implement CSR and trust development strategies is therefore a logical starting point to bridge the CSR/Finance divide. When CSR executives better understand how certain initiatives impact financial performance and ultimately share price, they gain a new lens through which to evaluate and pitch CSR proposals to the numbers guys. Learning to present important initiatives that develop brand value from a financial perspective will provide a win/win and accelerate the corporate shift to a more inclusive, longer term sustainable strategic outlook. At the same time, having CEOs and CFOs work closely with CSR executives to make important connections between CSR activities and profitability/risk will give the CEOs and CFOs valuable insights into the way their colleagues think about their responsibilities and overall place in corporate strategy. It will help to open everyone's mind around the importance of a wider range of objectives that can have a profound influence on how that business is perceived in the marketplace leading potentially to higher shareholder value[252].

This more inclusive approach also helps to build relationships with all stakeholders – including customers, suppliers/partners, investors, employees and colleagues.

It's not just customers who are demanding more from business, employees are also seeking a 'good' place to work, not just in the sense of a good job but an ethical place to work. They want to work for companies that do the right thing instead of making headlines for all the wrong reasons. People want to be proud of where they work, they want work that has purpose and to feel as though they have made a positive contribution to something bigger and more important than themselves. And this is especially true as the Baby Boomers and Gen Xers retire and Gen Y, and

---

[252] Bliss RT (2015) Shareholder Value and CSR: Friends or Foes? CFO.com http://ww2.cfo.com/risk-management/2015/02/shareholder-value-csr-friends-foes/

the Gen Z or 'Digital Natives' populate the workplace[253]. A BPW Foundation's Gen Y study published in April 2011 noted that by 2025, Generation Y will make up roughly 75 per cent of the global workforce[254].

A great deal has been written about the differences between these various population cohorts and whilst there are often variations between the date range that define each group there are clearly differences of mindset between each one. These differences are also cause for optimism that we can solve the problems we face.

Baby Boomers, as the name would suggest were born after WWII from 1946 – 1964. As of 2017 Boomers are therefore 53 – 71 years old. There are about 80 million Baby Boomers and many have already retired, are coming to the end or in the last third of their working lives. It wasn't just baby numbers that were booming for this cohort, economic growth was too. Life was good, the swinging Sixties, cradle to grave welfare, the Boomers were idealistic and uncynical, opportunity was everywhere and many grasped that opportunity and enjoyed unparalleled prosperity.

Gen X are the children of the Boomers born between 1965 and 1980 making them between 37 and 52 years old (2017). They watched their parents work hard for their success – often loyally working for the same company for 40 plus years. This often took a toll on relationships and the Boomers were the first to divorce in large numbers. The Xers therefore learned to look after themselves early as both parents often worked, or they were raised in single parent households. Xers were shaped by major political events such as the Vietnam War, the fall of the Berlin

---

[253] Asghar R (2014) What Millennials Want In The Workplace (And Why You Should Start Giving It To Them) Forbes http://www.forbes.com/sites/robasghar/2014/01/13/what-millennials-want-in-the-workplace-and-why-you-should-start-giving-it-to-them/#48ec1efe2fdf

[254] Dhawan E (2012) Gen-Y Workforce And Workplace Are Out Of Sync Forbes http://www.forbes.com/sites/85broads/2012/01/23/gen-y-workforce-and-workplace-are-out-of-sync/#3ec15d9d2579

Wall, the end of the Cold War and Thatcher Britain. This made them more diverse, open to difference and more tolerant and self-sufficient than their parents but also more skeptical. Gen X still believed that the way to success was to get an education and work hard for a company but they were more frequently laid off – amplifying their distrust.

Gen Y, or the Millennials born from 1981 to 2000 making them 17 – 36 years old, belong to another huge cohort of about 70 million people. This generation also known as 'Gen Why'[255] – watched their parents work hard but still get laid off. They realised that people are not always rewarded for their effort or loyalty. Gen Y are a lot more technologically sophisticated than their parents and are looking for purpose and fulfilment as well as a way to make a living. They don't necessarily feel loyalty to a company or brands and are happy to job-hop to a position they feel suits them and their ideology. As more and more Millennials move into the workforce and progress in those businesses or start new businesses they are looking for more than simply profit or a salary. They are looking for purpose, the ability to make a positive contribution to something they feel important – all while achieving a healthy work-life balance. This is going to be a positive force for accelerated change in the way business is viewed, its purpose and how it can attract and keep good people.

And if this is true of Gen Y, it's even more true of Gen Z, also known as 'Digital Natives'. Born from 2000 onwards this makes them 17 years old and younger (2017). They haven't entered the workplace yet but all they've known so far is a world proliferated by technology. They can't imagine their life without the Internet and political and financial turmoil are 'normal'. They see technology not as the waste of time or danger that their parents often see it as but as an opportunity to bring equality, education and information that can help right some of the wrongs they can

---

[255] Chester E (2002) Employing Generation Why: Understanding, managing and Motivating the New Workforce Tucker House Books, Boulder

already see in the world. No one knows yet how and where this population will seek and find work but they too are likely to follow in Gen Y's footsteps, seeking more balance and an opportunity to make money while also doing good.

This new 'workforce' will bring innovation and insight to business that will further accelerate our progress to a business model that goes beyond pure capitalism. At least that's the hope.

Smart business has realised that to attract and keep the most talented, disruptive and innovative people in a competitive world they need to do the right thing and make a positive difference to their stakeholders and wider community. Would-be employees, especially Gen Y high potentials are looking to work with a company with a strong employer brand – separate from the products or services that business may produce. Developing an employer brand is increasingly important in attracting and keeping the right people. A business will only achieve a strong employee brand if employees and potential employees perceive a corporate identity that is authentic, credible, relevant, distinct and aspirational. In the modern corporate landscape being considered an ordinary or generic employer is commercially constraining. Taking CSR seriously and stepping up to the challenge of making the world a better place is actually also shrewd business because not only do the businesses activities expand beyond pure capitalism but by doing the right thing that business is also more likely to attract talent which can in turn help to achieve strategic growth and shareholder returns. The two are now inextricably linked for any smart, forward thinking business.

Increased Transparency and Corporate Visibility

The final force for hope is the increased transparency and corporate visibility largely brought about by technology – specifically social media.

As mentioned above smart business recognises the need to evolve to a business model that moves beyond pure capitalism to deliver consistent sustainable returns while also doing its bit for people and the planet. This more inclusive, holistic view of business is also being accelerated by the advance of technology. Before the Internet a company would hold an Annual General Meeting (AGM) where the CEO would report to shareholders about the progress of the previous year and plans for the next year. Apart from this, the Executive Board could pretty much do what they wanted without a great deal of scrutiny or interference. Although this seems antiquated to us now, it could be argued that this approach held some significant advantages that are no longer possible today. The business was allowed to get on with running the business, meeting consumer needs and maximising shareholder value without having to constantly consider the narrative or spend inordinate amounts of time reporting to the City every quarter. But it would also be naive to believe that this laissez-faire, 'behind closed doors' approach didn't also facilitate some corporate bad behaviour or lead to ethically questionable strategic decisions. Business being unhealthily profit focused was, in many ways, made possible by the lack of transparency considered normal in pre-technology decades such as the 70s and 80s. The Internet changed business forever.

It is now no longer possible to keep corporate bad behaviour secret or to limit the experiences of one unhappy customer to a hostile letter back to HQ. One of the most famous examples of poor customer service ripping through an established brand is 'United Breaks Guitars'.

In the Spring of 2008, Canadian musician David Carroll and his band Sons of Maxwell were on tour heading from Halifax Nova Scotia to Omaha Nebraska. They booked their tickets with United Airlines which connected through Chicago O'Hare airport. As musicians, they obviously needed their guitars but were told that the instruments would have to be checked in to hold baggage as they were too big for hand luggage. While on the tarmac at Chicago, waiting to disembark and connect to their next flight the band and fellow passengers saw baggage-handling crew throwing guitar cases onto the tarmac. Most people don't travel with a guitar so Carroll and his band looked on in horror – assuming the worst. Sure enough, once reunited with their guitars in Omaha Carroll discovered his $3,500 Taylor guitar had been broken.

For almost a year Carroll tried to get United to accept liability and pay compensation. They refused, or at least they simply passed him around the company, each person denying liability and point to a variety of reasons why it wasn't their fault. Eventually Carroll realised he was fighting a losing battle and in his last email exchange to the company told them that he was going to write three songs about United and post them online. The person receiving the email probably thought – "Knock yourself out!"

The first song called *United Breaks Guitars* was posted on 6th July 2009. Within 24 hours it had been viewed by over 150,000 people. United decided they better pay attention but it was too late. Within three days half a million people had seen it. As of early 2017 over 16 million people have watched it! If you take the viewing figures for all three songs about 19 million people have learned all about how terrible United Airlines are at transporting odd shaped luggage or handling complaints. But it wasn't just about the online traffic; mainstream media also ran with the story further damaging the brand.

The *Times* Journalist Chris Ayres reported that four days after the video was posted United's share price dropped by 10 per cent wiping $180 million off the value of the stock. Although some analysts poured scorn of the idea that the two events were connected the damage the video did to the brand was significant. And yet before the Internet it wouldn't have even been possible.

On the upside for Dave Carroll, Bob Taylor who owns Taylor Guitars saw the clip and offered him two new Taylor guitars. He's also written a book on the subject and enjoyed success on the 'speaking circuit'. Carroll received a personal apology from Rob Bradford, United's managing director of customer solutions and United, for their part, use his video for internal training to ensure something similar doesn't happen again.

Of course, this capability to voice concern or shine light onto bad behaviour has since gone supersonic with the emergence and proliferation of social media. At least part of the reason that *United Breaks Guitars* was so successful was because it's also a really good, catchy song written and performed by professional musicians. The video clip is funny and it's just well done. Social media doesn't even need that. Social media and smart phones with good quality cameras and features such as Facebook Live are making everyone a potential journalist, critic or witness, and the quality of the post often doesn't even matter. In fact, as we wrap up this book United are embroiled in another PR disaster when a video, recorded on a smart phone by another passenger went viral. The video showed security staff forcibly dragging a man off an overbooked flight. One day later shares in United were down five per cent in premarket trading, potentially erasing as much as $1.1 billion off its market capitalisation[256].

Such, on the spot recording of corporate bad behaviour is helping to usher in a new level of transparency in business. If employees, customers, suppliers or any other stakeholder group can witness wrong doing, question decisions and freely share those concerns with the world via instant social media, anonymously or not, then there really is nowhere to hide for business. Often, it's no longer a case of one person's word against someone else's as video footage taken in the moment provides conclusive evidence. And this is only likely to increase as Gen Y and younger enter the workforce. This demographic is much more tech savvy,

---

[256] Wile R (2017) United's Stock Is Set to Plunge After Videos Show Passenger Dragged Off Plane Time Onlnie http://time.com/money/4734251/united-passenger-removed-dragged-violent-stock-price/

significantly more socially aware, more interested in personal purpose and working for 'good' companies that are helping others as well as their shareholders.

Social Media exposure is a very real threat (or opportunity) for business. Genuine moves toward collaboration and increased transparency can develop brand value and trust that often translates to bottom line results. At the same time, companies that have been used to doing things their own way without much interference can often struggle to negotiate the new corporate environment.

Nestlé, for example, no stranger to media controversy, found itself in hot water after Greenpeace launched a social media campaign to get them to be more discerning about their palm oil supply chain. Palm oil is an ingredient in a huge number of products from food to cosmetics to personal care products. Its ubiquitous nature makes it highly sought after and lucrative – so lucrative that huge swathes of habitat are being destroyed to make way for production. Greenpeace had written to Nestlé, urging them to stop buying their palm oil from a company that was consciously destroying Indonesian forests (Sinar Mas). They did not answer. What happened next is now a case study on how fast reputation can be damaged and also the opportunity that exists to do the right things and get back on track.

On March 17 2010, Greenpeace launched a YouTube video parodying the "Have a break; Have a Kit Kat" slogan, to highlight unsustainable forest clearing in the production of palm oil, used in products like Kit Kat. The video shows a bored office worker biting off a 'finger of Kit Kat' that turns out to be the bloody finger of an orang-utan, one of the many species threatened by the rising demand for palm oil. The campaign around it replaced the Nestlé logo with 'Killer', included an adorable orang-utan holding a placard asking Nestlé to "give rainforests a break".

Although Nestlé didn't respond to Greenpeace's letter at all they responded swiftly to the online campaign – demanding the video be removed from YouTube, citing breach of copyright. YouTube agreed and removed the video. Unsurprisingly, this perceived 'censorship' simply fuelled interest and attracted even more attention than it garnered in the first place. Greenpeace simply shared the video on Vimeo instead – within hours it had attracted 78,500 views. Interest moved to Facebook where Nestlé's own corporate page was inundated with negative comments. No doubt taken aback by the sudden outpouring of anger the moderator got defensive and helped to escalate the situation into a PR nightmare. Two days after the campaign launch it caught the attention of the mainstream media and countless articles appeared. By March 20 the blogosphere was running hot with over 4,000 blogs on the topic and Twitter was buzzing. Over *half a million* people were reading about the topic every day on Twitter. Greenpeace even used Google Ads to stoke the fire – "Have a Break – which chocolate company destroys rainforests for palm oil?" with a link to their website, and free downloads of the 'banned' video which they encouraged should be shared far and wide. By Saturday the video was back on YouTube – many times, with combined total views of 180,000[257].

Although Nestlé didn't handle the situation very well to start with, trying to stop the conversation rather than accepting responsibility and seeking a better solution – they came good. To deal with the short-term damage, Nestlé suspended sourcing from Sinar Mas and the company held meetings with Greenpeace where they provided details of their palm oil supply chains.

To address their longer-term agenda Nestlé sought a credible external partner, the Forest Trust, to certify the sustainability of its palm oil suppliers. The Forest Trust, a non-profit organisation then helped Nestlé liaise with Greenpeace as well as helping the company to audit its suppliers.

---

[257] Douglas S (2011) Nestle Kerfuffle https://prezi.com/kmrh4fmlzsen/nestle-kerfuffle/

In May 2010, Nestlé also joined the Roundtable for Sustainable Palm Oil, a partnership of companies and other parties aimed at eliminating unsustainable production.

A year later Nestlé had also changed its marketing and communications strategy including the initiation of a "digital acceleration team" - part of Nestlé's efforts to monitor social media sentiment 24 hours a day. Now, when the team sees problems, the communications unit co-ordinates the company's engagement with the relevant parties, such as suppliers, campaigners, governments and consumers. And finally, on the issue of sourcing, Nestlé announced the goal of using only palm oil certified as sustainable by 2015[258].

Clearly showing leadership on sustainability is becoming a business imperative – especially when the whole world can find out about failures in that area overnight! With the help of Greenpeace and social media, Nestlé discovered that engaging with its critics and addressing some of their concerns was more effective and developed more brand value than trying to shut down discussion on social media.

Large multi-national companies, like Nestlé often make for big, easy targets for groups like Greenpeace or any activist or committed consumer with an axe to grind. Sometimes this is unfair, sometimes it is not. Either way, these types of campaigns offer serious opportunities for business large and small to lift their game. Greater transparency ensures there is nowhere to hide so murky corners are cleared out, policy is clarified and positive moves toward an improved shared outcome can be achieved as evidenced by Nestlé's position on sustainable palm oil. In this context, big business may be under more scrutiny than smaller or medium sized companies but this also presents a real opportunity for these companies to lead the way in finding

---

[258] Ionescu-Somers A and Enders A (2012) How Nestlé dealt with a social media campaign against it The Financial Times https://www.ft.com/content/90dbff8a-3aea-11e2-b3f0-00144feabdc0

workable solutions to the challenges we face – including those in food.

It's clear that more and more people are becoming more informed and seeking ways to express their upset and exert pressure to change policy, improve business practise or shine light on unethical wrong doing. The US Minister of agriculture has even suggested that social media could replace regulation, where companies that don't meet high standards are named and shamed on social media. The dangers to this approach are however quite obvious – in an era where 'alternative fact' and genuine fact appear side by side in the online world, such an approach would be far too easy to manipulate. In the 'post truth era' whether something is true or not doesn't slow its dissemination around the globe, a company could be as easily destroyed by lies than by reality. It could certainly speed up innovation and improvement if the regulators themselves named and shamed bad behaviour but leaving that to potentially uninformed opinion would be unwise. As such regulation is almost certainly going to continue to play a crucial role in maintaining high food standards.

Where the internet does have merit is in mobilising and galvanising support for change. Anyone wanting to raise awareness of an issue and change the outcome can start an online petition on platforms such as change.org. Change.org, itself is a B-corp (Benefit Corporation) which has a bigger agenda than just profit. Originating in the US 181, 868, 057 global citizens have signed petitions for change resulting in over 21, 062 victories in 196 countries[259].

One example of how this activism can push through change in the food supply chain is an online petition started by 14-year old Lucy Gavaghan who wanted to see the end to the sale of eggs

---

[259] Change.org website https://www.change.org/impact [Accessed 29 March 2017]

from caged hens. After receiving 280,299 signatures and meeting with Tesco's head of agriculture Tesco agreed to stop selling eggs from caged eggs by 2025. This timeframe gave suppliers who had already invested heavily in 'enriched cages' (to meet a change in EU legislation to improve hen welfare) time to manage the transition. She is currently seeking similar commitments from the other UK retailers. We could argue that a universal move to free range only will simply push up the price of eggs or that even if eggs from caged hens are not sold in supermarkets the practise will still continue to supply food manufacturers and food service operators unwilling to pay for a premium product. But, the point is that consumers are more engaged and interested than they have ever been and the internet is allowing people to congregate behind ideas and push through policy change.

Taken together these four trends are significant forces for hope and we can start to feel a little more optimistic about our ability to meet and surpass our food needs so that everyone on earth has access to safe, healthy food now and into the future.

As we face these challenges it's also worth remembering just how far we have come. It's easy to watch the nightly news and feel quite despondent about the troubles that plague us but according to the World Economic Forum, the progress we have already made in the last few decades has lifted half the world's population out of extreme poverty.

At the start of the book we told you that this was a book of two halves. The first half is an exploration of the problems we face in relation to food – and they are significant. As a result, it probably wasn't an easy read. It can feel overwhelming to realise the true extent of any problem, but the good news is that many stakeholder groups, companies and individuals are seriously turning their attention to finding and implementing solutions. The last half of the book is a whistle stop tour of some of those solutions viewed through the wicked problem lens of multi-dimesionality.

You may remember from chapter one that every aspect of human experience and every second of that experience exists or is occurring in one or more of four critical dimensions – 'I', 'WE', 'IT' and 'ITS'.

It is often easier to think of these dimensions as systems/ innovation ('IT'), individual ('I') and collective ('WE'). In other words, what systems, processes and innovations are going to help us solve these problems (chapter six), what can we do as individual consumers and global citizens to help solve these problems (chapter seven) and finally, what relationships and collaborations between stakeholder groups could help us solve these problems (chapter eight).

All cause for even more hope.

Chapter 6:

Using Innovation, Technology and Wise Systems to Feed the World

Solving our food challenges is going to require multi-dimensional solutions. In this chapter, we are going to explore what innovations, technology and smart systems may help us to eat better, waste less and share more.

Product Innovations

There is little doubt that the food industry is changing. The changes themselves are being driven by multiple factors. On a macro level, there is increasing awareness of the challenges we've outlined in the book – existing food inequality, malnutrition (either from too little food or from too little healthy food), food waste, escalating population growth and the challenge of how we are going to feed everyone. On a micro level, consumers are demanding change. Consumers today are much more sophisticated than they were even ten years ago – they have far higher expectations and much lower levels of trust.

In an effort to understand the changing nature of the food industry and how their business could meet consumer needs and thrive into the future, Christian Hansen undertook a research project to discern the long-term, structural trends that would affect its industry and drive consumer decisions over the coming ten years. By seeking to figure out what the world might look like in 10 years they uncovered some very interesting insights for the whole industry. Perhaps what made this study so captivating was that it was not laboratory based and instead of looking at the various issues through the lens of their business they conducted the research through the consumer's perspective. They went out into the real world, interviewed and followed real consumers from multiple countries around the world while also gathering extensive expert opinion. Instead of just teaming up with scientists, academics and researchers they also involved anthropologists, sociologists and philosophers - people used to looking at the world a little differently in order to distil very solid directional intentions.

As mentioned in chapter one, what Christian Hansen found was that consumers were increasingly evaluating their food choices based on five different characteristics - tasty, healthy, convenient, authentic and safe.

Each of these characteristics were seen to be constrained by affordability and are known to already be altering consumer behaviour. As such they present a significant opportunity to any company that can deliver on these consumer demands.

Although the hierarchy may change from country to country the research indicated that tasty and healthy were always consumers first and second priority. Where tasty was first, healthy was usually second or when healthy was first, tasty was usually second. The only exception was China where safety is the number one priority and is likely to remain so until some of their most pressing food purity issues are solved.

Tasty is moving beyond the notion of 'I'm a savoury person' or 'I have a sweet tooth' to searching for new, unique diverse taste experiences. Consumers defined 'healthy' as nutritious, fresh, organic, unprocessed. At the same time, consumers don't want healthy to be a hassle, they want to be able to make healthy choices without having to think too hard about it. Convenience is moving from a 'guilty compromise' to an everyday strategy that helps consumers manage their busy lives. For consumers, a food is authentic when they can understand it, the food has a specific point of origin in nature, is relatable and maintains a tradition. Food produced by a 3D printer for example may struggle to catch on as a solution to our food challenges for this exact reason. It's just too far out the box for consumers to wrap their heads around and it also raises red flags around the last value driver – safety. Safety is a stand-alone driver that speaks of our drive to ensure that the product we are considering is not going to harm us today or into the future but safety also plays a part in what people consider healthy and authentic. As consumers, we may hear of a pill that helps us lose weight but is it safe? We may know that it's possible to print a beef burger but it's not 'real food' so how safe is it?

Interestingly the research indicated that while these are the five value drivers that motivate consumers and are likely to determine consumer behaviour for years into the future they also create dilemmas that people are struggling to resolve. A consumer may want something tasty and healthy. They may be able to find something that's tasty or something that's healthy, but it's currently pretty hard to find something that is both tasty and healthy. The same is true when searching for something that is both healthy and convenient. Healthy is available. Convenient is available. But there are far fewer products that are both healthy and convenient. Delivering to these consumer demands is almost certainly going to improve as producers, manufacturers and retailers increasingly tune into their customers' evolving expectations and what they say they are now looking for. The companies that can solve these dilemmas will be the ones who are going to start increasing their market share in the future.

Food innovations are already making an appearance, especially from start-up companies that can be more agile in meeting certain requirements within this shifting consumer demand. The fact that there are billions of consumers, with changing and multi-dimensional needs that are constantly evolving within their multi-dimensional lifestyles means that the market will continue to invite disruptive innovation. This will challenge the agility and responsiveness of the large global food companies.

There is little doubt that product innovation is playing an important role in solving the food challenges we face. *Chobani* is a protein rich yoghurt that tastes good. It started in 2007 and by 2015 was generating $1.6 billion in sales, no doubt helped because it meets the top two value drivers – tasty and healthy. It's also recognisable – yoghurt is a natural, authentic product, it's convenient and largely considered safe.

The Honest Company was founded in 2011 to provide eco-friendly baby products and was generating revenue of over $300 million by 2015. The business was valued at $1.7 billion in 2015!

Kind was founded in 2008 on the insight that consumers wanted a healthy snack bar with ingredients they could recognise and pronounce. Kind bars now generate sales of an estimated $200 – 300 million[260].

Problems breed innovation – as the saying goes, 'necessity is the mother of invention'. In many ways business is designed to solve a problem. If they do so successfully they thrive and when they stop solving the problem or the problem changes then they either adapt or start to die. Although many of the major food companies were founded by innovators they are now so large and so complex that innovation is far harder to achieve and many are finding the ground moving beneath their feet. In a separate report by Exane BNP Parabis, they too suggest that the innovation, certainly around product development, to meet changing consumer tastes

---

[260] Stent J et al (2016) Consumer Staple: Is M&A the new innovation? Exane BNP Paribas

is likely to come from smaller, more agile and flexible innovators rather than the large established companies.

Over the last couple of decades, almost without exception companies have been focusing on globalising their operations, leveraging efficiencies and concentrating on their big global brands. This focus can however stifle innovation. Unless a product can be shown to have global potential, it is often ignored, regardless of any local potential it may have. The implicit wisdom of this approach was that it was better to be good in 50 markets than excellent in one. Such a standpoint is not unreasonable when the local competition is poor. But today innovation is creating some truly excellent local competition in growing numbers. Plus, as the large companies sought to standardise and leverage efficiencies consumers increasingly wanted tailored products that allowed them to pick and mix around their various value drivers[261].

When making buying decisions consumers are constantly making trade-offs in the moment depending on what is most important around that purchase. It's not like we are looking for products that are always tasty, healthy, convenient, authentic and safe – all in the same product. And they may not even view their choices in these terms. Our drivers change in the moment depending on the problem we are seeking to solve in that moment. Are we looking for a quick healthy meal for the family dinner or are we looking for ice-cream as a Friday evening treat; or a cookie as a reward for a busy shopping trip? Innovation and smart product development is going to play a role in improving the quality of the food chain and bringing more options to consumers that meet their shifting demands.

Product or service Innovation is also going to include companies like Hello Fresh, Plated and Blue Apron. These services are already proving popular in larger towns and cities where people

---

[261] Stent J et al (2016) Consumer Staple: Is M&A the new innovation? Exane BNP Paribas

choose that they want to cook and the exact ingredients and instructions are delivered to their door in a chilled box. The customer then makes the meal with no waste in the home. This type of 'assisted' cooking is also prevalent in retail as more and more people are looking to meet their complex food needs without having to cook from scratch. Aimed at the customer who wants a home cooked meal without the hassle, these offerings are proving surprisingly popular. Mission based solutions such as Subway or Pret a Manger are also seeking to fill the gap of convenient, tasty and healthy food on the go.

Production Innovations

But innovation is not confined to meeting changing customer demands. There has been considerable innovation in food production in recent years. For example, the landscape for enhancing crop yields has changed significantly. Take chemical fertilisers. The use of chemical fertiliser is a complex and controversial issue. On one hand, chemically treating the soil or crops can deliver higher yields and can return some nutrients to the soil. In the developing world, their use is almost certainly going to play a role in expanding productivity and helping to regenerate cultivatable land.

On the other hand, conventional crop protection is facing a number of significant headwinds. There is growing concern from consumers about the impact of chemicals on the purity of their food and a drive toward more 'natural' food. As such pesticide use plays into consumers' health and safe value drivers and consumers are in turn applying pressure to retailers too. The UK's biggest food retailer, Tesco, works hard to ensure that their food, irrespective of where in the world it is grown, has been grown with a short list of pesticides that don't include the most controversial or toxic compounds. In the US, large retailers like WalMart are demanding suppliers reduce chemical residue because their customers are demanding it of them. Even the

European discount retailer Aldi is significantly expanding its organic range and removing eight of the worst pesticides from its stores to meet consumer demand[262].

There is also increased government regulation regarding their use - especially in Europe. There has been a partial ban on neonicotinoids for example as they are thought to be contributing to the loss of bee numbers. Many of the modern fungicides are also banned or in the process of being banned. Many of the pests these inputs are designed to combat are also developing resistance which is limiting their effectiveness. Climate change too is bringing more extreme weather events which stress crops. The continued use of many chemical fertilisers is unsustainable as the material used to create these compounds is also unsustainable. Finding alternatives to chemical fertilisers and pesticides is therefore going to be increasingly important over time.

So far, some of the suggested ways to reduce our reliance of chemical manipulation of crops include:

- Microbial Solutions

- Varietal Development

- Lasers, Drones and Precision Farming

- Vertical Farming

Microbial Solutions

One area that is showing significant promise is microbial research – using naturally occurring bacteria to make soil and plants more robust. The need for a better, more sustainable

---

262 Peterson H (2016) Aldi is fixing its biggest weakness, and that should terrify Whole Foods http://uk.businessinsider.com/aldi-is-fixing-is-biggest-weakness-and-that-should-terrify-whole-foods-2016-1?r=US&IR=T

solution has also coincided with rapidly accelerating knowledge and understanding of the role of bacteria and the microbiome in humans, animals, and plants.

The benefits of a bacterial solution for agriculture include:

- **Antagonism of pest and pathogens in plants**
  The bacterium colonises the growing root system and can deliver antibiotic molecules around the root, thereby harming pathogens that approach the root.

- **Stimulation of plant host responses in plants**
  For example. induced systemic resistance (ISR) which can result in protection of the whole plant against diseases caused by different organisms.

- **Promotion of host nutrition and growth in plants**
  For example, increasing accessibility of organic and inorganic nutrients and outcompeting pathogens in scavenging nutrients and in occupying niches on the root.

What is perhaps especially promising and inspiring about microbial innovations is that scientists working in this field are now discovering that many of the proposed microbial solutions could create benefit way beyond yield. Microbes or bacteria don't work like chemicals so they don't necessarily kill the disease that may, for example attack the plant and limit the yield. Far from being a disadvantage this could be a significant benefit. What experiments are showing is that the plants 'treated' with bacteria are more robust to abiotic stress or physical stress from the outside environment. Abiotic stress could include flooding or drought which is going to be even more important until we get the climate change wicked problem under control. Not only could bacteria hold the answer or at least part of the answer to greater yield but they could also help weather the various climate challenges we may face toward 2050.

Although it is still very early days, innovation in microbial research could deliver the trifecta in terms of potential benefits – it could help us to eat better, by reducing our reliance on chemical pesticides, herbicides and fungicides. It may also allow us to extend shelf life of products without chemical inputs in a much more natural way. This in turn could help us to reduce waste as food stays safe and nutritious for longer and it could help us to share more as we can maintain yield levels we need to feed a growing population while protecting the planet at the same time.

Varietal Development

Varietal development is also a well-established field of innovation that is making huge improvements to the food we eat. Varietal development is the genetic tinkering or breeding to alter varieties of fresh produce to improve all manner of desired characteristics. These varietal alterations can reduce the need for as many chemical inputs, increase the plant's disease resistance while also increasing or stabilising yield. All of which are important qualities if we are to meet the food demands of the coming decades.

Varietal development can also make changes in the variety of the product to deliver key customer requirements such as extra sweetness, easy peeling citrus fruit with no pips or longer lasting cut flowers with elevated scent levels.

As well as being a 3rd generation fruit producer Spanish company, AMC Group are varietal developers with over 20 years' experience in the area. One program, Citrus Genesis sequenced the DNA of the company's citrus varieties to ascertain which genes were responsible for the fruit's most desirable qualities, anything from disease resistance to vitamin and mineral content. The progression of technology itself is also helping in this area, with sequencing costs dropping from $150,000 to between $10,000 and $30,000 in 2014. Genotyping the sequenced DNA follows – breaking it down into smaller parts to determine how various genes are involved in the production of different attributes. Once this is completed it's possible to select the best varietals and discard those without value. This skill set speeds up the ability to launch varieties with the key attributes demanded by consumers: an attractive colour, easy to peel skin, good flavour, seedlessness, and, in the near future, characteristics that would contribute to consumers' health and nutrition. Citrus Genesis is actively working on the development and selection of citrus fruit with higher contents of vitamins, flavonoids, carotenoids and mineral nutrients with antioxidant, anti-inflammatory, anti-viral and anti-cancer properties[263].

Brussels sprouts are another example of a vegetable that has benefited from varietal development. Sprouts tend to divide us into those that love them and those that hate them. Like Marmite, there is rarely a middle ground with a brussels sprout! Most of the people who hate them however probably haven't eaten them for years, but the varieties that end up next to the Christmas turkey have changed considerably due to varietal development.

One company alone, Syngenta, has created 24 commercial varieties of the humble sprouts from the 'classic' old school variety without so much bitterness through to red-coloured sweeter, mild varieties especially for the festive table. Other varieties ensure year-round production and all of them still maintain the health benefits and nutrient content of the original brussels sprouts.

The bitter taste of brussels sprouts comes from a compound called glucosinolates and their degredation products. These bitter tasting compounds are an important defence mechanism against leaf-eating enemies. But they are also responsible for many of the health-giving properties of the brussels sprout and other brassicas, particularly their antioxidant and anti-cancer

[263] Alvarez JB, Lobb A (2014) Muñoz Group: Sustaining Global Vertical Integration Through Innovation Harvard Business School Case 515-011 (Revised August 2015.)

properties. Varietal development makes it possible to reduce the bitterness while maintain the health benefits[264]. A win/win for everyone.

Lasers, Drones and Precision Farming

Professor Simon Blackmore, director of the National Centre for Precision Farming at Harper Adams University, Shropshire, believes, "We need a paradigm shift—a new system to make crop production more efficient and good for the environment and society."

According to Blackmore, in the UK, up to 80 per cent of weeds have become herbicide-resistant and up to 90 per cent of the energy going into cultivation is being used repairing soil damaged by heavy machinery. Increasing precision by using smaller, unobtrusive technology could hold the key. Mini-robots have already been developed to move up and down the fields, inspecting plants, recognising the weeds and either zapping the weed via laser to make it dormant or administering dots of chemicals and fertiliser where needed. This more precise approach would mean a reduction in chemical input by 99 per cent as the treatment is only administered to the weed and not the whole crop, leaving the edible plant free from pesticide. Crops can now be monitored by aerial drones or compact ground vehicles using sensors and hyperspectral vision.

These innovations may bring huge improvements, without the use of soil-compacting tractors, there will be no need for ploughing (reducing CO_2 emissions), soil could stay absorbent longer and less fertiliser means healthier waterways[265].

---

[264] O'Driscoll C (2010) Brussels: a bittersweet story SCI Where Science Meets Business website http://www.soci.org/Chemistry-and-Industry/Cnl-Data/2010/24/Brussels-a-bittersweet-story

[265] Riley-Jones A (2017) The Machines are taking over Readers Digest http://www.readersdigest.co.uk/technology/thats-interesting/machines-are-taking-over

There are also prototype 'lettuce bots' which remove weeds from around the base of the plant and 'wine bots' which patrol vineyards and carry out precise pruning. Blackmore suggests that, "Crop robots might also mean we can keep value on the farm – grading, packing and sorting all at the point of harvest.

Although many of these innovations are still in prototype phase they are operational and could come online as demand for better solutions increases or regulation forces change.

One piece of technology already in use by farmers is aerial drones which offer a birds-eye view of their crops. Taking this one step further is a prototype called 'Robocrop' which hovers just above the crop, taking images using a digital camera. The images are immediately analysed by computer, which determine the health of the crop, what is plant and what is weed. Tiny blades then remove the weed leaving the crop to flourish[266]. This technology is already in use on some state of the art UK farms.

Vertical Farming

It's hard to imagine where production innovations will take us. Certainly, there are already some incredibly innovative production systems that are utilising significantly less space or repurposing space to create food. Vertical farms are popping up all over the world. Vertical farms, as the name would suggest are multi-story, usually hydroponic growing systems. They use less space, less water, less energy (mainly through artificial LED light) to grow fresh produce with less waste.

Vertical Harvest became one of the world's first vertical farms when they built a three-story hydroponic greenhouse on a 13,500-square-foot site next to car park in Jackson, Wyoming. The greenhouse uses 1/10th of an acre to grow an annual

---

[266] (2017) New Robots set to transform farming says Shropshire Expert The Shropshire Star http://www.shropshirestar.com/news/2014/01/28/new-robots-set-to-transform-farming-says-shropshire-expert/

product bounty equivalent to 5 acres of traditional agriculture. This includes greens, herbs and tomatoes. This system doesn't care about poor Wyoming weather, produce is not hauled long distance but delivered locally – providing fresh, pesticide free produce all year round. All while using about 90 per cent less water than traditional growing methods[267].

In London, although not vertical, one innovative company called Zero Carbon Food has repurposed World War II bomb shelters to create fresh hydroponic produce. A few hundred metres from Clapham North tube station, behind a padlocked gate is a dark, damp entrance to a spiral staircase leading 33 metres underground to a series of bomb shelters - large enough to fit 8,000 people. Today the company is growing pea shoots, rocket, red lion mustard, radish, tatsoi, pak choi and miniature broccoli for the local market. All with the tick of approval from Michelin Star chef Michel Roux Jnr[268]. These types of innovations offer real promise, not only in eliminating or reducing chemical input but for providing fresh healthy produce in locations where land is at a premium.

Changing our Behaviour and What We Eat

While technology will undoubtedly help us to create better food, improve yield and minimise chemical inputs over time, technology will also play an important role in helping us to eat better, waste less and share more.

It's already possible to monitor our own health using a variety of wearable devices and smart phone Apps that collect information such as heart rate, activity level, sleep patterns and calorie intake. Again, many of these are in their infancy and the ease and

---

[267] Vertical Harvest Wesbite http://verticalharvestjackson.com

[268] Smedley T (2014) Hydroponics used to grow salad in tunnels under London The Guardian https://www.theguardian.com/sustainable-business/hydroponics-grow-salad-tunnels-london-underground

accuracy of the data collected is sometimes questionable but they offer an important glimpse into the future of self-regulation and personal health management. US computer scientist Professor Larry Smarr states, "In a world in which you can see what you are doing to yourself as you go along the hope is that people will take more personal responsibility for themselves in keeping themselves healthy. We are at day zero of a whole new world in medicine and what will come out the other end is a far healthier society that is focused on wellness rather than fixing sickness when it's way too late." And he should know he used his own data to self-diagnose Crohn's disease - long before any physical symptoms emerged giving him the time and information to manage the condition appropriately. Access to knowledge we simply didn't have before gives us the ability to monitor our own health and heralds a new and exciting frontier of preventative medicine based on data[269].

The logic is quite simple, when we can see what we are doing or more often not doing and how those decisions are impacting how we feel these gadgets and smart phone Apps are providing us with new types of information that can support better choices.

Apps such as *Food Smart* which allow you to scan the barcode of a product and find out how much sugar, salt and saturated fat the product contains so as to help consumers make better choices. Although most of this information is already on the packet the scan presents the information graphically – which can help to drive home exactly what's in the product. So, as well as grams of sugar, there is a graphic representation of how many sugar cubes that is equivalent too – helping to make the contents more real for the consumer.

A US-based start-up, AVA, uses artificial intelligence and image recognition to allow users to take a photograph of their meal using their smart phone to learn the meal's nutritional content[270].

---

[269] BBC Two Horizon Monitor Me narrated by Dr Kevin Fong (2013)

[270] Martin D (2017) Improving Times British Airways Business Life Magazine
December 2016/January 2017.

With the accelerating pace of technological change and innovation it's inevitable that we will have a range of Apps and technology at our fingertips to improve our health and help us to make better decisions for ourselves and our families.

The Waste Hierarchy

In 1975, The European Union's Waste Framework Directive introduced the concept of the Waste Hierarchy into European waste policy. The emphasis and priority was to minimise waste, while protecting the environment and promoting human health. The Waste Hierarchy which applies to all types of waste is the result of a number of alterations, most notably in 2008 when the European parliament introduced a new five-step Waste Hierarchy to its waste legislation.

Figure 6.1 illustrates how the Waste Hierarchy relates to food. Waste prevention, as the preferred option, is followed by reuse, recycling, recovery including energy recovery and as a last option, safe disposal.

Figure 6.1: The Waste Hierarchy

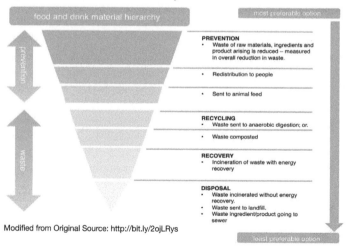

Modified from Original Source: http://bit.ly/2ojLRys

This legislative framework is an example of a strong system improvement ('ITS') to bring stakeholders together around a shared vision of how they should individually and collectively prevent as much waste as possible and dispose of what's left as well as possible. Figure 6.2 illustrates how each stakeholder is doing.

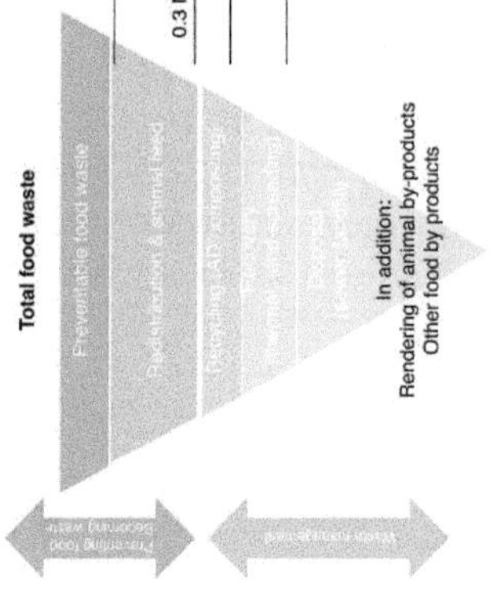

Figure 6.2: Summary of Waste (Figure 3.2) Relating to Waste Hierarchy

	Household	HaFS*	Retail**	Manufacturing	Farm	Total
Total food waste	7.0 Mt	0.9 Mt	0.2 Mt	1.7 Mt	nk	>10 Mt
Preventable food waste	4.2 – 5.4 Mt (£12.5 bn)	0.7 Mt (£2.5 bn)	0.2 Mt (£0.65 bn)	0.9 Mt (£1.2 bn)	nk	>6 Mt (>£17 bn)
Redistribution & animal feed	0.3 Mt (n/a humans) 0.3 Mt pets/other animals	nk	0.03 Mt	0.7 Mt	nk	>0.7 Mt
Recycling (AD) /composting	1.1 Mt	0.1 Mt	0.1 Mt	0.5 Mt	nk	>1.8 Mt
Sewer / recycling	1.0 Mt	0.2 Mt	0.1 Mt	1.2 Mt	nk	>2.5 Mt
Disposal (sewer/landfill)	4.7 Mt (1.6 Mt sewer 3.1 Mt landfill)	0.65 Mt (0.14 Mt sewer 0.51 landfill)	nk	0.002 Mt (nk sewer 2,000t land-fill)	nk	>5.4 Mt
In addition: Rendering of animal by-products Other food by products				0.6 Mt 2.2 Mt		0.6 Mt 2.2 Mt

Modified from Original Source: http://bit.ly/2ojLRys

As consumer's we are falling short – probably because most of us are unaware of the Waste Hierarchy. We also see the food waste we create ourselves in isolation of the challenge we face collectively. Where producers, manufacturers and retailers may see huge volumes of waste and be reminded of their need to do better we as consumers only ever see our own waste – the scraps off the plate from dinner, the brown banana that goes in the bin or the stale bread. It is easy therefore to underestimate our role in this problem.

There is clearly also still room for improvement across all stakeholder groups. Prevention is always the primary focus and most stakeholders are making strides in this area. What's frustrating is the length of time a good idea can take to spread. For example, you might remember some of the horrific waste figures from commercial fishing. These are largely caused by poorly-designed European regulation and fishing quotas along with consumer desire to eat only certain fish species. Bold and sensible laws have been passed in some countries such as Norway, Iceland and Namibia to prohibit discards altogether and new innovative ways of managing fish stocks are already working in parts of the world. Iceland has for example saved its fish stocks from over-exploitation by initiating a transferable share of the national allowable catch of each species. The EU system which is a classic example of failing to appreciate the unintended consequences of a strict quota system, effectively encourages discards because it is illegal to land more than a vessel's quota. In Iceland, it is illegal to dump any fish that is caught. Instead the vessel must land and record everything as part of the boat's quota. If the boat exceeds its quota it must either buy a share of another vessel's quota or 'borrow' part of its quota for the following year[271]. Surely this is a much wiser solution that ensures that we eat what we catch and don't waste millions of tonnes of nutritious fish. Rolling a similar system out around the world

---

[271] Stuart T (2009) Waste: Uncovering the Global Food Scandal Penguin, London

would make logical sense – especially as we face a growing need to feed an escalating population and maintain sustainable fish stocks for the future.

Beyond prevention, redistribution is also a key component in reducing waste now and into the future. It's unlikely we will ever reach a zero-waste scenario in any stakeholder groups so finding constructive and mutually beneficial ways to redistribute food is essential.

Innovations such as Too Good To Go (TGTG), mentioned in chapter three are certainly helping to redistribute food in food service. The TGTG App allows food service outlets to list what they have left at the end of service, the customer then chooses what they want to eat, pays a deeply discounted price and collect the food from their chosen outlet[272]. Not only does this provide a nutritious, affordable option to the consumer but it prevents that food from being thrown out and potentially ending up in landfill. It also saves the business money.

Food service, retail and manufacturing tend to pay particular attention to monitoring supply chains to increase forecasting accuracy to improve stock control which can help to prevent food waste in the first place. Where appropriate or possible some stakeholders will then seek to discount what's left over and finally redistributing food not sold as intended to people or for the production of animal feed. Most of the major supermarkets in the UK have for example, now begun to donate some of their surplus food to charity[273]. In the US, redistribution of food waste to needy causes is a very common practise across the industry[274].

---

[272] Too Good To Go website http://toogoodtogo.co.uk/about/

[273] Stuart T (2009) Waste: Uncovering the Global Food Scandal Penguin, London

[274] Stuart T (2009) Waste: Uncovering the Global Food Scandal Penguin, London

Food Redistribution

In the UK one of the largest redistribution charities is FareShare. Founded in 1994 as a co-venture between homeless charity Crisis and Sainsbury's, FareShare has since grown from one depot in London to 20 regional centres around the UK. As a member of both the European Federation of Food Banks and The Global FoodBanking Network, FareShare is a part of a global movement working to alleviate hunger by capturing surplus food and delivering it to the people who need it.

Figure 6.3: How FareShare FoodCloud Works

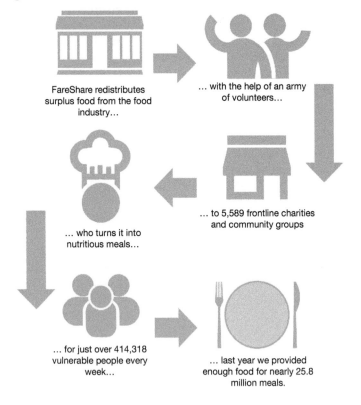

FareShare redistributes surplus food from the food industry...

... with the help of an army of volunteers...

... to 5,589 frontline charities and community groups

... who turns it into nutritious meals...

... for just over 414,318 vulnerable people every week...

... last year we provided enough food for nearly 25.8 million meals.

Modified from Original Source: http://bit.ly/2oHWNZs

FareShare now work with Tesco, Sainsbury's, Asda and the Co-op, four of the largest grocery retailers in the UK. Each providing large volumes of surplus food from their chilled distribution centres across the country. If finding ways to reduce waste and put food waste to good use is important to you then you may wish to take note of the retailers who are participating in this scheme and those that are currently missing and use your wallet to support behaviour you agree with.

FareShare has also expanded their partnerships with a number of manufacturers, brand owners and food processors who provide regular volumes of food. These include businesses such as AMT Fruit, G's Fresh, Kerry Food Group, Faccenda Foods, Friesland Campina, General Mills, Weetabix and Muller-Wiseman.

As a result of these and many other contributions FareShare was able to provide meals to 414,318 vulnerable people in 2016 (see Figure 6.3).

One of the biggest challenges with these food redistribution programmes is getting the food in time and making sure it gets to where it needs to go before the food spoils. This can be a considerable challenge when you consider the number of retail stores participating in the scheme and the distance those stores may be to a redistribution centre.

In an effort to solve this problem FareShare, in partnership with Tesco, joined forces with Irish social enterprise FoodCloud to deliver a safe and simple solution. This innovative scheme, known as FareShare FoodCloud, brings together the technology platform developed by FoodCloud and FareShare's knowledge of the UK charity food redistribution market.

The project works using the FoodCloud App that Tesco store managers use to alert charities about the surplus food they have at the end of each day. The charity will then confirm it wants the food and will pick it up free of charge from the store. Beneficiaries of the scheme will come from the wide range of charities, already in receipt of surplus food from FareShare who have been checked to ensure that they can use it safely and appropriately. This includes homeless hostels, women's refuges and breakfast clubs for disadvantaged children as well as projects supporting the elderly and people struggling with addiction.

Following a successful pilot scheme FareShare FoodCloud was launched in February 2016 and has provided over five million meals to more than 3,300 community groups and charities in just one year[275].

As of January 2017, the scheme is live in over 800 Tesco stores, and work is already underway to roll it out to a further 1,800 convenience stores. Waitrose have also announced that they will be trialling FareShare FoodCloud[276] so hopefully over time more and more retailers will get involved. See Figure 6.4 for how FareShare FoodCloud works.

Figure 6.4: How FareShare FoodCloud Works

STORE	CHARITY	PEOPLE
Tesco stores upload estimates of their good quality unsold food to theFareShare FoodCloud app.	A local charity or community group receives a text telling them about the available food.	The charity picks up the food they can use and turns it into meals for people in need.

Modified from Original Source: http://bit.ly/2ojDN0H

275 FareShare press Release (2017) FareShare FoodCloud celebrate 5 million meals with Tesco http://www.fareshare.org.uk/fareshare-foodcloud-celebrate-5-million-meals-with-tesco/

276 FareShare press Release (2017) Waitrose is latest retailer to trial FareShare FoodCloud http://www.fareshare.org.uk/waitrose-is-latest-retailer-to-trial-fareshare-foodcloud/

These types of schemes are also supported around the world including the US and across Europe and they play an important role, not just in preventing food waste but helping vulnerable people who may not have access to enough food any other way. Most modern retailers are teaming up with food distribution charities to help tackle the food waste problem but this approach, while a step in the right direction, barely scratches the surface. FoodShare estimate that they are still only accessing two per cent of supermarkets' available food waste. One UK retailer publicised that they donated nearly 3,000 tonnes of food in 2016 (up from 1,200 tonnes the year before) but 3,000 tonnes still only represented seven per cent of their surplus. Nine times as much went to anaerobic digestion, in part encouraged by subsidies that promote turning waste into fuel and fertiliser over actually feeding people[277]. The bigger hurdle often preventing more food waste from being redistributed is the physical challenge of connecting with charities seven days a week all over the country, when the waste occurs.

In 2016 France took a fairly radical step closer to large scale resolution by becoming the first country in the world to ban supermarkets from throwing away or destroying unsold food, forcing them instead to donate it to charities and food banks[278].

Clearly there is much more to do, not only in redistributing edible food but also reducing the waste in the first place. Currently too much food still fit for human consumption is being sent for animal feed or anaerobic digestion.

---

[277] Jarosz D (2017) Supermarkets should be cutting food waste, not relying on charities The Guardian https://www.theguardian.com/sustainable-business/2017/feb/03/supermarkets-food-waste-charities-tesco-sainsburys-fairshare

[278] Chrisafis A (2016) French law forbids food waste by supermarkets The Guardian https://www.theguardian.com/world/2016/feb/04/french-law-forbids-food-waste-by-supermarkets

The Role of Anaerobic Digestion

Anaerobic digestion (AD) is a biological process that happens naturally when bacteria break down organic matter found in wet biomass waste, such as sewage sludge, animal manure and waste food. This bacteria breakdown only occurs in environments with little or no oxygen and creates biogas. It is effectively a controlled and enclosed version of the anaerobic breakdown of organic waste in landfill which releases methane. It's the same process that occurs inside a cow too! Only with AD the output is not harmful to the planet but instead can be harnessed as energy. The resulting biogas consists of a mixture of around 60 per cent methane and 40 per cent carbon dioxide. It can be used to produce heat or burnt in a combined heat and power unit (CHP) to produce heat and electricity. Alternatively, it can be further processed to remove the carbon dioxide to produce biomethane which can be used in the same way as natural gas or used as vehicle fuel. Once processed the 'digestate' that's left over can also be used as a nitrogen fertiliser.

Just 5.5 million tonnes of food waste, treated by AD could meet the energy needs of up to 164,000 households[279], or a town the size of Leicester. Despite wasting about 15.1 million tonnes of food waste from farm to fork in the UK, we still only convert 1.8 million tonnes to energy via AD[280].

It is however not a blanket solution and should be the route of last resort. Currently it's not. FareShare have for example stated that manufacturers, processors, suppliers and retailers have opted to dispose of food surplus via AD or provide it for animal feed because this is a cheaper and easier option than redistribution to charities. Clearly being able to convert food waste to energy is a wise solution but only if all other avenues have been thoroughly

[279] Hogg D (2007) Dealing with Food Waste in the UK http://www.leics.gov.uk/dealing_with_food_waste_wrap_eunomia.pdf

[280] Estimates of Food and Packaging Waste in the UK Grocery Retail and Hospitality Supply Chains WRAP http://www.wrap.org.uk/sites/files/wrap/UK%20Estimates%20October%2015%20%28FINAL%29_0.pdf

exhausted beforehand. Getting smarter about what goes where is going to be a key part of the solution.

As a redistribution methodology sending food waste to feed animals is certainly preferable to recycling or energy recovery. It's also potentially much more productive.

Food waste that is sent to feed animals usually includes fruit and vegetables that are past their best but still edible, stale bread, bakery items or biscuits. These products are then mixed with other ingredients such as corn and fed to livestock. Animals, especially pigs have been fed 'swill' – food waste for centuries. They are extraordinary scavengers and can convert just about anything into protein. Unfortunately, following the mad cow outbreak in the UK, blamed on contaminated pig swill, there are now stringent laws preventing the use of most food waste for this purpose. Scraps from the table, food service waste or kitchen waste is now outlawed in Europe, Australia and some states in the US. Even allowing for this waste which could be diverted to anaerobic digestion it simply doesn't make sense to divert any other food waste to AD.

As is so often the case following a public health crisis it's likely the legislation went too far and too much food waste is diverted to AD or landfill that could be used to feed animals – especially pigs. UK waste campaigner and avid pig breeder Tristram Stuart suggests that allowing for all other factors feeding general swill to pigs is still 63 per cent better than using that waste for AD. It would be between 26 and 520 times better to eat a tonne of food waste with a similar nutritional quality to soymeal than it would be putting it in AD. Plus you don't have to make all the extra animal feed which adds strain to the production system. But it doesn't even end there – the potential value of one tonne of food waste in AD would be $37.20. If that food waste was converted into pork it would have a retail value of £330[281].

[281] Stuart T (2009) Waste: Uncovering the Global Food Scandal Penguin, London

Sometimes old methods can be viable solutions to modern problems and certainly making sure that food waste goes to animals before AD would make sense as that waste then creates more food as well as energy. Of course, for this to work effectively we need additional system solutions that link the people with the food waste with the people who raise the animals that could eat it. One such system solution is SugaRich, the UK leader in recycling surplus food products. SugaRich recover surplus materials from food manufacturers, food distributors and food retailers and turns them into animal feed that is environmentally friendly and cost effective. By recovering and up-cycling these food stuffs SugaRich also helps prevent unwanted food going to landfill.

Widespread System Improvement

The key to making these and many other individual improvements or innovations work is linking them up into an end to end system improvement. Unfortunately, this sounds a lot easier than it actually is. Food production has traditionally involved hundreds of thousands of individual producers and farmers doing their own thing, managing their own challenges and hoping for the best when the crop or animals go to market. It has also involved thousands of manufacturers, wholesalers and processors doing something similar. As a result, the multiple stakeholders in the food supply chain are disconnected and disengaged from each other never mind the system they are part of. This disconnection creates a great deal of waste and angst for everyone concerned.

But there is a better way – close collaborations that allow everyone to benefit while reducing waste and improving quality.

For example, Branston, one of the UK's biggest potato suppliers producing around 3,500 tonnes of potatoes each week for sale via Tesco. In the past, the retailer would typically buy 80 per cent of a crop for its shelves. Most of the rest would be out-grades - too big, too small or imperfect – perhaps with bad spots, blemishes or poor skin (see Figure 6.5).

Figure 6.5: Before Branston/Tesco/Samworth System Innovation

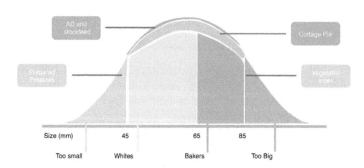

As we discussed in chapter three these out-grades are a common cause of waste in the food supply chain and are typical across producer/retailer relationships. Although edible they would not be considered suitable for the stores and would inevitably go for animal feed or into an anaerobic digester to create energy.

Today, Tesco purchases 100 per cent of the Branston crop and thanks to a new purpose-built peeling and cutting facility can ensure up to 95 per cent of the crop is used for human consumption (see Figure 6.6).

Figure 6.6: After Branston/Tesco/Samworth System Innovation

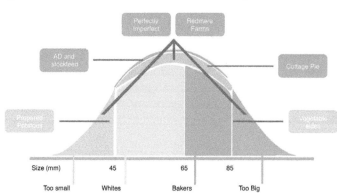

Rather than simply being a buyer Tesco collaborated with Branston and manufacturer Samworth Brothers to better understand the concerns and challenges each business had so they could solve them together for the benefit of all three parties and the customer – while almost eliminating waste.

State of the art peelers have the capacity to cope with potatoes of all shapes and sizes. The retailer also helped Branston facilitate a partnership with one of their existing added value food manufacturers, Samworth Brothers, so that they could have a reliable home for their out-grades. The out-grades now end up as mashed potatoes for the retailer's range of ready meals (e.g. cottage pies or fish pies). By March 2017 the producer will also have an operational 'slice and dice' line which can be used for other products made by the manufacturer, such as potato dauphinoise, or side plate parmentier potatoes. They are also working with the retailer to use peeled and sliced desiree potatoes that their partner fish processor and manufacturer will use in their fish cakes.

These types of collaborative partnerships add value to all the businesses concerned, provide stability and certainty for the primary producers and manufacturers while reducing waste and tightening up the whole supply chain. One of us (MS) was involved in this collaboration and we certainly believe that it heralds a new era. It's an inspiring example of a three-way partnership where growers, processors and retailers are working together as a team to give customers what they want while tackling business sustainability and food waste.

The partnership between Branston and Samworth Brothers and the new facility means that in addition to the retailer's Farms Brands and Perfectly Imperfect ranges, they are able to use up to 95 per cent of their growers' crops and prevent edible produce from being wasted[282]. It also means that the retailer can start to

[282] Draper A (2016) 20 new jobs at £5m Branston potato plant in Lincolnshire to supply Tesco
Lincolnshire Live http://www.lincolnshirelive.co.uk/branston-s-5m-investment-and-partnership-with-tesco-creates-new-jobs/story-29809840-detail/story.html#YlACmIZcuQyF7pkh.99

facilitate other relationships with growers of other crops, thereby helping to further utilise the facility at Branston for even greater efficiency.

The only way to usher in more of these types of arrangements that benefit multiple stakeholders is through open and honest dialogue and seeking to develop greater trust between stakeholder groups. Often the challenges for one stakeholder group have simply been unknown to the other stakeholder groups in the supply chain. For example, in another example I (MS) was visiting an iceberg lettuce supplier to better appreciate the challenges they were facing and how we could better work together. Icebergs are an incredibly seasonal product. When the sun shines, consumers clear the shelves of iceberg. If the weather is poor they don't move. This can be challenging for retailers and for the grower. When we started to really discuss these issues together it transpired that this grower routinely planted 130 per cent of what we committed to purchase, something we didn't know. The logic was simple – it was insurance for the supplier, but it also led to significant waste, especially if the weather was poor. Even though we had asked our partner supplier about waste figures they had repeatedly informed us that there was no waste. In their eyes the excess, which was ploughed back into the land, was not waste as it provided nutrients to the soil for the next season. Just by opening up a collaborative conversation, where we were genuinely looking for solutions that would benefit both parties, we were able to come up with a solution. As the retailer, we bought the whole crop. No lettuces were ploughed back into the land, instead we reduced the price of lettuce in store when we needed to in order to encourage consumers to purchase regardless of the weather, creating a win/win/win outcome. The consumer got an affordable, healthy product as part of their 5-a-day, the grower sold all his iceberg lettuces and the retailer sold more lettuces in a sustainable way.

Retailers can play a critical role in re-imagining these relationships. Often, as an important stakeholder with a helicopter view and influence over the end to end value chain, retail has an opportunity to show real leadership in opening dialogue with other stakeholder groups to solve collective challenges and create mutually beneficial arrangements that work for all concerned while also limiting waste.

To imagine system based improvements it is simplest to think about how we might organise resources if we were designing the end to end value chain from a blank sheet of paper. High quality data would be collected and utilised by all for the benefit of the chain. For example, consumer insight, would feed directly into research and development, branding, production systems, manufacturing and fulfilment, so that all activities would be focused on creating increased value (e.g. in terms of taste, health, convenience, safety and authenticity) at an affordable cost. Development capabilities would make long-term investments against the key consumer and productivity attributes possible. Growers would produce to defined consumer requirements at optimum productive yields with certain and clear, long and short-term, demand profiles. Manufacturers would run optimum sized facilities and production runs, supported by investment into technological innovation and continuous quality, efficiency and service improvement programmes. Stock and work in progress would be minimised across the entire chain. Product would flow efficiently through the system, only being touched when absolutely necessary to add value. This flow would satisfy consumers via whichever retail channel they wished to interact with to meet the needs of their busy lifestyles.

Of course, this all sounds a bit dreamy, but in the best and most competitive food value chains there are already great examples of better end to end system based improvements. After years of trying to incrementally squeeze the pennies from individual businesses to survive in an increasingly competitive and dynamic market place, companies are increasingly stepping back to think how they might collectively collaborate to step over the pennies and all pick up some pounds.

A great example of this sort of thinking is how retailers are re-evaluating their fresh food supply chains. Historically, because of the importance of always having the right quantities of product freshly available at the right time for their customers, whilst minimising financial waste, retailers set their systems up to order stock from their suppliers as late as possible. This allowed them to most closely meet the demand translated from each store, each day, across the country, thus both minimising waste and maximising availability. Through focusing on their own operations in this way, the retailers were ignorant to the 'costs' this would pass further upstream. Growers over-produced to meet uncertain demand. Suppliers created stocking points, physical stock and packing capacity close to retailers' distribution centres so that they could flex to meet this uncertain and untimely demand. All driving investment into the wrong places, adding costs into the chain, and actually increasing residency times (the time products are stored or housed in one location). All to the detriment of product quality and freshness while increasing the costs and wastage that the system was designed to avoid. More recently, retailers have increased their understanding of the end to end supply chains, and have started to try to link their annual grower programmes dynamically with real time demand as it develops. For example, by jointly planning supply and demand by combining data on crop yields with changes in seasonal and promotional plans and creating longer term, dynamic forecasting, and by ordering products earlier, not later, retailers have been able to ensure the production of more accurate quantities, and get them packed and date coded at source and delivered directly to distribution centres, thus avoiding the need to spend time in costly and inefficient warehousing in the UK. In such highly competitive industries where retailers and food manufacturers alike are struggling to achieve small, single digit margins, this sort of change can achieve cost reductions of over 10 per cent, whilst delivering two days of extra freshness for customers.

The more we can see food supply as a system rather than a constellation of disconnected stakeholders working in their own interest the more we can create better processes that allow us to manage and distribute the right food to the right people at the right price. And contrary to popular opinion that will mean sourcing products globally when it's smart to do so.

In recent years, more consumers have become interested in the airmiles that a product has travelled before arriving on their supermarket shelf. Airmiles have become a proxy for consumers to assess the carbon footprint of the food they are eating, but, like so much in the food industry, the airmiles argument is not as clear cut as we might, at first, imagine. Very often, the assumption is that if we want to keep our carbon footprint to a minimum we should buy locally sourced produce. And while that may be correct in some cases it's not always an accurate indication of the energy consumed in making that product and getting it to our local store.

Take New Zealand lamb as an example. This product travels around 11,000 miles to get the UK or European market (although it is almost always sea-miles not air-miles). None the less, it would be easy to assume that New Zealand lamb has a higher carbon footprint than British lamb. But this isn't always the case. New Zealand lamb is amongst the most sustainable lamb production in the world. The ewes are raised outside on grass. Depending on the weather during the winter they may receive supplementary hay but generally they are raised on grass and sunshine. The land rarely requires chemical fertiliser. The sheep give birth outside with little or no human intervention so minimal labour costs. There is almost zero carbon footprint up to this point. The only carbon footprint they incur is the transportation to the supermarkets on the other side of the world. It is therefore possible that New Zealand lamb could have a smaller carbon footprint than British lamb especially if the British lamb is grown 'out of season' or is transported a long way to the abattoir. In the UK, the most common 'lambing season' is Spring. Lambs are born just as the lush new grass is emerging in the fields after winter. The weather is warmer and the lambs, usually born inside, tended to by seasoned shepherds and lambing experts 24 hours a day, are then put out to grass with their mothers. This approach is more labour intensive but is still carbon low. However, some farmers plan for early lambing where the lambs are born in early January. This almost certainly means that the lambs are inside for longer, to escape the worst of the UK winter, they are fed additional feed which adds to their carbon footprint as does the lighting in the indoor housing. In addition, if those lambs are bought by a supermarket chain in say, the north of Scotland, but the abattoir and processing plant designated for the supermarket is several hundred miles away the additional road miles will add even more to the carbon footprint. When it comes to making a purchasing choice between New Zealand lamb and British lamb it may be very misleading to simply look at the airmiles travelled when considering the carbon foot print of the product.

Both production systems have their place in a global food supply system. But looking to airmiles as a simplistic assessment of carbon footprint is not always accurate.

If a farmer in Kenya can grow runner beans using the natural resources at his fingertips in that climate and then transport those goods to market this is almost always better for us, the environment and diminishing resources than creating polytunnel greenhouses where the beans require constant heating, lighting and irrigating to reach maturity. According to Professor Gareth Edwards-Jones of Bangor University, an expert in African agriculture, beans in Kenya are grown in a very environmentally friendly way, they are harvested manually by local labour, there are no tractors, cow muck is used as fertiliser and they have low-tech irrigation. These types of operations also provide vital employment to many people in the developing world which airmiles don't take into account[283]. According to James MacGregor and Bill Vorley of the International Institute for Environment and Development (IIED), "from a development and poverty reduction angle, the inclusion

---

[283]   McKie R (2008) How the Myth of Food Miles Hurts the Planet The
Guardian https://www.theguardian.com/environment/2008/mar/23/food.
ethicalliving

of sub-Saharan Africa in these high value markets has been a success story. Food miles as a concept is blind to these social and economic benefits associated with trade in food, especially from developing countries[284]."

Research by the Centre for Environmental Strategy at Surrey University has shown that British apples are better for the environment during autumn and winter, but in spring and summer it is 'greener' to import them[285].

Clearly what we need is to improve supply chain efficiencies and utilise a mix of both local sustainable production and international sustainable production rather than seeking to manufacture growing conditions and markets. It has been argued by UK farmers for example that if the market just tells them when they want lamb they can produce lamb for that time of year but this is not a helpful solution. While it is perfectly straightforward to bring the lambing season forward or push it back, raising lamb through the winter requires significantly more energy which makes the move counterproductive. Instead it would make more sense if the market stock sustainable local produce – meat, fruit and vegetables, when available and stock alternate sustainable stock when it's not. Considering the mounting pressure on the environment and the additional pressure climate change and escalating population is going to add to our ecosystem, the key must be sustainability rather than geography.

We need to be much more mindful of looking at the whole picture not just a snapshot and find wise sustainable solutions that ideally solve multiple problems at once. One example of such an approach is Standhill – a 205-hectare dairy farm with 220 milking cows in the Scottish Borders. The Shanks family have farmed Standhill since 1951 producing milk, beef, lamb, arable crops and

---

[284] Gardner B (2013) Global Food Futures Bloomsbury Academic

[285] (2007) Greener by Miles The Telegraph http://www.telegraph.co.uk/news/uknews/1553456/Greener-by-miles.html

more recently, a range of distinct cheeses. In 2014, they installed an anaerobic digester and now produce natural methane and CO_2 from the manure of the dairy cattle and some biomass in the form of silage. The methane powers a combustion burner and generates electricity, heating and powering the farm, including the farmhouse. Surplus electricity is fed back into the National Grid. Surplus heat is used to dry biomass wood chips. As of 2017 the energy, made largely from cattle waste will also be used to grow tomatoes in purpose built greenhouses[286].

The project is designed to rely entirely on rainwater collected from the roof of the greenhouses, with excess stored in two huge rainwater storage tanks which could feed the tomatoes for up to two months during dry spells (which are rare in Scotland anyway). The digestate from the AD plant is also used to fertilise nearby fields through an umbilical cord pump system. Not only is this farm making food, it's generating energy from waste and not using additional resources to do so. This type of sustainable 'closed loop' system is now widespread in the supply chain and represents a significant step in the right direction as we seek to solve our food, waste and energy challenges[287].

System efficiency, effectiveness, diversity and collaboration is going to be crucial. We need a balance of large and small scale, with different farming and food systems, working to meet the needs of local consumers and the developmental needs of local economies, as well as the planet as a whole. Growers, suppliers and retailers must connect and partner more so that consumers receive both the quantity of food that they require and the diverse variety of food that can sustainably deliver better quality nutrition for all. With the right innovation, technology and wise systems we will all be able to eat better, waste less and share more.

---

[286] Renewable Development Initiative Website http://www.
renewableenergyonfarms.co.uk/project/standhill-farm

[287] Border Telegraph (2014) Drought fears as tomato enterprise takes root
http://www.bordertelegraph.com/news/13544439.Drought_fears_as_
tomato_enterprise_takes_root/

Chapter 7:

Making Better Choices – What We Can do as Individuals

They say ignorance is bliss and it's easy to see why. Sometimes once we know about a problem we can wish we didn't. You may feel a little like that after reading this book. But if you've made it this far then you will also know there is plenty for us to be hopeful about. If you are a member of an influential stakeholder group then we hope this book will help direct your actions toward positive, inclusive outcomes. However, we are all consumers. As a result, this chapter will focus on what we can do as individual consumers to help solve our food supply challenges now and into the future, improve our health and help protect the planet.

Cultural anthropologist, Margaret Mead once said, "Never doubt that a small group of thoughtful, committed citizens can change the world. Indeed, it's the only thing that ever has." We, as consumers have a responsibility to ourselves to take care of our health, reduce our waste and remain mindful that our excess really does take food off the table of those who currently struggle to feed themselves and their families.

Tackling Obesity

The numbers of people currently overweight and obese suggest that far too many of us don't know what eating better actually means. Or we are ignoring the advice. Or we simply don't have adequate access to the right types of food due to availability, cost or time constraints.

Obesity is a massive problem. And it is not just a food problem stemming from our inability to supply the growing population with enough quality food at an affordable price. It is also an enormous health and productivity problem.

As mentioned in chapter one, in the UK the direct NHS costs of treating overweight and obese patients was estimated at £4.2 billion in 2007[288]. Estimates of the indirect costs – those arising from the impact of obesity on the wider economy such as lost work days or reduced productivity is estimated to be between £2.6 billion[289] and £15.8 billion[290]. Relatively, these types of figures are likely to be experienced in most developed countries. Ironically, those who eat too much of the wrong type of food and those who eat too little food often both suffer from malnutrition of some type. The foods that contribute to obesity are usually high in sugar, salt, fat and cheap carbohydrate but the human body needs much more to be healthy. We need the vital vitamins and minerals contained in a variety of food groups. Refined carbohydrate such as white bread or white rice may fill us up but, alone they don't nourish us.

---

[288] National Obesity Observatory (NOO) (2010) The Economic Burden of Obesity http://www.noo.org.uk/uploads/doc/vid_8575_Burdenofobesity151110MG.pdf

[289] National Audit Office. Tackling Obesity in England. London: The Stationery Office, 2001

[290] Butland B, Jebb S, Kopelman P, et al. Tackling obesities: future choices – project report (2nd Ed). London: Foresight Programme of the Government Office for Science, 2007. www.bis.gov.uk/assets/bispartners/foresight/docs/obesity/17.pdf

We tend to view obesity as simply a mismatch between calories in and energy expenditure. In other words, if we eat more calories than we burn we will put on weight. Do that consistently and obesity will follow as sure as night follows day. Whilst that may be true, the real question is why people consume more calories than they burn, and the answer to that question is far more complex than it seems. It is very clear that demonising people who are overweight or obese is counterproductive in that it does not increase the likelihood that they will lose weight. Like most issues, obesity is not just a simple matter of calories in versus calories out. Thus, there are no simple, one size-fits-all solutions to obesity. There are multiple factors that contribute to the problem from poverty, lack of education and limited access to affordable healthy options, to lack of emotional regulation or our evolutionary inability to inhibit our impulse to eat when faced with a bounty of food. Some people misread hunger signals or are insensitive to satiation signals. The problem may be further compounded by our inability to separate the reasons why people become obese from the reasons people remain obese. There are genetic factors and a whole host of physical activity issues that may prevent effective calorie burn. There is even some new research suggesting that the health and balance of our gut bacteria may be contributing to the obesity epidemic.

The rapidly developing science of gut bacteria is particularly interesting and is shining new light on the obesity challenge. Every living organism, including human beings, are teeming with bacteria and microbes and the resulting bacterial 'community' is known as the microbiome. The human microbiome consists of around 39 trillion microbes. This is likely to make you feel uncomfortable and rush for the disinfectant gel because most of us still view microbes and bacteria as germs – unwanted bringers of illness or disease that we must avoid at all costs. This stereotype is however grossly misleading. At worst, they are hitchhikers. At best, these microbes are the guardians of our health. They help us digest food, educate our immune system, protect us from disease, sculpt our organs and guide our behaviour[291]. In fact, it has been shown that bacteria contain more than 100 times more genetic information than our human DNA.

The wide-ranging influences of bacteria on human health has made microbiome science one of the hottest areas of biological research in the last decade. Professor Jeff Gordon, arguably the most influential scientist in the field, is trying to unpick exactly how the microbiome is connected to obesity and malnutrition. His lab is leading the exploration of which bacterial species increase the risk of obesity and how our microbiome is influenced by our diet, immune system and our emotional life[292]. In 2004, Fredrik Bäckhed, a member of Gordon's team, transferred gut microbes from conventionally raised mice to specially bred germ-free mice. Normally the sterile mice can eat as much as they want without putting on weight but this ability disappeared after they were inoculated with bacteria. The previously bacteria-free mice didn't eat more, in fact they ate less but they converted more of their food into fat and became obese.

Mice biology is similar enough to human biology for this experiment to imply that, our gut microbes may be influencing the nutrients we extract from food and therefore body weight. When this research was published, it was certainly considered a breakthrough. In the same year, another scientist on the team, Ruth Ley found that obese people (and mice) have a different microbiome in their gut. The most obvious difference was the ratio of two major groups of gut bacteria – the firmicutes and the bacteroidetes. Obese people had more of the first and fewer of

[291] Yong E (2016) Gut reaction: the surprising power of microbes The Guardian https://www.theguardian.com/science/2016/aug/25/gut-reaction-surprising-power-of-microbes

[292] Mayer EA et al (2014) Gut Microbes and the Brain: Paradigm Shift in Neuroscience Journal of Neuroscience 34 (46) 15490-15496; http://www.jneurosci.org/content/34/46/15490.full
Hoben AE et al (2016) Regulation of prefrontal cortex myelination by the microbiota Translational Psychiatry 6, e774 http://www.nature.com/tp/journal/v6/n4/full/tp201642a.html

the second. Further experimentation by then graduate student, Peter Turnbaugh, showed that when microbes harvested from fat mice were given to germ free mice the mice packed on 47 per cent more fat. Other researchers demonstrated that the weight changes could also work in the other direction, making mice thinner rather than fatter. *Akkermansia muciniphila*, one of the most common species of gut bacteria, is over 3,000 times more common in lean mice than in those genetically predisposed to obesity. If obese mice eat it, they lose weight and show fewer signs of Type 2 diabetes.

Of course, this science has huge implications and the world's media was quick to extrapolate early results into the inevitable discovery of a miracle microbial pill that will allow us to eat what we want and stay slim[293]. But before we all get too excited the microbiome does not replace or contradict other long-understood causes of obesity.

Clearly, if changing the microbiome in the gut could trigger weight loss then there would be an opportunity, at least theoretically, for a pill or potion that would keep us endlessly slim. But that simply did not happen in experiments. In 2013 another of Gordon's students, Vanessa Ridaura staged battles between the gut microbes of lean and obese people in germ free mice. She loaded human microbial communities of lean subjects into one set of mice and communities from obese subjects into another set of mice and put both sets of mice together. You may not realise this but mice often eat the droppings of other mice so they are constantly populating their own microbiome with their neighbours. What she discovered was that it was not just about the microbes in the gut but the conditions of the gut itself that made the difference. When all the mice were fed plant-heavy food, the 'lean' microbes could successfully colonise the gut of the mice with 'obese' communities and stopped their new

---

[293] Highfield R (2007) Fat? Blame the bugs in your guts The Telegraph http://www.telegraph.co.uk/news/science/science-news/3295620/Fat-Blame-the-bugs-in-your-guts.html

hosts from putting on weight. And yet the 'obese' microbes could never establish themselves in the gut where the 'lean' microbiome were already present. But when Ridaura changed the mice's food to mimic the worst extremes of the Western diet – high fat, sugar and low-fibre the lean microbiome communities couldn't establish themselves or stop the mice from getting fat. They could only infiltrate the gut of mice that were already eating a healthy diet[294].

Although there is clearly much more science to be done in this area, these results would certainly indicate that there may never be a point where we can eat a poor diet and not pay the consequences for those choices with weight gain and ill health. Microbes matter but so do the choices we make individually about what we choose to eat and drink. If we eat poorly most of the time, even if we eat the occasional piece of fruit we may not even be able to absorb the nutrients from that food because our microbiome ecosystem is out of whack. This may also explain why taking supplements may simply create nutrient rich stools rather than real nutritional benefit. If the complex, internal ecosystem of the gut is thrown out of balance then it is simply not able to use and absorb the nutrients we give it, either from food or supplements and they pass straight through.

It would therefore seem that we really can't escape sound dietary advice and common sense. We need a balanced, varied diet, rich in plant food (fruits and vegetables), ideally those harvested with minimal chemical interference so as not to kill any of the good gut bacteria. Despite what some of us might like to believe the chances that we will someday reach a point of innovation where we can take a few micronutrient supplements for the good stuff and then eat whatever we want and our body will use the good and simply discard the bad is probably nothing more than blind hope and science fiction.

---

[294] Yong E (2016) Gut reaction: the surprising power of microbes The Guardian   https://www.theguardian.com/science/2016/aug/25/gut-reaction-surprising-power-of-microbes

What we choose to eat and drink has a profound impact on our health and well-being. We need to understand that and take personal responsibility rather than looking to science for a quick fix. And that means wading through some of the confusion around what we should be eating so we can make better choices.

In chapter one we explored the various stakeholder groups connected to food production and consumption from the farmers, growers and agribusiness through to processors, manufacturers and retailers and finally us – the consumer. Specifically, we unpacked a little of what these various stakeholder groups consider to be the main problems in the food chain. One of the characteristics of a wicked problem is that there are multiple stakeholders and each stakeholder group tends to see the problems from their own specific perspective, often identifying the causes, symptoms and potential solutions from that single viewpoint. This insular, narrow style of thinking is partly why collaborative solutions are so challenging. Each stakeholder tends to privilege their own concerns above the often-competing concerns of other stakeholders while also having to prioritise their own commercial interests.

Thus, fresh produce growers may be aware of the need to cut down pesticide and herbicide use but at the same time, they will, understandably, not want to reduce yield and therefore income. So, finding a solution that doesn't financially penalise them may come before consumer concerns about pesticide use. Similarly, beef farmers may appreciate the need to cut the population's consumption of red meat, but as their livelihood depends on that consumption they may wish to direct consumers' attention to other potential solutions first. Many retailers are embracing their responsibly to reduce waste and promote healthier living but they also feel their priority is to meet customers' demands (which are not always healthy) and if they don't then they could easily lose customers to their competitors. Each stakeholder is juggling their own range of competing priorities and these priorities are almost always changing for each stakeholder and across all stakeholders. This is part of the reality of wicked problems, and why they are so challenging to solve.

As we have suggested one of the major problems facing consumers is confusion. Over the years, we have been told we should avoid all fat, now it's trans fats, hydrogenated fats and saturated fats that are the enemy. But the truth is we all need some fat in our diet. The issue is what type of fat. We have been told that we should give up butter and move to margarines only to have that advice overturned, and even manufacturers of margarine look like they may be backing out of its production[295]. We've been warned about too much salt, but again we need salt in the diet. Ironically, the message to cut back on salt is now so pervasive that iodine deficiency in the developed world has increased more than fourfold over the past 40 years. Nearly 74 per cent of normal, "healthy" adults may no longer consume enough iodine[296]. We've also been told to cut back on sugar and that advice at least seems to be holding water. The point is, it's probably now possible to find a study done somewhere by someone that tells us what is good or bad about just about every possible food group. Often there is contradictory information in the public domain which simply adds to consumer confusion and fuels apathy toward making better, healthier choices. Why make better choices when even the experts are arguing about what those better choices are?

So, given all of that what should we, confused consumers, be doing?

---

[295] Cox J (2017) Unilever confirms sale of spreads business which includes Flora and Stork butter The Independent http://www.independent.co.uk/news/business/news/unilever-sale-spreads-flora-stork-butter-shareholder-kraft-heinz-a7669461.html

[296] Gunton JE, Hams G, Fiegert M, McElduff A. Iodine deficiency in ambulatory participants at a Sydney teaching hospital: is Australia truly iodine replete? Med J Aust. 1999 Nov 1;171(9):467-70.
Hoption Cann SA. Hypothesis: dietary iodine intake in the etiology of cardiovascular disease. J Am Coll Nutr. 2006 Feb;25(1):1-11.

The purpose of this book is certainly not to morph into a diet, healthy eating or recipe book. Nor do we intend to get into the details of what constitutes healthy eating. Nevertheless, considering the challenges we face, in terms of the escalating obesity and diabetes crisis, it's worth taking a quick look at the largely agreed upon facts and basics of what it means to eat better.

Eat Better: The Eatwell Guide

Considering there is so much competing information in the public domain it can be hard to know what to believe but there are still some solid and reliable sources that provide a framework for healthy eating so we can eat better. One such guide is the UK government's Eatwell Guide (see Figure 7.1).

Figure 7.1: The Eatwell Guide

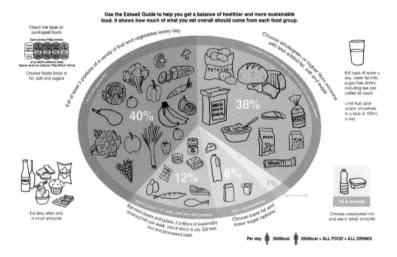

The Eatwell Guide was launched in March 2016 and replaced the 'Eatwell Plate' as the UK's healthy eating tool. The change incorporated the latest dietary recommendations, specifically around reducing sugar intake and the concern about escalating obesity. Originally a plate with a knife and fork on either side, this graphic style, also used in the American 'MyPlate' version was changed to encourage people to consider health beyond just what they ate, but also hydration, how to read food labels more effectively and how to make more sustainable choices.

The segment names changed to place emphasis on certain food products within a food group that can be considered more environmentally sustainable. For example, the 'meat, fish, eggs and beans' segment was renamed 'Beans, pulses, fish, eggs, meat and other proteins' to highlight the contribution non-meat sources make to protein intake. These other protein sources are more sustainable. In fact, the Carbon Trust's sustainability assessment of the Eatwell Guide indicated that should we eat a diet in line with the guide it would lead to an appreciably lower environmental impact than the current UK diet[297]. The segment previously known as 'Foods and drink high in fat and/or sugar' was changed to reflect the fact that some fat is essential for a healthy balanced diet where as other foods high in fat, salt or sugar are not and should be eaten rarely and in small amounts. These foods are now located outside the main graphic to indicate their occasional nature.

The segment sizes of the Eatwell Guide were modelled using linear programming with the most up-to-date data including robust nutrient content of foods. The modelling, conducted independently by the University of Oxford, took the most commonly consumed foods in the UK (according to the National Diet and Nutrition Survey, NDNS), applied the revised government dietary recommendations to those foods and modelled the fewest possible changes needed to achieve the proposed dietary recommendations. This ensures recommendations are as realistic as possible and not too far removed from the current

[297] Public Health England (2016) From Plate to Guide: What, why and how for the eatwell model https://www.gov.uk/government/uploads/system/uploads/attachment_data/file/579388/eatwell_model_guide_report.pdf

dietary habits of the UK population[298]. The border of the Eatwell Guide also helps to remind consumers of average calorie intake.

To meet the revised UK dietary recommendations, average consumption of potatoes, bread, rice, pasta and other starchy carbohydrates together with fruit and vegetable categories would need to increase, with a corresponding reduction in all other categories. But, if we take the advice on board we can be assured that all current government dietary recommendations are met, helping us to ensure we are getting all the macro and micronutrients essential for health and well-being, including adequate hydration[299]. An additional, very helpful, online resource is the Micronutrient Information Center at the Linus Pauling Institute – part of Oregon State University. The website (http://lpi.oregonstate.edu/mic) provides a detailed insight into all the vitamins, minerals and other nutrients that we need, why, symptoms of deficiency, recommended daily intake and food sources that provide each micronutrient.

There are, of course, multiple additional contributing factors to health that we still don't fully understand. For example, we don't yet know how gut bacteria, social affiliation and ethnicity alter how food interacts with our individual body. But the Eatwell Guide is a scientifically robust starting point, especially if we are determined to eat better, have better health and do our bit to help solve the complex challenges of food supply moving forward. Not only will these guidelines help us to achieve better health but they will help the planet too.

---

[298] Public Health England (2016) The Eatwell Guide: How does it differ to the eatwell plate and why? https://www.gov.uk/government/uploads/system/uploads/attachment_data/file/528201/Eatwell_guide_whats_changed_and_why.pdf

[299] Public Health England (2016) From Plate to Guide: What, why and how for the eatwell model https://www.gov.uk/government/uploads/system/uploads/attachment_data/file/579388/eatwell_model_guide_report.pdf

Eat Less Meat

As consumers, we love meat. Greater affluence is almost always accompanied by a shift from staple carbohydrates to more animal protein. Fifty years ago, global consumption was 70 million tonnes a year. By 2007 it had risen to 268 million tonnes, a nearly four-fold increase. Similarly, the amount of meat eaten by each person, per year has leapt from around 22kg in 1961 to 40kg in 2007[300]. Figure 7.2 illustrates how, by 2015, meat consumption has skyrocketed, globally.

Figure 7.2: Top Meat Eating Countries (2015)

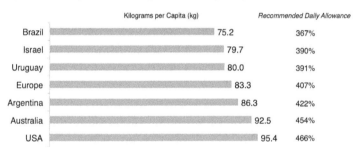

Created from Original Source: http://bit.ly/2pO7xU4

The RDA of protein is 56 grams per day from a mixed diet, meaning all the 56 grams shouldn't come from meat. And yet, clearly far too many of us are now eating significantly more meat than the recommended daily allowance (RDA). For the populations of the countries highlighted in Figure 8.2 above, often three or four times as much as the recommended daily allowance.

The production of meat, especially red meat is also resource intensive. The FAO state that it takes:

* 100 calories of feed to produce one calorie of beef – one per cent conversion ratio.

---

[300] The Economist (2012) Kings of the carnivores http://www.economist.com/blogs/graphicdetail/2012/04/daily-chart-17

- 8.8 calories of feed to produce one calorie of pork – 11 per cent conversion ratio.

- 6.5 calories of feed to produce one calorie of chicken or turkey meat - 15.3 per cent conversion ratio.

These feed inputs come from grass, hay, grains, feed concentrates etc. Most livestock farming systems use a combination of these feedstock. The amount of grains used in feedstock varies across the world but academic research endorsed by the World Resources Institute (WRI) estimates that on average cattle consume about seven kilograms of grains in their feed to produce one kilogram of beef. Pigs consume four kilograms of grains and chicken two kilograms of grains to produce one kilogram of meat respectively[301].

As mentioned in chapter one, the 'food system' – i.e. from growing food and animal feed, making and transporting food, cooking, eating to throwing food away - accounts for just under a third of greenhouse gas emissions. This means that food alone has the potential to use up the entire Paris climate agreement's carbon budget to keep climate change to well below two degrees centigrade. Figure 7.3 shows the amount of food needed to produce one kilogram of greenhouse gas.

Clearly, the most potent way to "decarbonise" the food system is therefore to reduce the amount of greenhouse-intensive food we produce – most notably meat[302]. And especially red meat (see Figure 7.4).

[301] White T (2000) Diet and the distribution of environmental impact Ecological Economics 34 (234) 145–153 http://ipidumn.pbworks.com/f/White_DietandEnvironImpact.pdf

[302] Benton T (2016) What will we eat in 2030? World Economic Forum https://www.weforum.org/agenda/2016/11/what-will-we-eat-in-2030?utm_content=buffer5ac1f&utm_medium=social&utm_source=twitter.com&utm_campaign=buffer

Figure 7.3: Amount of Food Needed to Produce 1Kg of Greenhouse Gas

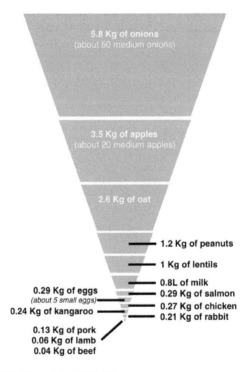

Modified from Original Source: http://bit.ly/2oIeXso

Greenpeace Brazil have estimated that cattle ranching is the biggest driver of deforestation in the area. Seventy-five per cent of the loss of the Amazon rainforest is caused by land clearing to make way for 'concentrated animal feeding operations' (CAFOs), otherwise known as 'factory farming' or 'feedlots'. Between 1990 and 2003, Brazil's cattle herds grew from 26.6 million to 64 million head of cattle[303]. This is a double blow to our planet. Not only

---

[303] Cattle ranching biggest driver of Amazon deforestation (2009) http://www.greenpeace.org/international/en/news/features/cattle-mapping/

Figure 7.4: Carbon Footprint of Various Protein Options

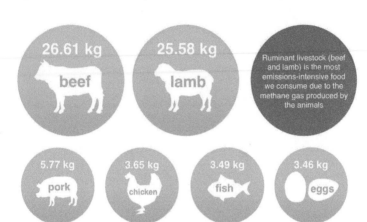

Modified from Original Source: http://bit.ly/2oleXso

does that number of cattle create a huge amount of Greenhouse Gas but the trees that could mitigate much of the damage we are creating are being destroyed to make way for the cattle or crops to feed the cattle which is exacerbating the problem still further.

Most of the meat, eggs and dairy products we consume, especially in the US are derived from livestock raised intensively. In the case of cattle, often thousands of animals are raised in confined conditions with no access to grass, which is their natural diet. Putting aside the considerable animal welfare concerns for a moment, this type of production is incredibly energy intensive[304]. Without the grass, the animals need enormous quantities of feed which use a great deal of water, land and energy to create in the first place. Typically, it takes three units of fossil fuel-based energy to produce one calorie of food energy for most US agriculture

---

[304] Energy and Agriculture. (n.d.). Network for New Energy Choices. http://newenergychoices.org/index.php?page=EA_Intro&sd=ea

products combined. For intensively raised beef, that ratio soars from 3:1 to as high as 35:1[305].

It also raises health concerns for the cattle and consumers who eat meat raised in this way[306]. Grass fed beef is higher in conjugated linoleic acid (CLAs)[307]. Various studies have shown that CLAs have cancer fighting properties[308], help tackle obesity[309] and lower 'bad' cholesterol (LDL) levels[310]. Cattle that eat grass also eat soil which is full of essential bacteria for the animal. There are 40 million bacterial cells in one gram of healthy soil. To cattle, grazing on grass is similar to us drinking a probiotic yoghurt every day and helps to maintain healthy gut bacteria which is essential for human and animal health.

[305] Halden. R. U. & Schwab, J. K. (n.d.) Environmental Impact of Industrial Farm Animal Production. Pew Commission on Industrial Farm Animal Production. http://www.bigcovecreekalliance.org/wp-content/uploads/2016/01/PewComissionReport212-4_envimpact_tc_final.pdf

[306] Sapkota, A. R., Lefferts, L. Y., McKenzie, S., & Walker, P. (2007). What do we feed to food-production animals? A review of animal feed ingredients and their potential impacts on Human Health. Environmental Health Perspectives, 115:663-670. http://ehp03.niehs.nih.gov/article/info:doi/10.1289/ehp.9760

[307] Dhiman, T. R., G. R. Anand, et al. (1999). "Conjugated linoleic acid content of milk from cows fed different diets." J Dairy Sci 82(10): 2146-56. http://bewholeagain.com/wp-content/uploads/2011/11/Conjugated-Linoleic-Acid-Content-of-milk-from-pastured-cows.pdf

[308] Aro, A., S. Mannisto, I. Salminen, M. L. Ovaskainen, V. Kataja, and M. Uusitupa. "Inverse Association between Dietary and Serum Conjugated Linoleic Acid and Risk of Breast Cancer in Postmenopausal Women." s 38, no. 2 (2000): 151-7.)
Ip, C., J. A. Scimeca, et al. (1994). "Conjugated linoleic acid. A powerful anticarcinogen from animal fat sources." Cancer 74(3 Suppl): 1050-4.

[309] Riserus, U., P. Arner, et al. (2002). "Treatment with dietary trans10cis12 conjugated linoleic acid causes isomer-specific insulin resistance in obese men with the metabolic syndrome." Diabetes Care 25(9): 1516-21.

[310] Hunt WT et al (2010) Protection of cortical neurons from excitotoxicity by conjugated linoleic acid J Neurochem. Oct v115(1):123-30. http://www.ncbi.nlm.nih.gov/pubmed/20633209
Riserus, U., P. Arner, et al. (2002). "Treatment with dietary trans10cis12 conjugated linoleic acid causes isomer-specific insulin resistance in obese men with the metabolic syndrome." Diabetes Care 25(9): 1516-21.

In addition, intensive farming means animals are raised in confined conditions. To combat disease the feed or water supply often includes antibiotics and it is this overuse of antibiotics that has been attributed to the emergence of antibiotic resistant superbugs in human health[311]. Considering that antibiotics also kill good bacteria in our gut[312] they will do the same for cattle.

Beef raised in this way is unsustainable. It requires 28 times more land to produce than pork or chicken, 11 times more water and results in five times more climate-warming emissions. When compared to staples like potatoes, wheat, and rice, the impact of beef per calorie is even more extreme, requiring 160 times more land and producing 11 times more greenhouse gases. Beef's environmental impact dwarfs that of other meat, with one expert saying that eating less red meat would be a better way for people to cut carbon emissions than giving up their car[313].

It is these types of numbers and our growing awareness of sustainability that prompted a UN report urging us toward a vegan diet. According to the report such a move is likely to be vital to save the world from hunger while reducing poverty and the worst effects of climate change[314]. However, such a solution is unlikely to reach mass scale among a population who clearly enjoy meat. The most ambitious solution may

[311] McEachran AD et al (2015) Antibiotics, Bacteria, and Antibiotic Resistance Genes: Aerial Transport from Cattle Feed Yards via Particulate Matter Environmental Health Perspectives http://ehp.niehs.nih.gov/1408555/

[312] Blaser M (2011) Antibiotic overuse: Stop the killing of beneficial bacteria Nature v476:393–394 (25 August 2011) http://www.nature.com/nature/journal/v476/n7361/full/476393a.html

[313] Carrington D (2014) Giving up beef will reduce carbon footprint more than cars, says expert The Guardian https://www.theguardian.com/environment/2014/jul/21/giving-up-beef-reduce-carbon-footprint-more-than-cars

[314] Carus F (2010) UN urges global move to meat and dairy-free diet The Guardian https://www.theguardian.com/environment/2010/jun/02/un-report-meat-free-diet?CMP=share_btn_link

come from science. Biochemist, Pat Brown left his Stanford position to join 80 fellow scientists is the hunt for the meat free beefburger. As mentioned in chapter one the very idea of 'synthetic meat' is problematic for consumers because it's not 'authentic' – one of their value drivers. But, this is largely because previous attempts at synthetic meat are focused on growing vats of animal-derived muscle stem cells – which sounds pretty hideous to most people. However what Brown and his colleague are doing is using nature itself to create a meat free alternative. The red meat colour and much of the flavour from beef comes from haem, a molecule at the core of the blood protein haemoglobin. Soybeans make a version of this molecule too, leghaemoglobin, and it's this protein that makes Brown's burgers so realistic. Mixed with wheat protein and other chemicals to mimic the texture and taste of beef the burger looks and tastes like a burger you would buy in a fast-food joint. Only it uses ⅑th of the water, ½th of the land and ¼ of the greenhouse gases of a real beef burger[315]. Who knows maybe in time we will come to accept this type of alternative to beef- especially if it looks and tastes similar.

In the meantime, another, perhaps more realistic and consumer friendly option comes from different scientists. This time, from the Rowett Institute of Nutrition and Health at Aberdeen University in collaboration with WWF who have created the Livewell Plate as an adaptation of the Eatwell Guide that focuses on nutrition and sustainability[316].

Livewell Plate

The LiveWell Plate is a visual representation of food that is good for people and the environment (see Figure 7.5). It conveys the

[315] Zoloth L (2017) Philosopher's Corner Cosmos: The Science of Everything Magazine Feb-Mar 2017 P24.

[316] Macdiarmid J et al (2011) Livewell: A balance of healthy and sustainable food choices http://assets.wwf.org.uk/downloads/livewell_report_jan11.pdf

types and portions of food we need to eat more of – cereals and vegetables; and what we should eat less of – meat, both red and white.

Figure 7.5: **The Livewell Plate**

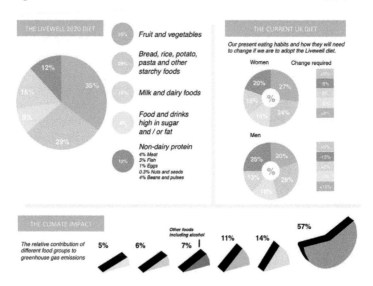

Modified from Original Source: http://bit.ly/2ol8obf

Further research into the consequences of eating along the lines of the Livewell Plate have shown it is possible to develop a Livewell diet that:

- Decreases greenhouse gas emissions by 25 per cent from the current average diet.

- Costs no more than the current dietary patterns.

- Complies strictly with national nutritional requirements.

- Closely resembles the current dietary patterns.

If we are serious about finding sustainable solutions to our food production so we can feed the planet while not simultaneously killing the planet, then eating less meat, especially non-grass fed intensively reared beef is probably going to be part of the solution. And with a little effort it may not be as hard as we imagine. We could easily swap beef mince for pork or turkey mince the next time we make spaghetti bolognese or lasagna or try going meat free for one day a week.

It's also worth pointing out that the diets favoured by some of the countries experiencing the fastest population growth (e.g. in the East) eat more fish and lower impact meats like chicken than red meat. Perhaps we will see that the impacts of globalisation will not only flow from West to East but also East to West as we use the new insights to evolve our diet and make better, sustainable choices.

Become a Better-Informed Consumer

If we are to eat better, waste less and share more we need to become better-informed consumers and make buying decisions that reward behaviours that are beneficial and penalise behaviours that aren't.

Food production is not a black and white issue. In almost every area it's impossible to make sweeping generalisations about the way food is produced or what is being produced. For example, it would be easy to dismiss all intensive food production as 'bad' and organic as 'good', or 'processed' as bad and 'natural' as good, or locally sourced as intrinsically better than food from overseas. The truth is rarely so simple, and often somewhere in the middle, or containing a combination of both.

If we are to meet demand efficiently from our growing population then intensive production is going to be not only necessary, but critical. Intensive farming, by definition, describes farming systems that are characterised by higher yields per unit land area. There are many productive food systems supplying the UK's requirements both domestically and from overseas, that are both efficient and also sensitive to broader consumer requirements such as welfare. The UK food market is sophisticated and consumers are offered a wide choice of foods from a variety of different production systems. Strict regulation around the production of food means we can choose high quality, affordable and convenient chicken or pork products that have been produced in agricultural systems all of which deliver to high food safety and animal welfare standards. Consumers who wish to differentiate more can do so by selecting products from specific systems, breeds and/or 'extensive' farming methods such as 'organic' or 'free range'. Many of these alternatives are higher in price, reflecting the higher production costs inherent to these farming systems. The key point being that choice, and a balance of systems is a required ingredient of the solution.

If a consumer is concerned about pesticide use, then organic is a valid option but it will usually be more expensive. Most people believe that organic means no pesticides or herbicides but that isn't necessarily true. Organic producers can still use pesticides, but the list of approved chemicals is much smaller and they include the least toxic varieties which the grower can only use as a last resort. In addition, there is often no point paying more for organic produce if that produce has a tough outer skin that will be removed before eating anyway such as an avocado or pineapple. It is also worth remembering that fresh fruit and vegetables can be washed, pealed or cooked to remove at least some of the residue and their inclusion in our diet is always beneficial in helping move us towards a fuller, more balanced Eatwell or Livewell diet. The single biggest change we could make toward a healthier life would be to eat more fresh fruit and vegetables and those benefits are always greater than the possibility of a little pesticide residue. Of course, consumers choose organic products for lots of different reasons. Some people think organic products taste better, and some know that organic certification will often guarantee a higher set of specifications in relation to stocking densities, or feed, for example.

Processed food has a bad rap but a huge amount of food is processed in some way so to make sweeping statements that all processed food is bad for us is not true. Most of our food has gone through some type of transformation from its initial form in the field. When foods such as ready meals first came to the market in the 1970s they were meeting consumers needs for convenience, as lifestyles became busier and more pressured. Since then, advances in chill chain technology enable higher quality, better product solutions to the existing ambient ranges. Sometimes convenience, whether it comes in a tray or a can or a packet, can take priority over nutritional value, but today, consumers want convenient and healthy options and manufacturers and retailers constantly strive to meet that demand.

Retailers will only stock products that sell so, as consumers become more educated and more demanding, poorer quality processed food will increasingly give way to healthier alternatives. There is little doubt that home cooked food, made from fresh ingredients will always be healthier and more nutritious than pre-prepared alternatives, simply by virtue of the fact that it doesn't need to include preservatives or additives to ensure a sufficient 'shelf-life'. That said, not everyone wants to, can or has time to cook everything from scratch so healthy ready-meals and pre-prepared foods can often provide a really positive solution that ticks more consumers' requirements (tasty, healthy, convenience, authentic and safe.)

We all want 'natural' food and food produced by nature is always preferable to something that is highly processed. But we need to be mindful of marketing – a granola bar from the local bakery may have 'natural' ingredients that may deliver more nutrients than a glazed donut but it will probably have much the same amount of sugar. Just because something is marketed as a healthy option doesn't necessarily always mean that it is healthy. Food writer David Freedman tells the story of purchasing a 'healthy' apple, blueberry, kale and carrot juice smoothie only to calculate it probably contained about 300 calories. That's about 80 calories more than McDonald's blueberry-pomegranate smoothie which was also $6 cheaper[317]! We buy products that we simply assume to be healthy based on where we buy them or what the packaging says without really questioning those assumptions. Many consumers are unaware that products branded as 'low-fat' for example often achieve the 'low fat' branding requirement by adding extra sugar or artificial flavourings. Clearly removing one 'bad' ingredient and replacing it with another 'bad' ingredient doesn't actually improve the health of that product.

Locally bought products may be better than products that have travelled longer distances, especially if they are fresh from the fields. Fresh produce starts to lose nutritional value from the moment it's harvested so that product needs to be quickly frozen to seal in the goodies or purchased by a consumer as soon as possible. But if the quality of the local produce isn't as high as the imported goods in the first place then such blanket statements are unhelpful. Plus, as mentioned in chapter six, if you are buying a product based on the airmiles it's travelled it may not be an accurate indication of sustainability. Food is a product of land, water and energy. The most natural source of energy for growing things is the sun, and certainly in the UK and parts of Europe we don't see much of it, particularly in winter. But, there are plenty of other places in the world that do. It would never be a good idea to try to grow bananas or pineapples in the UK, it's definitely a better idea to grow citrus in Spain (or Brazil, or Florida for juice), and it's almost certainly beneficial to grow broccoli in the UK in the summer and Spain during the winter.

---

[317] Freedman DH (2013) How Junk Food Can End Obesity: Demonizing processed food may be dooming many to obesity and disease. Could embracing the drive-thru make us all healthier? The Atlantic http://www.theatlantic.com/magazine/archive/2013/07/how-junk-food-can-end-obesity/309396/

Ultimately it comes down to personal choice, what we as consumers want and value and what we want to avoid. Transparency and clear labelling can help us do that but we still need to be better informed about the food and drink we are eating and the nuances of what is good for us and what is bad for us. There is usually a great deal of middle ground to explore. This is especially true when we already know that too much saturated fat, salt, refined carbohydrate and (especially) sugar is not good for us.

Carbonated soft drinks are a good example of a product we could all do with less of. They may be enjoyable from time to time, but anyone struggling with weight issues should steer clear. A 330ml can of either of the two premium cola brands contains about 140 calories and 40 grams of sugar – that's almost 10 teaspoons of sugar in a single can. But don't be fooled by all of the 'healthy' options either. Some of the freshly squeezed orange juice products or popular 'natural' smoothie products have even more sugar than that, although they do have more nutrients! The World Health Organisation states that the daily allowance for sugar should be no more than six teaspoons[318]. These calories, especially for carbonated drinks are also 'empty' calories which means they have no nutritional value beyond basic hydration but considering that water is free and contains no calories surely moving to water or even water with sugar free cordial is a simple, 'hack' that can easily help reduce calorie intake while also helping the planet. Most of us don't realise that it takes between 150 – 300 litres of water to make one single litre of fizzy soft drink[319]. That is a heart-breaking amount of a rapidly depleting scarce

---

[318] Malnick E (2014) World Health Organisation advises halving sugar intake The Telegraph http://www.telegraph.co.uk/news/health/news/10677712/World-Health-Organisation-advises-halving-sugar-intake.html

[319] Boseley S (2017) No evidence sugar-free soft drinks aid weight loss – study The Guardian https://www.theguardian.com/lifeandstyle/2017/jan/03/no-evidence-sugar-free-diet-soft-drinks-aid-weight-loss-study?utm_source=esp&utm_medium=Email&utm_campaign=GU+Today+main+NEW+H+categories&utm_term=206857&subid=2689330&CMP=EMCNEWEML6619I2

resource to make something that delivers no nutritional benefit and significantly contributes to obesity and diabetes. Just drink the water.

Like most things in life diet is about balance. If you enjoy carbonated soft drinks, then have one every now and again. But if you care about your health or the planet they should be considered an occasional indulgence rather than a regular part of your diet and this is true for all drinks of this type – not just cola products. And before you congratulate yourself that you are drinking the 'diet' variety – they are still empty calories, they still use huge quantities of water to manufacture and recent research has also shown that they do not help consumers lose weight[320]. Plus, the diet products use artificial sweeteners such as Aspartame or high fructose corn syrup (HFCS) – both of which have their own health issues.

We need to use some common sense. Pay attention to what is in the products we purchase. Ingredients are listed according to what the product contains most of. If you don't know what that ingredient is, can't pronounce it, it's fat, sugar or salt, then chances are you shouldn't be making that product a significant part of your diet.

Often people buy branded products because they 'know what they are getting' but few people realise that the same branded product may have different ingredients depending on where it's produced and the regulation that is relevant to that jurisdiction. You could for example buy Heinz Tomato Ketchup in the US and the ingredients are listed as:

---

[320] Boseley S (2017) No evidence sugar-free soft drinks aid weight loss – study The Guardian https://www.theguardian.com/lifeandstyle/2017/jan/03/no-evidence-sugar-free-diet-soft-drinks-aid-weight-loss-study?utm_source=esp&utm_medium=Email&utm_campaign=GU+Today+main+NEW+H+categories&utm_term=206857&subid=2689330&CMP=EMCNEWEML6619I2

- Tomato concentrate

- Distilled vinegar

- High fructose corn syrup (HFCS)

- Corn syrup

- Salt

- Spice

- Onion powder

- Natural flavourings

In the UK

- Tomato concentrate

- Spirit Vinegar

- Sugar

- Salt

- Spice & Herb Extracts (contains Celery)

- Spice

The key difference is HFCS which is a cheaper and sweeter substitute for sugar made from the waste product of the cereal industry and has been linked to increased levels of obesity.

We need to pay attention and educate ourselves about the food we eat.

Sometimes when problems seem insurmountable it's easy to be despondent as though our individual contribution can't make a difference, but it can. Just look how far we've come with climate change, our ability and willingness to recycle is a measure of our individual willingness to learn new information and adapt our behaviour accordingly. Individually we can make a huge difference not just to our own health and wellbeing but we can reduce waste and help the planet as well.

Reducing Waste

It's likely that there are social and evolutionary forces that contribute to our willingness to waste food. When there is abundance we as human beings are frequently lulled into a false sense of security that the abundance is infinite. This is especially true for many Western consumers who have never experienced shortage. They have never walked into their local store and found empty shelves. They have never gone to buy meat but been turned away by the butcher because there was none left. The older generation is often more naturally frugal, probably because many of them still remember rationing in the Second World War and would never leave anything on their plate as a result. They may still remember the propaganda slogans such as "Food is a weapon: don't waste it! Buy wisely – cook carefully – eat it all[321]". The younger generations don't. They assume because the shelves of their local supermarket are always full that they will always be full (instore, online or via their mobile device).

In the past, when faced with abundance we have often reproduced exponentially and gorged ourselves on all available resources with little thought to their sustainability. Indeed, when anyone has tried to remind us of the finite nature of natural resources we have ignored them. During his term as the 39th President of

---

[321] United States, Office of War Information Poster Division of Public Enquiries (1943) https://digital.library.unt.edu/ark:/67531/metadc156/

the United States, Jimmy Carter made four televised speeches warning the population of shrinking resources[322]. Carter urged the American people to appreciate that the US was not a land of limitless resources and that learning how to manage those limited resources sustainably was the key to long-term prosperity. The people didn't want to hear it so they elected Ronald Regan who delivered the Hollywood version of reality instead. He refuted the science pointed to by Carter and swept to power by telling the American people what they wanted to hear (sound familiar?). What followed was instrumental in the serious challenges we now face in the world.

This over-exuberance, over indulgence and unwillingness to see the writing on the wall has led to the ultimate demise of many civilisations as their resource base became depleted. American scientist and author Jared Diamond gives many examples including the Maya of Central America, the inhabitants of Easter Island, the Anasazi of New Mexico's Choca Canyon and the Mediterranean civilisation surrounding Pera in the fertile Crescent itself[323]. On the upside, if the civilisations are not wiped out the strain on resources often triggers new levels of ingenuity – let's hope we take the second option.

We need to become smarter with the resources we have. We must innovate and reduce the waste we create.

The changes we can individually make must start in the home. When we go shopping and when we go out to eat or order take-out there are many things we can do to reduce food waste.

---

[322] Miller Centre of Public Affairs University of Virginia Transcript of Jimmy Carters Address to the Nation on Energy April 18 1977 http://millercenter.org/president/speeches/speech-3398

[323] Stuart T (2009) Waste: Uncovering the Global Food Scandal Penguin, London

Here are just a few ideas to consider to reduce waste:

- Too often, whether in the home, ordering take-out or eating out we are preparing or ordering too much food. Order a steak today and chances are you are going to receive a slab of beef that is three or four times the recommended portion size. This wouldn't be so bad if we then saved what we didn't eat for another day or repackaged the take-out for lunch the next day. But too many of us don't. Instead we simply put the left-over food in the bin.

- Buy smaller dinner plates. The plate will still look full (which is important so you don't feel deprived) but you will be less likely to waste food.

- If you make too much food put the extra into single portion sizes and freeze it as a future ready meal.

- When you order take-out consider sharing a smaller order – especially if you always have leftovers that go into the bin. When we buy take-away the outlet knows they need to give us a decent portion otherwise we might feel short changed. If this is true of your favourite take-out, order less or use the left-overs for lunch or a snack the next day.

- If you are eating out, ask for a doggy-bag to take home what you didn't eat and consume it later or the following day.

- Shop in places that allow you to buy what you need - single, loose items rather than larger pre-packed quantities. Sometimes we don't need a bag of onions we just need two. Buy two and not the bag.

- Learn how to store food properly so that it keeps fresher for longer:
    - Tomatoes like breathing space and shouldn't be put in the fridge.

- Cut the ends off the stalks of asparagus and place in a glass of water.
- Cucumbers and onions stay on the counter, cut onions go in the fridge.
- Don't store onions with potatoes – they make potatoes sprout.
- Don't keep bananas in the fruit bowl with other fruit
- Store potatoes (and garlic) in a dark place.
- Fresh herbs will keep for at least five days if you cut the ends off the stalks, place them in a glass of water and cover with a loose-fitting plastic bag over the top. Parsley and coriander is better in the fridge, basil prefers the warms so keep it outside the fridge.
- Vegetables like it humid, fruit likes to be dry.

- Plan your weekly meals and shop accordingly. For many this idea can seem restrictive but most of us eat a rotation of much the same meals week in week out. A study conducted by Merchant Gourmet amongst 4000 UK consumers found that most families relied on just nine recipes that they would make on rotation[324]. Even if we pre-plan for three or four of those meals a week then we will always reduce waste.

- Learning how to use our freezer more effectively can also help us to reduce waste. If you don't enjoy cooking or don't have time, consider bulk cooking and freezing meals for the working week. This provides convenience and is also likely to reduce waste.

- If you have time, work out when your local supermarket discounts food that is approaching use-by dates. Use what's on offer to determine the evening meal. This can save money and reduce waste.

---

[324] (200) How mothers rely on just nine recipes to feed their families The Daily Mail http://www.dailymail.co.uk/news/article-1228162/Mothers-rotate-recipes-feed-families.html

- Consider being a little less stringent on 'best before' and 'use by' dates. Remember best before dates are simply an indication of when the item is at its optimum quality, it is usually perfectly edible for a few days afterwards. This is especially true for bread that can easily be used for toast without any detrimental effect on quality or nutritional value. Even use by dates have some lea-way built in so don't just automatically throw something out that has passed the date. Use your judgement about whether the food is good to eat or not. Obviously, if the food looks different, has changed colour or smells unpleasant then don't eat it.

- Learn to use left-overs. Our grandmothers did this all the time but the skill has been somewhat lost as our affluence has grown. If you have a Sunday Roast, consider using the left-over meat to make curry. If you find you have bought too many vegetables, cut them all up and make soup. It's almost impossible to mess up soup, boil up the vegetables with some stock and seasoning. Done.

- If you have a food waste bin – use it. If you don't have one, make one from an old plastic tub with a tight-fitting lid. Compost the waste for your garden or a neighbour's garden.

And don't worry, all bets are off for Thanksgiving, Christmas or any other major festival where over indulgence is part and parcel of the celebration! Just don't do it every day.

Who We Are

This chapter has so far focused on what we as individual consumers can do to eat better, waste less and share more. From a multi-dimensional perspective, these suggestions are almost exclusively focused on the individual exterior world of 'doing' ('IT') and not on the individual interior world of 'being' ('I'). We've deliberately written it this way because it's much easier to appreciate what action we could or should be taking so that each of us can do our bit to improve our own health and ensure there is enough food for everyone.

What is not so obvious however is that what we are willing to do in the first place is directly influenced by interior attitudes, values and belief that are invisible to the outside world and sometimes even obscured from ourselves.

What we do, what we eat, what we choose to buy in the supermarket may be visible to others, but the choices we make every day about food are driven by what's happening on the 'inside'. Think of this like an iceberg (see Figure 7.6).

Figure 7.6: What's Really Driving Behaviour and Results

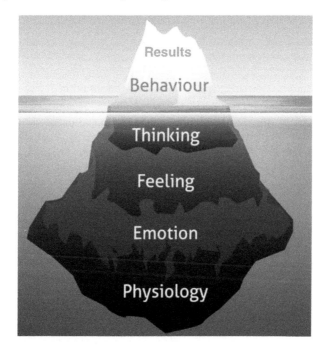

As you've read through this chapter have you found yourself thinking, "Yeah I could do that" or perhaps you found yourself in the middle of a "Yeah right" moment when you knew immediately that you were never going to give the suggestion a try. In the spirit of transparency both of us love meat so the prospect of eating less red meat is not something either of us are super enthusiastic about, but we will try.

When you go shopping you will often think about what you want to buy and then go out and buy it. You may create a list of your thoughts on what to eat that week. So, your thinking and your beliefs about what you need in the weekly shop will drive your behaviour. But your thoughts are invisible to others. They are below the 'waterline'. Other shoppers can see what you put in your trolley but they can't see whether your choices were based on your initial thinking or not. Thus, what ultimately determines your decisions about food and whether you will eat better, waste less and share more are the thoughts that drive your behaviour. But the story doesn't stop there.

Whether you decide to act on any of the information in this book or not isn't just determined by what you think. When we buy food many of our purchases are unconscious. Our choices are often driven by impulse or habit. Our decision to pick up a product off the shelf may not be that conscious. Sometimes we just feel like chocolate. We don't put any thought into it. Sometimes a special offer catches our eye. The moment of choice is not rational. All our decisions are ultimately driven by the feelings[325] we have and then we may recruit our logical minds to justify what we feel is correct[326]. Thus, we feel excited at the 'buy one get one free' offer that has caught our eye. Then we engage in an inner dialogue about our own frugality. Our belief is that we shop carefully and this is a good deal so we go with our feeling.

[325] Damasio A (2000) The Feeling Of What Happens: Body, Emotion and the Making of Consciousness random House, London

[326] Watkins A (2014) Coherence: The Secret Science of Brilliant Leadership Kogan Page, London

So, what we think and how well we think it is determined by how we feel. Of course, thinking and feeling reciprocally affect each other. But if the two were to get into a fight, our money is on feeling! Feeling wins out over thinking almost all the time because feeling is faster and more powerful than thought. This may come as a surprise, especially if you pride yourself on being a clear-thinking rationalist but just take a moment to consider this. If you think you should go to the gym but you don't feel like it – what wins? If you think you are going to make grilled chicken salad and quinoa for dinner but feel like a pizza when you pass the take-out – what do you end up eating? Feeling wins almost *every* time. Even if by some miracle, you manage to pass the take-out store you are likely to feel so deprived that you didn't eat what you really wanted that you will go and get the pizza for supper instead!

Clearly, as adult human beings we can all make ourselves do stuff we don't want to do if we think it's important enough but such choices often don't last unless we really feel like doing it and "feel it is important". What we feel has a far bigger impact on what we do than thinking does. We all know this. When we put on weight for example we know we need to eat less and exercise more but after an initial flurry of well-intentioned activity, we just don't feel like going for a run. Besides, we ran five kilometres last time so we really deserve that mint choc chip ice-cream.

If what you do in the shop or what you do as a result of reading this book is ultimately down to how you feel, then we simply need to control our feelings to change behaviour? Well no. Because how we feel is determined by something even deeper in the human system – and that's our raw emotion or more accurately e-motion (energy in motion). The reason it is so hard to control or change how we feel is because of the raw emotion that is occurring in our body without us realising it. And the reason this raw energy is coursing through our body in the first place is because at an even deeper level, down in the basement of the human system is our physiology, or our biological reactions and processes.

It all starts with physiology. Physiology is just data or information streams that are occurring inside your body all the time. As you read these words your body is taking care of a million little details that keep you alive – there is constant activity. Vast streams of data are being sent and received from one body system to another in the form of electrical signals, electromagnetic signals, chemical signals, pressure, sound and heat waves. Thankfully, we don't have to think about this information or put it in our diary, but we do need to appreciate what's influencing that process.

And guess what, the food choices we make can seriously impact our physiology which can in turn influence our emotional reactions, how we feel, how and what we think and then what we do. The food and drink we consume affects our entire life.

Considering how important food is in relation to how we behave, think and feel, we give our choice of food very little thought. Perhaps it's time we give food the respect it deserves as an important tool for keeping us healthy, happy and active as well as altering the quality and content of our consciousness. We have to stop approaching food as though it was just fuel we pour into our bodies in the same as we fill up a car with petrol. The quality of that food changes the performance of our system dramatically.

And if we are to make positive changes and do our bit to solve the wicked problems we face then we must evolve and develop as human beings. This means we must appreciate the need for change in sufficient numbers to effect the change.

Ten years ago, the mainstream didn't really know about climate change or recycling. Today most homes, certainly in Europe recycle their waste. They split their paper and plastic from other waste and more recently they separate their food waste. We have done so because individually and collectively we have become more informed about climate change. We've changed what we think, with the help of new information. This new information makes us feel that maybe we could do something constructive and so we change our behaviour. There is no reason why we can't do the same with food waste.

This will require us individually and collectively to change our mind, how we feel and the attitudes that are currently driving wasteful behaviour, otherwise the change won't stick and we will simply revert to what we were doing before. We need to ask ourselves who are we being in relation to this food challenge. Are we going to embrace the need to change course and do our bit to help or are we going to continue to be part of the problem? It's not just about what we are 'doing' individually and collectively it's about who we are 'being', day in day out and the choices we make. A recent review of behaviour change strategies suggested there were at least 93 different approaches but all of them boil down to two main choices[327]. Behaviour change through setting external goals and targets or behaviour change because of how we see ourselves. Our immunity to change is ultimately driven by whether we see ourselves as capable of change[328].

Think Balance and Diversity

When it comes to our health and wellbeing the key is balance and diversity.

If we eat a diverse range of healthy food, then we will increase the possibility of our getting the macro and micronutrients we need. If most families eat just nine recipes on rotation, together with around 10 take-aways a month[329], we could quite easily increase our food diversity by adding a few more staple recipes to the rotation. If we seek to mix the type of meat (beef, lamb,

---

[327] Cobain M 2017. Personal communication to AW based on Younger Lives report for AXA Insurance

[328] Kegan R and Lahey LL (2009) Immunity to Change: How to Overcome It and Unlock the Potential in Yourself and Your Organization Harvard Business School Press, Boston

[329] Channel 4 (2016) Tricks of the Restaurant Trade Series 2 Episode 4

pork, turkey, chicken or even a meat free day) with a variety of vegetables, depending on what's in season with a variety of carbohydrate (potatoes - mashed, boiled, or chipped; with rice, pasta, egg noodles etc.) we will eat a more diverse range of food.

Balance is also key. There are very few foods that are inherently bad. If you would like something that you know is not terribly healthy, then have it. Just make sure it's an occasional indulgence rather than a staple part of your daily diet.

And finally pay attention to how you feel once you've eaten certain foods. Because of the contributing factors that influence how we digest food and how that food impacts with our internal environment, gut bacteria, genetic markers or our emotional wellbeing there really is no one-size-fits-all approach to diet. We have to pay attention to what we eat and how that food makes us feel. If you eat bread and feel sluggish, consider removing bread for a few weeks and seeing if it makes a difference. Consider trying gluten free bread or brown bread to see if that makes you feel better. In short, you need to experiment with food to see what works for you and makes you feel good and what robs you of energy and makes you feel sluggish.

Use that information to fine tune your diet to one that supports you individually. For example, one of our researchers for this book has a daughter who was really struggling with her skin. She'd always had very good skin growing up but as a student it had gone downhill. Her mother suggested 'poor living' was to blame, poor diet, perhaps vaping, or too much alcohol. The daughter systematically cut each of these 'potential causes' from her lifestyle but nothing made any difference. Eventually someone suggested she may be lactose intolerant. As a student, living away from home her cheese intake had spiked so it seemed plausible and she cut cheese from her diet. Her skin returned to normal within a few weeks.

Part of eating better is paying more attention to what we put into our body through the food and drinks we consume and connecting the dots between those choices and how we feel. No book can tell us that – it's an individual journey.

If we educate ourselves, we can improve our own health while also doing all we can to reduce the food waste in our own home. By doing so we can make a huge difference to ourselves, others and the planet and do our bit to help solve the food challenges we face.

Chapter 8:

Wise Collaborations – What We Can Do Collectively

We have explored a number of innovations, technological and systems solutions ('IT') that can give us cause for hope that we may yet change the future of food. We have also considered what we need to do individually in terms of our actions ('IT') as well as embracing new knowledge to alter our beliefs and behaviour that can change our destiny ('I'). But ultimately all of these efforts will fail if we do not work together in a wise and collaborative fashion ('WE') on a sufficiently large scale to make these possibilities a reality. Working together is the final common pathway to solving the wicked problem of food and it is probably the single most difficult dimension of all. We unpacked part of the reason for this in chapter four when we looked at the waste of human potential, now it's time to take a closer look at the 'WE' dimension.

Cleary there are examples of effective and productive collaborations in the food supply chain that can help us to eat better, waste less and share more. Many of the system improvements we discussed in chapter six were only possible because the people in those systems chose a more inclusive, transparent and collaborative approach that would benefit all the stakeholders and reduce waste. Such collaborations are often more likely and easier to establish with private label manufacturers than established brands, because the stakeholders tend to be more interdependent, but they are gradually happening across the board. Retail collaborations with charities to distribute unsold food is an example of a constructive system improvement made possible by the willingness of people to implement that solution. The potato producer's collaboration with retail and manufacturing was also made possible by the willingness of key decision makers to implement a better solution. Interestingly all three decision makers in that collaboration had already worked with each other and this elevated trust and the existing relationship was certainly instrumental in its success. It is these 'people and relationships skills' that are so crucial in constructive collaboration and yet they are not common.

These types of constructive collaborations are still not the norm in the corporate sector. Despite the fact that there are now over a million NGOs in the world and the internet is facilitating global connection we still live with a commercial model that is centred around a Darwinian model of competition and survival of the fittest[330]. In this chapter, we will take a closer look at how we can change that. We will explore how we can work together more effectively and what it takes to establish strong partnerships than can benefit all parties. This chapter is different from the two preceding solution chapters, simply because plucking a few rare examples of genuine collaboration from a sea of siloed behaviour does not mean we have or are making progress. Far from it. The paucity of examples of such collaborations reveals how far short we are of being able to work effectively together to deliver sustainable solutions. We will need to change a lot if we are to have any hope of real progress in this 'WE' dimension. This chapter, therefore, looks at where we are right now and what we need to appreciate and change in order to make inspirational collaboration the rule and not the exception.

Wicked problems are wicked because at their heart they are about people, and feeding the planet will require people to work

---

[330] Hawkins P (2008) Blessed Unrest: How the Largest Social Movement in History Is Restoring Grace, Justice, and Beauty to the World Penguin, London

with each other in a positive and productive fashion. As we've mentioned, this is particularly difficult because those people come from multiple stakeholder groups – each with their own agenda. The fact that people with different opinions or beliefs find it difficult to collaborate in the interest of the greater good is the perennial stumbling block that prevents us from solving many of the problems we face - from what to have for dinner tonight to keep all the family happy, to how to reverse climate change or ensure we all have access to safe, affordable food as the global population expands.

We need to take a very serious and sober look at the way we relate to each other. Basically, the whole field of human relationship needs a serious upgrade - a complete overhaul for the modern era. This overhaul must go way beyond subtle changes in meeting planning or group dynamics to embrace a much more profound change in our understanding of ourselves as social beings; a much more sophisticated awareness of our interdependency and how we see each other; and a mature acknowledgment that we all live our lives together in an intimately entwined complex matrix of human connectivity. In fact, our very survival on the planet requires us to 'wake up' and 'grow up' to this reality. So, before we get together to discuss our differences or convene meetings to explore the varying views of the many stakeholders we must change the way we prepare individuals, teams and organisations for such conversations, otherwise our interactions will fail. Most of the time we compete, we conflict, we comply or we capitulate, but we never deeply connect and cooperate in a way that will resolve the wicked issues we face. And with each successive meeting we certainly don't develop an increased capability to collaborate compassionately and coherently. If we did each new meeting would move faster, be more energising and accelerate us toward delivering genuine progress.

As we have said solving wicked problems requires us to adopt an equally complex yet wise approach. This means that from the start of the process, we must take a multi-dimensional stance. We must involve multiple stakeholders, address the multiple causes, multiple symptoms and recognise that there is never one single answer, there are always many. And the answers must constantly evolve as we solve and re-solve the issues which themselves are evolving.

That's no easy task.

The Importance of 'Stage' and 'State' in Effective Collaboration ('WE')

Before we even start a conversation with any stakeholder, or frankly anyone whose opinion might differ from our own, there are two key conditions that must be understood that will determine whether that conversation is likely to succeed or not. These two conditions can be described as 'stage' and 'state'. 'Stage' and 'state' are relevant to individuals, stakeholder groups, business, NGOs, government departments or any other entity tasked with finding solutions.

But, let's take business as an example. Whether business is, or will become, a positive force for good is dependent on what 'stage' of development that business, the key leaders within the business and the shareholders operate from, as well as what emotional 'state' that business, leaders and stakeholders are in. If a CEO is solely focused on financial return they will make different decisions to a CEO who embraces a 'triple bottom line' philosophy.

The decision the CEO makes is largely a product of their developmental 'stage'. If shareholders are angry and losing confidence in a Board the 'state' those shareholders are in will most certainly alter corporate behaviour. In addition, our ability, as individuals, to interact with stakeholders is also dependent on the 'stage' of maturity we operate from and the emotional 'state' we are in at the time. If we fail to understand that the outcome of all our conversations is dependent on both the 'state' and 'stage' of development of the person or group involved in the conversation, we are at a high risk of failing.

This is an incredibly important point and it's crucial that we appreciate its significance. In the process of writing this book we have talked to many people and have enjoyed some lively debates about the role of various stakeholder groups in solving the numerous problems we face. For example, many people, genuinely believe that business is trying to do the right thing, and that people inside business are seeking to make good decisions that look at more than just profit. The challenge however is that the definition of 'the right thing' changes depending on the level of development those inside that business are operating from. It's not that people are inherently good or bad and it's not that they make good decisions or bad decisions – the issue is human development.

Developmental 'Stage'

Let's take a simple example. Most four-year-old children have developed to a stage where they can recognise that they are physically separate from other human beings and they also understand to some degree that their emotional needs are also unique to them. However, they have yet to develop a sophisticated understanding of ethics and the rules around ownership. Therefore, they often enter a stage where they think everything belongs to them. Everything is "mine". They own every pencil, every toy and every idea. So, when you see a child steal their sister's pencil, they will flatly deny that they did so. How can they steal something that belongs to them? They are not lying or being 'bad' when they claim they did not "take the pencil", they genuinely have not yet developed the ability to understand the point you are making. Similarly, when stakeholders are intransigent and refuse to negotiate they are often not being deliberately difficult (although we should never exclude this as a possibility) they are often at a developmental stage which cannot see the counterproductive nature of the stance they are taking or they have not matured sufficiently to enable them to understand the other person's point of view. If you live in a binary black and white world where either "I am right and you are wrong" or "you are right and I am wrong" then there will only ever be two outcomes of any conversation – namely I force you to submit to my answer or I must capitulate to yours. Anything else is just an unhappy compromise which I may tactically retreat too but in reality, I've simply withdrawn to fight another day when I will be able to "win the argument". People operating from such a binary view will struggle to achieve a 'win-win' outcome or find the 'best of both worlds'. In their mind the 'best of best worlds' outcome is seen as a 'cop out' or a 'whitewash' of what they believe to be a defeat. As such win-wins are usually perceived, at this stage of development, as some sort of surrender.

Let's explore a real-world example - the 2008 global financial crisis (GFC). There is good evidence that the problem was caused by as few as 50 individuals[331]. Were those people evil? Did they set out to trigger a chain of events that would bring the global financial system to its knees; double American debt in one year; cause 30 million people to lose their jobs and cause thousands of suicides globally as people's lives imploded? Or did they just see a personal profit opportunity without ever considering the wave of human suffering their actions could unleash? We could argue which is more likely. We may like to demonise these individuals, with due cause, but it's more likely that they were just not sufficiently vertically developed or have the altitude to anticipate the unintended consequences that their own actions would create. They were almost certainly operating from 1st tier thinking. You may remember we discussed this in chapter four when unpacking value systems. First tier thinking (beige to green)

---

331   Lewis M (2011) The Big Short: Inside the Doomsday Machine Penguin, New York

is characterised by the drive to service our own needs with little or no regards for the needs of others. If you imagine each stage of development is a rung of a ladder – with each progressive developmental step upward we can see further, appreciate more of the landscape before us and consequently make better decisions. When our development is arrested at a 1st tier developmental stage we can only see the world from that 'rung of the ladder'. We are driven by the corresponding values and motives of that stage and anyone who is driven from a different value set is simply mistaken. We can't effectively step into other people's shoes and we don't fully appreciate the complexity, depth or breadth of the challenges we face. We see a partial view of the whole picture and make choices that often make matters worse or create new problems. If people arrested at this stage of development are in positions of authority, power or influence then it becomes imperative that they develop individually to give us any chance of establishing effective collaborations capable of creating wise answers to wicked problems.

And the critical importance of stage development is perhaps especially true in government, NGOs and business where decisions can have far reaching consequences as evidenced by the GFC. There is zero doubt that business can and must play a critical role in solving wicked problems – including food. However, whether these critical stakeholders solve or exacerbate those issues largely comes down to how vertically developed they are across the commercially relevant lines of development outlined in chapter four. We need many more stakeholders to be operating at 2nd tier so they can see further, appreciate more of the complexity and bring more sophisticated thinking to the solutions. We need these people to be able to appreciate the inherent value in each of the 1st tier stages while also acknowledging the built-in myopia of each stage. This broader appreciation for where people bring most value and where they can easily de-rail the process or create catastrophe is critical in finding the best solutions.

Consider one study for a moment... it looked at 43,060 transnational corporations and suggested that there were only 147 companies that determine global outcomes across the planet[332]. Due to their share ownership, these companies, many of which are banks or financial institutions, control what happens in most of the other companies. For example, a few pension funds, insurance companies, mutual funds and sovereign wealth funds hold $65 trillion, or 35 per cent of all the world's financial assets[333]. If we consider within each of these 147 companies there are a small number of people who are actually calling the shots, say three (and they may not necessarily be the CEO, CFO or COO, they may be others behind the scenes). This means that in effect less than 450 individuals run the planet. These 450 people pull the ownership strings of 147 companies which indirectly control the other 43,060 companies which in turn drive the global economy and determine the destiny of over 7 billion people[334]. Imagine what the world could be like if those 450 individuals were operating from 2nd tier thinking. Imagine what could be achieved?

Emotional 'State'

We have outlined how many of the wicked problems don't get solved because their solution requires the human beings involved to be operating from a more sophisticated stage of development. But developmental stage is just one of two critical conditions that must be in place for people to be able to effectively collaborate. The second is emotional 'state'.

Human beings have evolved to respond to the environment based on how each moment of our lives makes us feel. We,

---

[332] Vitali S, Glattfelder JB, Battiston S. (2011) The network of global corporate control. PLoS One. 2011;6(10): Epub 2011 Oct 26.

[333] Barton, D (2011) Capitalism for the long term Harvard Business Review March 2011

[334] Rothkopf D (2009) Superclass: The Global Power Elite and the World They Are Making Farrar, Straus and Giroux New York

and others, have outlined in detail how we are not, contrary to popular belief, in conscious control of the choices we make[335]. Our decisions are driven first and foremost by our feelings and then we look for the evidence, facts and logical justification to rationalise what we feel[336].

Every second of every day we evaluate our environment to determine the level of threat we face. This threat detection and processing occurs in the amygdala - two bundles of cells, one in each hemisphere, clustered deep within the emotional circuitry of our brains. This threat evaluation is superfast in order to save our life. If we detect a threat, then our amygdala triggers an emotional response that drives our behaviour. Specifically, under threat our amygdala trigger an emotion laden with chaotic physiology. This chaotic physiology then shuts down our frontal cortex, and creates a binary response – fight/flight or play dead. This rapid reaction has been variously described as an "amygdala hijack"[337], the "chimp brain"[338] or a "DIY lobotomy"[339]. Basically, if we feel threatened then we become reactive and make very simplistic decisions without access to all the smart processing and the power of our neocortex that has evolved over thousands of years. Essentially, unchecked emotion can make smart people do very stupid things.

[335] Watkins A (2014) Coherence: The Secret Science of Brilliant Leadership Kogan Page, London
Watkins A (2016) 4D Leadership Kogan Page, London

[336] Damasio, A (2006) Descartes Error Vintage, London

[337] Goleman D and Dalai Lama(2004) Destructive Emotions: And how can we overcome them Bloomsbury, London
Goleman D (1996) Emotional Intelligence: Why it can matter more than IQ Bloomsbury, London

[338] Peters S (2012) The Chimp Paradox: The Mind Management Programme to Help You Achieve Success, Confidence and Happiness Vermilion, London

[339] Watkins A (2014) Coherence: The Secret Science of Brilliant Leadership Kogan Page, London
Watkins A (2016) 4D Leadership Kogan Page, London

If we want to breakthrough on wicked problems we need to address the issue of emotional 'state'. Mismanaged emotions are a significant obstacle to effective collaboration partly because of the subtlety of their interference when human beings sit down with each other. The 'threat system' can just as easily be activated by mild or seemingly innocuous subconscious signals as it can to a genuine threat[340]. Often there is no logical rhyme or reason to it[341]. If we perceive a threat to our self-esteem or even our point of view our amygdala can respond by shutting off all of our smart thinking. What makes matters worse is we don't realise when our smart thinking has shut down because realising it would require the very parts of our brain that have been shut down!

When working with teams, groups of stakeholders and crowds as a facilitator it is vital to monitor the degree to which people may feel threatened even mildly if we want to unlock the wisdom of the crowd and generate better quality answers[342].

The Ability to Effectively Cooperate is a Sign of Evolutionary Maturity

Human beings have become one of the most successful species on the planet, arguably second only to bacteria! A large proportion of that success has come down to our ability to collaborate. Evolutionary biologist and futurist, Elisabet Sahtouris, has written and lectured widely on the evolutionary benefit of cooperation. Thus, as she has pointed out, it took single-celled bacteria a billion years to learn that cooperation was more energy efficient than conflict and killing each other. One of bacteria's early cooperative

---

[340] Declerck CH, Boone C and Emonds G (2012) When do people cooperate? The neuroeconomics of prosocial decision making Brain and Cognition 81(1):95-117

[341] Watkins A (2014) Coherence: The Secret Science of Brilliant Leadership Kogan Page, London

[342] Watkins A and Stratenus I (2016) Crowdocracy: The End of Politics Urbane Publications, Kent

manoeuvres, when they still had the planet to themselves, was to share some of their cytoplasmic DNA with each other. This enabled a colony of bacteria to create a library of DNA giving the colony a greater adaptive capability and advantage. This library of DNA was walled off and ultimately developed into a cell nucleus. This nucleation is one of the greatest breakthroughs in evolution. But the newly emerged nucleated cells had to start at square one again and despite their new found adaptive capability nucleated bacteria reverted to killing each other once again. It took them another billion years to realise, for the second time, that cooperation between all nucleated cells was more beneficial and energy efficient than competition and killing. This led to the second great breakthrough in evolution - the emergence of multi-cellular organisms, and ultimately homo sapiens[343].

Sahtouris points out that the realisation that "feeding your enemy is more intelligent and energy efficient than killing them" occurs once a species moves out of its adolescent phase of evolution into a more mature adult phase. She argues that species and communities that learn and then apply this lesson are significantly more sustainable in the long-term. Those that don't develop the ability to effectively cooperate ultimately become obsolete.

This is not to say that some degree of competition is bad. Darwin's idea of survival of the fittest is not wrong, it is just that in our excessive drive for individualism we have taken this idea to the extreme and it has overly influenced how we live, particularly in the West, and particularly in relation to our approach to business and financial markets. Even in Darwinian moments there is some degree of cooperation. For example, in the predator-prey relationship there is a kind of cooperation. The predator's task is to weed out the week in the herd and the prey's task is to get stronger to avoid the predators. Such Darwinian cooperative dynamics have an evolutionary benefit. If the predator binges

---

[343] Sahtouris E (2016) The Secret To Human Coexisting YouTube https://www.youtube.com/watch?v=qMAPIIUJwmQ

in periods of abundance, then their ability to hunt may be diminished and they may themselves become the prey. Thus, when Darwinian imperatives are not taken to extremes there is a degree of cooperative dynamic balance or coherence in the system[344].

Let's take the human body as a metaphor for a mature highly evolved decentralised cooperative economy. It has fifty trillion cells and nearly every single cell is as complex as a modern large city. In the human body one cell type doesn't seek to dominate the others. The lungs don't seek an unequal advantage over the liver. There is no inequity between the kidney and the spleen. All the 'wealth' is not concentrated in the muscles at the expense of the bones. No, the human body has thrived because it has matured into an extraordinary cooperative economy.

In contrast communities of human beings are still largely at a very adolescent stage of development. We still have a lot of growing up to do if we are to work effectively with each other without seeking to dominate or create excessive privilege for the few at the expense of the many. In the human body, unchecked growth where all the resources are consumed by a few cells in one part of the body is basically cancer. As mentioned in chapter five, in 2017, the World Economic Forum stated that eight men have the same wealth as 50 per cent of the planet[345] - surely an example of the same unchecked growth on a macro level. This level of inequity is destructive and counterproductive to the evolution of humanity.

Thus, the notion that the only valid mode for the evolution of human communities is competition rather than cooperation is an

[344] Sahtouris E (2015) The competitive and cooperative aspects of evolution YouTube https://www.youtube.com/watch?v=JolR8Diig-o

[345] Elliot L (2017) World's eight richest people have same wealth as poorest 50% The Guardian https://www.theguardian.com/global-development/2017/jan/16/worlds-eight-richest-people-have-same-wealth-as-poorest-50?CMP=twt_a-world_b-gdnworld

adolescent or immature idea. But unfortunately, we are largely still stuck at that immature phase of human community and society development. The world is still run by national empires, religious empires or corporate empires. But if we are to solve the wicked problems we have created we must move beyond the Hero's Journey mythology and its focus on individual prowess and develop a much more sophisticated, more mature story. One that understands the evolutionary benefits of prosocial cooperation. A story of working together for the greater benefit of us all. A story that unites us all and brings us home to who we really are – beautiful multi-dimensional beings who can experience so much more joy when we come together than when we live fragmented lives.

The Post-Truth Spanner in the Collaborative Works

Collaboration has always been challenging, but it has become significantly more so as the world has become more complex, with multiple sources of information and many different views being broadcast all the time. Who do we believe in this 'post-truth era'? Who do we trust? The evidence suggests that we no longer trust politicians, we don't trust the media, we don't even trust experts and scientists anymore. So, who do we trust? The research points to the fact that we only trust ourselves and people we know personally. But, unfortunately, if we disregard information from all other sources than ourselves and those nearest to us we are at serious risk of creating a distorting 'echo chamber' where all we hear are our own views and opinions mirrored back to us. Of course, if those views and opinions are rooted in misinformation or lies then we can't break through confusion. If we want to learn and develop a wiser answer the most useful opinion in any conversation is the one that disagrees with our own view[346]. But if we are still operating from 1st tier thinking and don't have a handle on our emotional state, then contrary views can become distorted and we easily become lost in a world where we don't trust anyone or anything. In such a world, all facts can be refuted or viewed with deep suspicion and little progress is made as everyone simply reinforces their own unconscious bias in their own echo chamber. This is partly what has led us to the 'post-truth' era. In a world of echo chambers when we trust no-one but those closest to us it is easy to see how we can start to believe there is no absolute truth.

But the 'post-truth' world we find ourselves in is not new. It is an entirely predictable outcome of the 'green' value system being the leading edge of human development. You may remember from chapter four that the emergence of each stage of cultural development, either individually or collectively is triggered by the dysfunction or dark-side of the previous stage. The evolution from a 'red' power based value systems to a 'blue/amber' order and rules value system is often an attempt by the collective to curb the excesses of the 'red' leader with their autocratic, 'my way or the highway' dominance. The evolution from a 'blue/amber' order value systems to the 'orange' wealth creation systems is often triggered by an attempt to break free from the excessive bureaucracy, constraints and rigidity of disciplinarian rules that stifle innovation and growth. It's the dark-side of each developmental stage that continually drives evolution and spawns more personal or cultural development.

At the beginning of 2017, the cutting edge of cultural development in most industrialised societies is the green value system. But it is failing on a grand scale. Although green may be the cutting edge the vast majority of the population in developed nations still operate well below this green cutting edge. And because the green cutting edge is currently failing to do its job and find

---

[346] Peppers D (2012) Entropy can be good for you Fast Company https://
www.fastcompany.com/1843201/entropy-can-be-good-you

new ways to embrace diversity, create cooperation across stakeholders and society significant numbers of people are feeling excluded and left behind. Ironically, making people feel included and heard is meant to be a strength of the green value system. But when people feel they no longer have a voice and those in power ignore them then we create the conditions for backlash where there is a large-scale rejection of the status quo (i.e. the green cutting edge). The failure to create a more inclusive cooperative narrative in society where we can transcend and include the immature, excessively competitive Darwinian model with is financial and social inequality is at the root of the UKs vote to leave the European Union, the rise of extreme right wing political parties in mainland Europe and the election of an exceptionally 'red' leader in Donald Trump as the 45th President of the United States.

Green Chaos

Although the 'green' value system has been the leading edge of cultural evolution for several decades, the chaos caused by the GFC almost certainly helped to cement the battle lines between the green value system and all earlier value systems. A rash of books such as Reinventing Capitalism[347]; The Ascent of Money[348]; When Money Runs Out[349]; The Road to Ruin[350]; How Much is Enough[351]; Post Capitalism[352] and Greed Inc[353] all detail

---

[347] Freeman J (2015) Reinventing Capitalism: How we broke Money and how we fix it, from inside and out Spiralworld, London

[348] Ferguson N (2008) The Ascent of Money: A Financial History of the World Penguin, London

[349] Kind SD (2014) When the Money Runs Out: The End of Western Affluence Yale University Press, New Haven

[350] Rickards J (2016) The Road to Ruin: The Global Elites' Secret Plan for the Next Financial Crisis Portfolio Penguin, London

[351] Skidelsky E, Skidelsky R (2012) How Much is Enough?: Money and the Good Life Penguin, London

[352] Mason P (2016) PostCapitalism: A Guide to Our Future Penguin, London

[353] Rowland W (2012) Greed, Inc.: Why Corporations Rule the World and How We Let It Happen Arcade Publishing, New York

how the orange value system failed us. Several books such as Minding the Markets[354]; The Big Short[355]; Fixing the Game[356]; The Conscious Guide to Macroeconomics[357]; Wikinomics[358] and IOUSA[359] suggest the failure is systemic. The GFC brought that failure into conscious awareness for all. The global collapse increased the anger within the green value system at what they considered to be excessive capitalism. As a result, we have seen a whole flurry of academic and leadership books exploring the failures of capitalism. Thus, Conscious Capitalism[360]; Full Spectrum Economics[361]; Conscious Business[362]; Sacred Economics[363]; Caring Economics[364] and Circular Economy[365] all advocate a new greener, more inclusive tomorrow.

[354] Tuckett D (2011) Minding the Markets: An Emotional Finance View of Financial Instability Palgrave Macmillan, New York

[355] Lewis M (2011) The Big Short: Inside the Doomsday Machine Penguin, London

[356] Martin RL (2011) Fixing the Game: How Runaway Expectations Broke the Economy, and How to Get Back to Reality Harvard Business School Press, Boston

[357] Moss DA (2007) A Concise Guide to Macroeconomics: What Managers, Executives, And Students Need To Know Harvard Business School Press, Boston

[358] Williams AD, Tapscott D (2008) Wikinomics: How Mass Collaboration Changes Everything Penguin, London

[359] Wiggin A, Incontrera K (2008) IOUSA: One Nation. Under Stress, In Debt John Wiley & Sons, New York

[360] Mackey J, Sisodia R (2014) Conscious Capitalism: Liberating the Heroic Spirit of Business Harvard Business School Publishing, Boston

[361] Arnsperger C (2010) Full-Spectrum Economics: Toward an Inclusive and Emancipatory Social Science Routledge, London

[362] Kofman F (2014) Conscious Business: How to Build Value Through Value Sounds True, Boulder

[363] Eisenstein C (2011) Sacred Economics: Money, Gift, and Society in the Age of Transition Evolver editions, Berkeley

[364] Singer T (Ed), Ricard M (Ed) (2015) Caring Economics: Conversations on Altruism and Compassion, Between Scientists, Economists, and the Dalai Lama St Martins Press, New York

[365] Webster K, MacArthur E (2016) The Circular Economy: The Wealth of Flows Ellen MacArthur Foundation Publishing; 2 Edition

These books, and many others testify that we are in the middle of a cultural tipping point. The green cutting edge is becoming increasingly desperate and dismissive of the behaviour and self-centredness of red leaders or the blatant greed of orange leaders which led to the GFC.

The election of Donald Trump brought the battle lines into sharp focus. The reaction to this appointment from the green cutting edge has been extreme, visceral and loud. The same polarised visceral and vocal opposition between two strongly opposing cultural views was also experienced in the UK before and after the referendum on leaving the European Union in 2016. Both sides pointed fingers and mocked the 'stupidity' and short-sightedness of the other side. Identical polarisation and extreme opposition could be witnessed in France, Netherlands, Italy and many other European countries who are seeking a regression back to a more insular, nationalistic value system. The point here is we are still operating from a largely competitive and immature 1st tier perspective and the green cutting edge which should help us unlock a more mature cooperative and collaborate viewpoint is failing us. The green cutting edge is operating from its own dark side of judgment. The net effect is we are stuck. Every stage of development is elbowing each other for a position at the table. Excessive competition and domination is still widespread as each stage vies for supremacy, just as bacteria did for two billion years.

So how will we breakthrough to a more mature adult phase of cooperation? Will the green leading edge of cultural evolution (generically referred to as 'postmodern') save us? In fairness to those operating from the green value system there have been some pretty wicked new problems to deal with from huge migrant numbers entering Europe to failing democratic process to elevated terrorism threats from so called ISIS[366].

[366] Watkins A and Stratenus I (2016) Crowdocracy: The End of Politics Urbane Publications, Kent

Green overtook orange as the 'growing tip[367]' in the 1960s and delivered some stunning global successes in the form of the civil rights movement, the worldwide environmental movement, the rise of personal and professional feminism, a heightened sensitivity to any and all forms of social oppression of virtually any minority, and allied to that the emergence of the diversity and inclusion agenda. As the years went by, the negative traits of the green value system also started to emerge.

Remember all values systems or developmental stages have positive, constructive characteristics that can, if taken too far, flip into negative characteristics. These negative characteristics can block evolution and progress for generations, although they will ultimately be the catalyst for the emergence of the next evolutionary stage.

In its desire to be as 'inclusive' as possible the green value system promoted the critical importance of 'context' in understanding any knowledge claims. Unfortunately, the positive broad-minded inclusivity of green slipped into rampant and runaway relativism (which then collapsed into nihilism). The notion that all truth is contextual (or gains meaning from its cultural context) slid into the notion that there is no real universal truth at all, there are only shifting cultural interpretations (which eventually slid into a widespread narcissism).

Key ideas, which began as important 'true but partial' concepts, collapsed into extreme and deeply self contradictory views, including the idea that all knowledge is, in part, a cultural construction; all knowledge is context-bound; there are no privileged perspectives; what passes for "truth" is little more than fashion.

You may recognise this scenario as the 'post truth' 'narcissistic' era we now find ourselves in where truth is whatever we want it to

---

[367] Maslow A (1968) Overcoming Evil: An interview with Abraham Maslow, founder of humanistic psychology. https://www.psychologytoday.com/articles/199201/abraham-maslow

be – nothing more than a cultural fiction. Science, fact and rigor has given way to fake news, click-bait, 'alternative facts' and twitter. Believing that climate change isn't real because we don't want to believe it doesn't alter the fact that 97 per cent of climate scientists concur that it is very real. What's true for you may be true for you and what's true for us may be what's true for us but there is also some measure of objective, verifiable, scientific fact that does not change depending on any one person's cultural context.

Each developmental stage, left unchecked has the capacity to create a monster. The 'green' monster – emerging from the collapse and failure of the green value system to lead, is the 'post truth' culture, and the twins of nihilism and narcissism[368]. The green drive for equality, inclusiveness and fairness have become distorted and degraded into the notion that nothing should be better or more real than anything else because all is dependent on and rooted in context. In this post truth vacuum the floor is clear for the biggest self-promoting nihilist or narcissist to take over. The failure of green has therefore created the condition for nationalistic, 'Brexit' and 'America First' style politics to succeed. Plus, the green judgment and vocal denigration of early stages of development is self-destructive and certainly will not help us to evolve still further or solve wicked problems. We all have to experience each level and transcend and include that level in our evolution – judging and ridiculing those operating at an earlier level is a little like laughing at those that can walk when we can run. In order to be able to run at all we had to first learn to walk and we don't suddenly lose the walking ability when we can run. The same is true of values levels.

We have arrived at a uniquely confusing albeit predictable juncture in human history. This moment is equally laden with the possibility of triumph and disaster. It's widely acknowledged that

[368] Wilber K (2017) Trump and a Post-Truth World: An Evolutionary Self-Correction Integral Life https://integrallife.com/trump-post-truth-world/

postmodernism as a philosophy is now dead – the big question is what is going to come next. Are we going to make the quantum leap up to 2nd tier thinking, which can unlock enough human potential so that we can finally solve these challenging problems or are we going to collapse back down to egocentric, power based, nationalistic systems?

Leadership Breakthrough Requires Kinder Green and 2nd Tier Cutting Edge

When we are at such a crossroads whether we breakthrough to a new more mature cooperative phase or not, normally requires a widespread realisation that the leading edge is failing – usually badly, obviously and often. Paradoxically the fact that there is such considerable unrest, particularly amongst those operating from the current leading edge of green is cause for optimism.

Green has no idea where it's going, exactly because of its 'everything is equal' stance. If everything is equal and there is no truth except contextual truth it's very hard to imagine a 'right course of action', it's also incredibly difficult to know who to trust and to build genuine win/win collaborations. Needless to say, when a leader emerges, even if they are from a much earlier stage of development, and suggests they do *know* what that answer is then people will often flock to that certainty in uncertain times.

This regression we are now seeing throughout the world is actually a paradoxical sign of progress. The primary and central cause is a failure of the green leading edge to be able to lead at all. Nihilism and narcissism derails evolution entirely. This halt in the progress of humanity is, itself, a necessary and evolutionary self correcting dynamic. The evolutionary current itself stops, reassesses, and reconfigures itself and this move often includes various degrees of temporary regression. There often needs to be a retracing of steps to find the point green began to collapse in order to enable it to reconfigure a new, more constructive way forward from there[369].

For green, that almost certainly means no more characterising earlier stages of development as a 'basket of deplorables[370]'. Green must move past their judgement to genuinely connect effectively with everyone and take people with them, which is one of their primary capabilities. In short, the green value system needs to heal itself and the rest of us need to stop contributing to the polarisation. However, we also need a second evolutionary move and that is for the cutting edge to leap forward into the 2nd tier where disruptive innovation combined with technology could create new models of genuine cooperation and collaboration to deliver real change and better governance[371].

The encouraging news, regardless of your political views, is that all this green chaos is quite normal. It is part of the cyclical nature of evolution. The green collapse becomes the catalyst for regression and ultimately a leap forward allowing the evolutionary process to continue. When faced with the choice of regression or boldly pushing into unknown territory, regression may appear easier. The ethnocentric regressive drift we are witnessing in the UK, Europe and the US simply reflects people's desire to get back to a world they recognise. If we get stuck with this regression, we are almost certainly in for a rough ride. Evolution doesn't go backwards. However, if we opt for upward evolution, then we can unlock a transformation the like of which the world has never seen. Whether it happens tomorrow, or years from now, the collapse of green will still help to push us collectively toward the 2nd tier. What makes 2nd tier thinking so exciting for

[369] Wilber K (2017) Trump and a Post-Truth World: An Evolutionary Self-Correction Integral Life https://integrallife.com/trump-post-truth-world/

[370] Clinton H (2016) Comments made at a New York Presidential Fundraiser http://time.com/4486502/hillary-clinton-basket-of-deplorables-transcript/

[371] Watkins A and Stratenus I (2016) Crowdocracy: The End of Politics Urbane Publications, Kent

collaboration is that it's the first stage where we can deeply step into another person's shoes. We can see the 'true-but-partial' nature of all our earlier mindsets and we are naturally more inclusive, tolerant of differences, appreciative of diversity and willing to collaborate. That evolutionary step forward will make all the difference.

Bright Spots on the Collaborative Horizon

These inclusive, supportive and mutually beneficial perspectives and the collaborations they can create are already happening. It would therefore be remiss to leave this chapter without at least one concrete example of positive collaborations that is already helping us to eat better, waste less and share more…

In 2013 Tesco was the largest retailer in the UK and the third largest in the world behind Walmart and Carrefour[372]. Customers made 78 million shopping trips a week across convenience stores, hypermarkets and online orders across 11 countries[373]. Just accounting for the fresh food and own-branded grocery items, the retailer had thousands of suppliers across more than 70 countries. Traditionally each country had been responsible for sourcing products and all in-store decisions including pricing and promotion. For years, this approach worked well because it allowed each geographical market to meet local product preferences and keep prices low. New entrants, a move to more online shopping and tougher competition challenged the business model and Tesco created a new centralised sourcing department for food in 2010. The purpose of the new Group Food initiative was to develop a global approach to sourcing

---

[372] Alvarez JB, McLoughlin DP and Shelman M (2014) Tesco Food Group Harvard Business School Case 514-022

[373] Tesco Website Our Business https://www.tescoplc.com/about-us/our-businesses/

and an end-to-end supply chain system, including integrated forecasting and logistics, which would allow the company to be faster, nimbler, and more efficient.

Having previously moved to group buying for store-brand non-food products such as clothing and electronics with good results it was recognised that this was 'easier' because the non-food sourcing operation was centrally located in Asia. In comparison food sourcing was run by 11 separate country commercial buying teams that sourced products and were responsible for margins. The consequence was a transactional business model based on tough price negotiations and frequent switches between suppliers to keep costs down. When the company was in growth and opening new stores regularly in the 1990s and early 2000s this approach worked but it also created adversarial relationships with suppliers and resulted in a very fragmented supply chain. As one senior manager said of the system at the time, "We operated like a football team with no defense but 10 strikers."

Another problem was that Tesco's intense focus on operational efficiency encouraged supply chain teams to delay finalising orders until the very last minute, when there was the greatest insight into customer demand. This approach created additional cost and waste in the system because suppliers would have to overstock to ensure they could meet the company's changeable demands. As another senior manager pointed out, "We didn't provide forecasts and changed our orders at very short notice. As a result, there was no ability for our suppliers or us to drive efficiency in the supply chain. We did not have visibility or understand the impact we were having on end-to-end costs by making sure the store shelf was always full[374]."

I (MS) believed that Tesco would benefit from a new approach to food procurement that would include centralising supply chain

---

[374] Alvarez JB, McLoughlin DP and Shelman M (2014) Tesco Food Group Harvard Business School Case 514-022

operations, getting closer to producers, and better information sharing. It required a complete mindset change as well as many alterations to traditional procedure. For example, supermarket buyers typically rotated between product categories every 18 months as they moved up in their career. The rationale for this strategy was that this kept negotiated prices down, as buyers did not have time to form personal relationships with suppliers. Group Food required exactly these relationships in order to be effective. Moving away from transactional buying (i.e., where each contract was negotiated with the short-term goal of minimising costs on that particular deal) towards supplier partnerships that would ultimately deliver lower total costs and differentiated products. Real collaborations that would benefit everyone – the producer/ supplier, the retailer and the customer.

And, the results have been astonishing.

Take Tesco's citrus fruit partner MMUK, part of the AMC group. MMUK is a very entrepreneurial, successful grower, importer and supplier of citrus fruit to Tesco UK. I (MS) met them first when they were supplying our UK business and we were transitioning buying responsibilities to the Group Food team which I was heading up.

Alvaro Munoz, one of the brothers who owned the family business in Spain, came to listen to us to share our vision for the future at a supplier conference in 2012. He was worried that we were setting up a direct sourcing operation that was seeking to cut importers out of the supply chain. Open dialogue soon cleared that up and allowed us to appreciate how good a supplier they were in terms of both supply chain and category management. At this point, MMUK was managing around 80 per cent of Tesco's citrus business and had designs on delivering 100 per cent of the citrus category and expanding into grapes, ice cream and smoothies from across the AMC Group.

Personally, I'd always favoured two suppliers for each major category thus maximising our volume efficiencies whilst maintaining some competitive dynamic to keep suppliers hungry to invest and innovate for growth. I had explained this to Alvaro several times, but he was persistent and on a flight to China with him and Jon, his MD, in 2013 we finally concurred that if we were to align our interests any further we would need to evolve the business model, and try out a different, virtually integrated partnership - no physical change in ownership, but a joint Board overseeing the transparent activities of the value chain. Alvaro, Jon and I were immediately excited by the opportunity and during the flight we strategised over what a true partnership might deliver. By the time we touched down in China, we had agreed that the virtual partnership would combine our respective capabilities, and we had chosen six directors to run it, three from each business. The venture would be called AMT Fruit.

In the early days, there were some challenges. We believed that all our partnerships should be completely open book, but it was the first time MMUK had opened everything up, and there were initial trust related concerns for both parties. But soon, having unpacked everything, we were re-building a more transparent and sustainable system for us both. We agreed transparent joint investments into a long-term varietal development program, put 100 per cent of the Tesco citrus business into AMT, expanded into grapes, brought in the ice cream, smoothies and flowers joint ventures, and extended their role and oversight across other direct suppliers, including melons and pineapples, so that we could collectively avoid duplication and optimise supply chain efficiencies.

So far, this open, transparent and constructive collaboration has delivered:
1. Collaborative virtual end to end partnership with the customer at the core including:
   - Genetics and plant breeding; Long term R&D and innovation.
   - Global farming and security of supply; varietal development; direct grower commitments.

- Optimised packing (at source and destination); consolidation of the supply chain.
- Retail partnership (fully transparent and visible model; joint risk management).
- Customer engagement (insight; joint planning; brand activation).

2. Significant financial improvements including:
   - Over £5 million in supply chain savings (with sight to a possible further £20 million).
   - +£6.7 million in increased like for like annual sales.

3. Significant operational improvements including:
   - Greater product consistency.
   - Up to 2-days additional shelf life of products from improved supply chain efficiencies.
   - Less road miles travelled resulting in 13 per cent transport cost reduction.
   - Increase of imports from Spain delivered direct (from 27 per cent to 69 per cent) to distribution centres.
   - Longer term order commitments.

4. Increased R&D and Innovation including:
   - Direct investment into long-term development of new citrus fruit varieties.
   - Improved flavour and key attributes such as easy peeling or seedless.
   - Focus on health (replacing bad sugars with good sugars; pigmentation)
   - Reduced farming costs.
   - Longer product life.

5. More Sustainable Farming including:
   - Long-term approach which encourages investment.
   - Planting trials of new varieties and systems.
   - Increased density/yields and reduced pesticides and water use.

- Global risk profiling (e.g. sustainable availability of water) with Anthesis

6. Reduced Food Waste including:
   - End to end food waste preventions via wider product specifications and wider portfolio of available brands/channel options; forward ordering and direct deliveries to reduce on farm waste, reduce supply chain residency and increase consumer shelf life.
   - Crop utilisation via the Tesco Global reach extending supply for Tesco CE
   - Greater emphasis on alternative use via prepared produce; processing; juicing; animal feed supplements; high value compounds for cosmetics/personal care.
   - Redistribution to charities such as Fareshare.

On the supply side, this type of partnership means better prices, better products, less waste, and long-term supply security. On the demand side, it means companies that seek out this collaborative, mutually beneficial approach can develop innovative and unique products and re-build customer loyalty all within the framework of sustainability and finding global solutions to the food challenges we face.

Encouragingly, even though Tesco went through a very significant financial crisis and subsequent organisational upheaval in late 2014, the mindset around partnerships and collaboration was not only held onto, but was further developed and integrated across all of Tesco's key suppliers by the new CEO, Dave Lewis, as a key part of the business turnaround plan. As a result of significantly writing down profits and their store asset base Tesco needed to streamline the number of directors by 50 per cent and management by 30 per cent. In this process, the Group and the UK food teams were integrated, but care was taken to maintain all of the newly developed capabilities and thinking. In fact, the incoming CEO further challenged all its most capable supply partners and the Tesco teams to imagine they were running one, end to end, business, having none of the distractions and barriers created by individual ownership – collectively, how would we run our food value chains? It was an open invitation for a fresh perspective and a different dialogue, sponsored and supported from the very top of the Tesco organisation. And, encouragingly, it was readily and enthusiastically accepted and personally sponsored by the CEOs of the food manufacturers and processors too.

With the right mindset of collaboration amazing things are possible in food and beyond. Increased transparency and information sharing can change corporate culture. By building a producer network—an online community of over 1,600 members (and counting) across all agricultural categories—and introducing a number of working groups, everyone learns from each other. For example, one of Tesco's Asian growers had a defect that he hadn't seen before. He put the question up on the network (many of whom could easily be considered competitors) and there was an incredible response from growers across different continents. Within two hours, the problem was identified and he had a number of different suggestions as to how to solve it.

That's collaboration and it can change the world.

Conclusion:

A Sustainable World of Health and Plenty

Let's imagine a new world.

What would happen to us as individuals if we chose to make better eating decisions, move a little more and take more personal responsibility for our health? How many extra years of good quality life could we expect[375]? Where could we go? What could we do and who would we become with so much more time and energy?

In the next thirty years, our lives will change beyond all recognition. The access to disruptive health technology will accelerate and massively increase our personal connectivity which will enable us to understand our bodies and ourselves in ways that are barely imaginable now. People will instantaneously benchmark their own data, be plugged into advanced medical artificial intelligence (AI) that can interpret abnormalities faster and better than any physician. We will easily be able to make adjustments to our diet to optimise our health and performance based on rapid assessment of multiple internal systems including blood and microbiome health. Thus, enabling us to customise our nutritional choices from a vast array of seasonally available,

---

[375] Gratton L (2016) The 100-Year Life: Living and working in an age of longevity Bloomsbury, London

environmentally sustainable, real food from our local area and further afield. We will be continuously tracking many biometric markers embedded in our clothing and homes that will enable us to adjust our lifestyle years before problems are likely to arise – allowing us to eat better, exercise in a way that keeps us trim and manage our emotional life to optimise how we feel in any given moment.

With this new wave of preventative medicine, information, knowledge and personal health data we will be able to precisely identify and appreciate the quality and impact all food and drink has on our mental and physical health. Internalised and circulating nanorobotics will advise us when we need more or less calories. Our phones will alert us when we have reached and exceeded our daily calorific requirement, in the same way that our bank currently texts us when we are running out of money. We will be alerted when our Vitamin C levels are too low or when we need more protein, together with suggested food options that would help redress the imbalance. Such real-time information would allow us to make small daily adjustments to easily get back on track without medication or outside intervention – simply a prompt to eat more or less of a particular food. We could still enjoy our 'guilty pleasures' from time to time, whether that's chocolate, pizza or a bowl of ice cream but we would no longer be under any illusion of their impact on our health. Much of the technology we have mentioned already exists and we are only a few years away from having such integrated health and wellbeing guidance. When it arrives, it will offer game-changing opportunities for us to manage our own health, while simultaneously reducing our dependence on prescription medication and rolling back the excessive pressure on our global health care systems. Finally, we will stop underestimating or trivialising the impact our food and drink choices are having on our physical and mental wellbeing – our own data will make sure of that.

If we chose to aggregate our data or remove any individual identifying markers, and share it with scientists and researchers this type of innovation and optimised personal health system could liberate all of us, not just improve our own future. The data could be benchmarked so that we can collectively learn how to eat better, waste less and share more therefore transforming health care around the world.

Human beings are not stupid. When faced with the evidence poor eating choices and lack of activity are having on our body on a daily basis we will be far more motivated to change our behaviour and take an active role in our health and well-being. Imagine a world where we could roll back Type 2 diabetes. Where people are alerted to that potential outcome so far before the condition develops that changes to diet and lifestyle ensures that it never develops. Imagine if we eradicate obesity and famine – where we are all able to get the food and information we need to make better decisions for ourselves and those we love. Glowing skin, boundless energy, supple strong bodies made possible by the right food, the right activity and the right information – provided at the right time. Not after illness or poor health has occurred but long before it emerges. What would we do as a species if we were all healthy, active and bursting with energy. What would we create? What would we be able to fix? What other wicked problems could we solve?

What would happen if we wasted less. Less of everything – not just food. Imagine if all the millions of tonnes of food we waste throughout the world, especially in the West, was not wasted. Where we come to respect the journey, effort and resources used to make the food that arrives on our table and act accordingly. Where we consider what we buy and eat all that we buy. What could be done with the land, water and energy that is used to create the food we currently waste? Could we turn back deforestation, plant the trees again and reintroduce the animals, biodiversity and indigenous communities that have been pushed out to make way for our gluttony. What if we enjoyed the abundance that the world has to offer but remember it's fragility and that it is not just our home. What if we made space and opened our hearts to all the species - plant and animal that live on earth. How many species could we save from extinction?

What if we shared more. Could we actively reduce the number of times we eat alone, reach out to others and enjoy that connection and companionship. We are social creatures and you just can't enjoy a meal with someone on Snapchat! Besides, we need someone to help us eat that cheesecake otherwise we all know what happens to it!

We live in an extraordinary world. Mother Nature has given us access to a rich cornucopia of food options. Human creativity and innovation has multiplied that bounty to a point we have an indescribable diversity of food and drink to choose from. Science has added its weight and knowledge to improve varieties of produce, increase yield and provide disease resistance. The demands of science may change but its ability to deliver is unquestioned. What we can already achieve today would have been considered science fiction even a decade ago.

Imagine a world where the food supply system was efficient, connected and coherent. Where small and mid-range producers all over the world worked hand in glove with large agribusiness to manage risk, mitigate the weather and organise and distribute supply so as to ensure a continuous flow of safe, tasty, nutritious, affordable food available for all – regardless of how many people occupied the planet. Where we could cook from scratch, buy a healthy ready meal, learn to cook using 'assisted' meal solutions, order take away, eat out, shop in-store, shop online or via our phone and still enjoy affordable food that supports our health and well-being… most of the time.

Imagine collaborations where no one party was seeking to out-manoeuvre another. End to end teams of experts and integrators energised around common goals, striving to make a real difference; transactional negotiations would become a bewilderingly wasteful thing of the past. Imagine a world where investment decisions considered all significant implications. Where capital and resources were allocated and deployed efficiently and effectively around the world, and innovation was the lifeblood of differentiation and healthy, dynamic competition. Where diversity, sustainability and cooperation were truly valued and where all stakeholders from growers to consumers prosper. Where all stakeholders took a more inclusive, expansive long-term view – constantly mindful of people, planet and profit. What could we achieve with constructive, open and honest dialogue within and between governments, businesses and NGOs – could we roll back climate change? Absolutely we could, even if we reduced our food waste we could make a huge difference to climate change.

Let's make it happen – it starts with you, me and all of us.

About the Authors

If we are to solve the wicked problems we face we need to understand them in much greater depth from as many perspectives as possible. That is the purpose of this book – to do so regarding the future of food. As such the views presented here are not always views shared by the authors. Instead we took an integrally coherent approach and went where the sources and verifiable research led us in an attempt to present as many of those different perspectives as possible. Only when we can hold a space for difference, seek out all the 'true but partial' viewpoints and stitch them together into a cooperative, collaborative wise solution will we ever address these complex issues.

Alan Watkins

Alan is recognised as an international expert on leadership and human performance. He originally trained as a physician and has a first class degree in psychology and a PhD in immunology. He worked in the UK's National Health Service for 11 years. He also worked as a physician in Australia and the USA before ending up in neuroscience research. Over the last 20 years he has been a coach to many of Europe's top business leaders, including his co-author Matt. He is currently the CEO of a leadership consultancy, Complete Coherence, that works predominatly with large muti-national organisations helping them to improve their results and make a greater social impact. He is a sought after key note speaker and his three TEDx talks have attracted over 3.5 millions views. He is a frequent contributor to BBC Radio 2 and 4 and was the sole expert in a TV series, Temper your Temper, helping people with mental health and anger issues. He has written numerous scientific articles in peer-reviewed journals and this is his sixth book, the third in his Wicked and Wise book series. In addition to his corporate work, Alan works closely with a number of Olympic Sports and Professional Sports clubs. He is also working with a number of partners to improve mental and emotional health in schools.

Matt Simister

Matt joined Tesco in 1996 following his graduation from The University of Sheffield with a BA in Business Studies and Marketing and a short spell at a London marketing agency. Having initially joined the company in the marketing department, he quickly moved into the commercial team working across a number of product categories in the UK business before his promotion to Category Director of Meat, Fish and Poultry in 2003. He subsequently ran the Household category, before setting up the International Buying Office, which was a natural stepping stone to his promotion to Commercial Director for the Czech and Slovak businesses in 2007, where he lived with his wife Karen and two daughters in Prague. In 2010, he returned to the UK to set up Tesco's Group Food capability, managing regional fresh food and Tesco Brand sourcing, buying and inbound supply chains for the UK, ROI, Central Europe and Asia. Following Tesco's financial problems in late 2014 and subsequent restructuring, Matt integrated these Group capabilities and the associated developing supplier partnerships into the UK business and led the UK Fresh Food and Commodities business to successful turnaround. He was promoted to the Executive Committee in April 2017, and is now responsible for Tesco's business in Central Europe.

THERE ARE TWO FURTHER GROUND-BREAKING VOLUMES IN THE WICKED AND WISE SERIES:

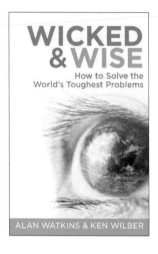

Many issues, whether social, cultural, political or business-led, seem completely resistant to change. In the first book in the series, the co-authors Alan Watkins and renowned social thinker Ken Wilber, suggest that many 'wicked' problems can be philosophically and practically challenged through the application of a 'wise' Integral Coherence model, providing a platform to engage with issues in a highly developed, enlightened and selfless way.

Paperback: 320 pages

ISBN-13: 978-1909273641

Price: £12.99

WICKED & WISE SERIES

CROWDOCRACY

The End of Politics

ALAN WATKINS & IMAN STRATENUS

'I predict Crowdocracy will come to be seen as a landmark book; not for totally getting it right, but for being the first to get enough of it right to help launch a movement for fundamental democratic renewal. Our global polls show citizen trust in established democracies at an all-time low. A tipping point is nigh and this book will help shift the balance much as a crystal lowered into a supersaturated solution transforms liquid into form.'

Doug Miller, President,
GlobeScan Foundation

The second book in the series, Crowdocracy: The End of Politics discusses one of the world's most debated and critical issues - who decides our future and how should we be governed. Democracy is struggling to produce solutions to the many challenges of our time. Populations feel disenfranchised with the political process. Crowdocracy offers a radical new way forward, one that allows all of us - not just the privileged few to participate in how we are governed. Using technology and the insights of crowd wisdom, the authors describe how we can ultimately shape and govern our communities. A revolutionary idea that can be implemented in an evolutionary way.

Paperback: 288 pages

ISBN-13: 978-1910692158

Price: £12.99

Index

URBANE

Urbane Publications is dedicated to developing new author voices, and publishing fiction and non-fiction that challenges, thrills and fascinates.

From page-turning novels to innovative reference books, our goal is to publish what YOU want to read.

Find out more at
urbanepublications.com